AF352443

THE OVIDIAN VOGUE: LITERARY FASHION AND IMITATIVE PRACTICE IN LATE ELIZABETHAN ENGLAND

The Ovidian Vogue: Literary Fashion and Imitative Practice in Late Elizabethan England

DANIEL D. MOSS

UNIVERSITY OF TORONTO PRESS
Toronto Buffalo London

ISBN 978-1-4426-4868-5

Library and Archives Canada Cataloguing in Publication

Moss, Daniel David, 1979–, author
The ovidian vogue : literary fashion and imitative practice in late
Elizabethan England / Daniel D. Moss.

Includes bibliographical references and index.
ISBN 978-1-4426-4868-5 (bound)

1 English poetry – Early modern, 1500–1700 – History and criticism.
2. Ovid, 43 B.C.–17 A.D. or 18 A.D. – Adaptations – History and criticism.
3. Ovid, 43 B.C.–17 A.D. or 18 A.D. – Parodies, imitations, etc. – History
and criticism.   4. Ovid, 43 B.C.–17 A.D. or 18 A.D. – Appreciation – England.
5. Ovid, 43 B.C.–17 A.D. or 18 A.D. – Influence.   6. Imitation in literature.
7. English literature – Roman influences.   8. Literature and society –
England – History – 16th century.   I. Title.

PR549.N3M68 2014   821'.309   C2014-901690-5

University of Toronto Press acknowledges the financial assistance to its
publishing program of the Canada Council for the Arts and the
Ontario Arts Council, an agency of the Government of Ontario.

University of Toronto Press acknowledges the financial support of
the Government of Canada through the Canada Book Fund for its
publishing activities.

For my grandfather, Ralph Wolman

Contents

Acknowledgments

In addition to Publius Ovidius Naso, the author would like to thank:

These Three Fates: Oliver Arnold, Leonard Barkan, Jeff Dolven

These Three Graces: J.K. Barret, Abby Heald, Dave Urban

These Nine Muses: Irina Dumitrescu, Dennis Foster, Ezra Greenspan, Tim Rosendale, Nina Schwartz, Lisa Siraganian, Willard Spiegelman, Rajani Sudan, Marjorie Swann, and Greg Brownderville (Orpheus)

These Twelve Virtues: Angela Ards, Rick Bozorth, Tim Cassedy, Darryl Dickson-Carr, Mike Holahan, Ross Murfin, Jasper Neel, Beth Newman, Jayson Gonzales Sae-Saue, Martha Satz, Steve Weisenburger, Bonnie Wheeler

These Seven Wonders: Harry Berger, Patrick Cheney, Andrew Escobedo, Heather James, Stephen Orgel, Anne Lake Prescott, M.L. Stapleton

These Nine Worthies: Denis Feeney, Marjorie Garber, Philip Hardie, Sean Keilen, Maggie Kilgour, Jerry Passannante, Ayesha Ramachandran, Suzanne Rancourt, Colleen Rosenfeld

The Following Streams and Rivers: Tim Albrecht, Jason Baskin, Elizabeth Bearden, Roger Bellin, the Bridwell Library, Douglas Bruster, John Bugg, Angeline Chiu, Rick Cogley, Sean Cotter, Hannah Crawforth, Dan Crown, Larry Danson, Billy Flesch, Erin Forbes, Renee Fox, John Garrison, Shari Goldberg, Ken Gross, Brooke Guelker, Pat Guglielmi, Charles Hatfield, Briallen Hopper, Aaron Hostetter, Anna Swartwood House, Billie Hubbard, Lorna Hutson, Paul Kelleher, Jason Leubner, Alan Levitan, Lia Lynch, Joe Moshenska, the Seeley G. Mudd Manuscript Library, Nick Mycklebust, Cynthia Nazarian, Rachel and Josh Newburn, Mary Noble, Joe Ortiz, Andrew Oshman and Amy Berger, Krzys Piekarski, Kyle Pivetti, Lyra Plumer, Rebecca Rainof, Erwin x Acknowledgments

Rosinberg, Leslie Reid, Sarah Sage, Janice and Bruce Saulnier, Kyle and Brooke Saulnier, Melanie Saulnier, Deneen Senasi, James Shapiro, Jacky Shin, Jerry Singerman, Nigel Smith, Richard Strier, Frances Subbiondo, Jenn Tinker, Bill Tsutsui, Stefan Vander Elst, Jen Waldron, Brad Watson, Keri Walsh, Leah Whittington, Lina Wilder, David Wolman, Don and Joan Wolman, Mike Wolman and Tamela Williams-Wolman, Can Yeginsu

My Gloriana Sandra Moss, my Arthur Robert Moss, my Artegall Ken Moss, my Britomart Anne Eakin Moss, my Cambel and Triamond Isaac and Aaron, my Marinell and Florimell Rick and Tania Oshman, my beloved Una Lindsay Oshman, and her lion Loki.

A version of chapter 2 has appeared in the journal *Modern Philology*, under the title, "'The Second Master of Love': George Chapman and the Shadow of Ovid" (© 2014 by the University of Chicago Press).

Abbreviations

Except where otherwise noted, references to the poems of Ovid and Virgil are to the most recent editions in the Loeb Classical Library, and are provided parenthetically throughout the manuscript according to the following abbreviations:

Ovid, *Amores*: *Am.*
  – *Ars amatoria*: *Ars am.*
  – *Heroides*: *Her.*
  – *Metamorphoses*: *Met.* (references to Arthur Golding's 1567 English translation will be preceded by the name "Golding")
  – *Tristia*: *Tr.*
Virgil, *Aeneid*: *Aen.*
  – *Eclogues*: *Ecl.*

References to other classical texts are provided parenthetically, as are references to Natale Conti's *Mythologiae* (abbreviated *Myth.*), and the specific editions and translations used are identified in the bibliography. Biblical references, employing the standard abbreviations for individual books, are to the 1560 edition of *The Geneva Bible*. References to Edmund Spenser's poems are provided parenthetically, according to the abbreviations listed in *The Spenser Encyclopedia*, 2. References to Ben Jonson's works are to Herford and Simpson's edition.

THE OVIDIAN VOGUE: LITERARY
FASHION AND IMITATIVE PRACTICE IN
LATE ELIZABETHAN ENGLAND

Introduction: "Note how she quotes the leaves"

With the exception of one fatally illiterate clown, the hapless characters trapped in the helical revenge plot of William Shakespeare's earliest tragedy, *Titus Andronicus*, are all well-read. Even the play's barbarians – the Gothic princes Chiron and Demetrius, their bloodthirsty mother Tamora, and her lover, the sinister Moor Aaron – appear to have received the equivalent of an early modern humanist education, predisposing them to cite classical precedents almost as obsessively as their Roman foes.[1] The Andronici themselves, however, prove Shakespeare's most determined bibliophiles. In desperate circumstances – Titus's daughter Lavinia has been raped and mutilated, and the patriarch himself has severed his own hand in a failed effort to ransom his two sons, framed for the murder of his son-in-law Bassianus – the family turns to the classics for consolation:

> Lavinia, go with me;
> I'll to thy closet, and go read with thee
> Sad stories chancèd in the times of old.
> Come, boy, and go with me; thy sight is young,
> And thou shalt read when mine [eyes] begin to dazzle. (3.2.80–4)[2]

The young scholar whom Titus addresses is his grandson Lucius, and by reading to Lavinia, the child will return a favour his aunt has often performed for him, for as Titus recalls in the following scene, "Ah, boy, Cornelia never with more care / Read to her sons than she [Lavinia] hath read to thee / Sweet poetry and Tully's *Orator*" (4.1.12–14). The family library begins to take shape as Titus reminisces; the matronly virtue of Cornelia Africana, made famous by Plutarch, is exemplified by her act of reading Cicero and "sweet poetry" to her sons. Which poets? Presumably Seneca, whom Titus quotes in the same scene (80–1); Horace, whose odes provide the motto for the vengefully emblematic weapons the grieving patriarch later sends to his daughter's rapists (4.2.20–1); above all the Roman laureate Virgil, whose Aeneas's surname, Pius, has become Titus's honorific title in recognition of his victories against the Goths (1.1.23–4). Otherwise domineering in his attitude towards his daughter – he attempts to marry Lavinia to the vicious emperor Saturninus against her will – Titus proves a singularly obliging father when it comes to literature, offering Lavinia "choice of all my library" and noting how she is "deeper read and better skilled" than the schoolboy Lucius (4.1.33–4). Before Lavinia lost her hands and tongue, presumably she too read and recited Plutarch, Cicero, Seneca, Virgil, and for that matter the historian Livy, whose account of Virginius's mercy killing of his own daughter provides the model for Titus's murder of Lavinia in the play's final massacre.

But here in the play's central scene, Lavinia cares only for one book: Ovid's *Metamorphoses*. Indeed, she is desperate to cite a particular passage from it, having pursued the terrified Lucius on to the stage and singled out Ovid's authoritative compendium of myths from among the books abandoned by the fleeing boy. "Some book there is that she desires to see," Titus observes, and demands, "Which is it, girl, of these? – Open them, boy" (31–2), but despite her disability, Lavinia is too impatient to let her nephew act as page-turner. Never was literary citation so animated: "what book is that she tosseth so?" asks Titus again, as he and his brother Marcus marvel at how "busily she turns" and "quotes the leaves" with her bleeding stumps, perhaps even with her teeth (41, 45, 50). Heroically, she finds her place in the epic poem, just as her father finally intervenes, "Help her; what would she find? Lavinia, shall I read? / This is the tragic tale of Philomel, / And treats of Tereus' treason and his rape; / And rape, I fear, was root of thy annoy" (46–9). At last, Titus recollects the specifically Ovidian scene of the crime:

> Lavinia, wert thou thus surprised, sweet girl?
> Ravished and wronged, as Philomela was,
> Forced in the ruthless, vast, and gloomy woods?
> See, see; ay, such a place there is, where we did hunt –
> O, had we never, never hunted there! –
> Patterned by that the poet here describes,
> By nature made for murders and for rapes. (4.1.51–7)

The tragedy of *Titus Andronicus* is an iteration of Ovid's "tragic tale of Philomel"; all along, the stage itself has been an extension of the *Metamorphoses*.

Amid the bombastic verse and gory spectacle of the scene, it is easy for an audience to lose sight of Lavinia's allusive precision. Lacking the means to cite – the hands to point, the tongue to "quote" – she nevertheless advances Ovid's poem literally to centre stage, distinguishing the *Metamorphoses* most immediately from the pile of titleless props at her feet, and more broadly from the play's allusive ghost library: the various authorities constantly invoked on this stage, but never consulted. Lavinia is named, after all, for the long-suffering heroine of a very different poem, for as Heather James observes, "the Andronici virtually claim the *Aeneid* as family history," yet she must now overcome her father's exasperating tendency to interpolate himself and those around him into a narrow and irrelevant Virgilian paradigm.[3] As recently as the previous scene, Titus has resumed his accustomed role as Aeneas, obliged to "tell the tale twice o'er, / How Troy was burnt and he made miserable" (3.2.27–8), and Lavinia herself has long participated dutifully in this ponderous theatre of imperial dialectic; her first act upon entering the play was to kneel in devotion, shedding "tributary tears" for her "brethren's obsequies" alongside "tears of joy" for her father's triumph (1.1.159–62). As she cites the *Metamorphoses*, however, Lavinia not only substitutes a single, manifestly Ovidian identity for her father's Virgilian delusions, but narrows the play's allusive field of reference to a particular passage within that unique source – one myth from among hundreds the poem makes available. Momentarily at least, for Shakespeare's audience as for the Andronici onstage, Ovid's Philomela stands at the centre of the whirling literary tradition.

"Take choice of all my library"

This study primarily concerns the narrative poetry of the English 1590s; expressly literary adaptations of Ovid by Edmund Spenser, George Chapman, Michael Drayton, John Donne, Thomas Nashe, and Shakespeare himself. I begin by close reading a pivotal scene in the popular drama of the early 1590s, however, because in *Titus Andronicus* Shakespeare stages the dynamics of the Ovidian imitative mode then at the heart of literary fashion. As she elevates the *Metamorphoses* above the rest of her father's library, preferring Ovid to the competing authorities in her nephew's curriculum, Lavinia embodies, represents, and re-enacts a broad shift in English secular culture, away from the classical models long approved by humanist scholars and educators – Virgil's *Aeneid*, most pervasively – towards the less stable and less coherent, but more vivid and pliable Ovidian corpus. Taking centre stage as Philomela, Shakespeare's earliest tragic heroine effectively makes an allegory of the Ovidian vogue itself: the conditions under which it occurred, its historical relevance and broad aesthetic appeal, and its immediate and far-reaching effects on Elizabethan literary culture.

Lavinia's actions and onstage motivations correspond to the first part of my broader thesis: for the Elizabethans, Ovidianism was not primarily a retrospective mode, but an immediate allusive language, through which poets competed with one another in the literary marketplace, addressing readers, patrons, and audiences increasingly familiar with Ovidian materials and styles. Consequently, Ovidianism was not a single literary movement, but a compounding set of individual authors' selective bids for rhetorical control over the various cultural forms and functions Ovid represented – that is, not only those found among Ovid's own works, but also in the many subsequent commentaries on his corpus, in the Roman poet's semi-legendary biography, and in widely disseminated post-classical imitations. As I will demonstrate, what strikes today's scholars as the ambivalence of particular Elizabethan poets towards Ovid on the one hand, or as a cacophony of Ovidian voices resonating through the 1590s on the other, largely arises out of these constant readjustments of imitative posture. Indeed, many of the late Elizabethan poets turned to Ovid repeatedly over the course of their careers, not merely for the convenience of a familiar source, but in order to replace an initial imitative posture with increasingly sophisticated ones. By means of this serial self-revision, an enterprising poet could chart his individual progress towards poetic maturity, and in the process register his keen sense of evolving literary fashion in advance of his own imitators. Shakespeare, Spenser, and Drayton, respectively the subjects of the first, third, and fourth chapters of this study, all self-revised in this way throughout the 1590s, reconstituting fresh Ovidian models so as to distinguish the stages of their professional development. In turn, the most successful of these individual metamorphoses of Ovidian imitation, such as Shakespeare's *Venus and Adonis* or Drayton's *Englands Heroicall Epistles*, concomitantly transformed literary fashion more broadly considered, altering the rules of the game for everyone. This study therefore relies on stereoscopic analyses of at least two works by each author, as the logical extension of the phenomenon of serial imitation.[4] The Ovidianism of the 1590s, in other words, must be described in relative terms, and its intertextual constellations located not only among multiple authors, but within each poet's evolving body of work.

On her own, then, Lavinia can hardly represent sufficiently the self-revisionary imitative choices of rising poets like Shakespeare, let alone the laureate Spenser, especially as she becomes an accomplice to her father's most notorious stage antics (e.g., "Bear thou my hand, sweet wench, between thy teeth," 3.1.281). As I show in the second half of this introduction, Lavinia proves less a paragon of late Renaissance Ovidianism than a farce of that increasingly popular allusive process; more precisely, she parodies the vogue in dumbshow. To be sure, her newfound Ovidian sensibility, however painfully compelled, strongly impresses those around her, as first Titus, then Marcus, then the rest of her family subscribe to her new mania for the *Metamorphoses*, producing apace their own allusions to the epic. Yet their united reproduction of the Philomela myth – a story containing only losers – ultimately satirizes Ovid's viral appeal to private patrons and public audiences alike, and the hapless Lavinia becomes the prototype for the gullible slaves of fashion in all of us. Meanwhile, the brevity of the play's central scene exaggerates the apparent speed with which a single poet had ascended from centuries of mere significance to cultural pre-eminence.

As an onstage vivisection of the young Shakespeare's cultural moment, Lavinia's maltreatment testifies most immediately to Ovid's inherent limitations as an imitative model, more broadly to the pitfalls of the allusive process itself, and finally to the ephemerality of all literary fashion. Indeed, the prescient satirical aspect of Shakespeare's *Titus*, which I discuss in detail below, points towards a crisis in literary fashion later in the decade, as the Juvenalians of the Inns of Court and the vitriolic playwrights of Elizabeth's final years incorporate this sense that all things Ovidian have long gone stale, even the most basic allusions. The early date of *Titus*, however, suggests that this sense of Ovidianism's functional obsolescence already formed part of the intellectual discourse of the early 1590s, hence the second core concern of this study: to account for the relentless critical and self-critical indictments of Ovidian excess and inconsequence, prominent even in manifestly Ovidian texts, as fundamental to imitative practice throughout the period. Scholars of Shakespeare and Spenser, in particular, have overlooked this paradoxical element in the composition of Ovidian poems, while most discussions of critical and self-critical imitative postures have remained limited to accounts of the late-century satires.

Accordingly, this introduction closes with a discussion of Shakespeare's more proactive and sardonic Ovidian villain, Aaron, whose allusive intrigues ultimately compel Lavinia to reach for the *Metamorphoses*. Directing his fellow villains away from the dialectical myths of empire, towards the self-consuming myth of Philomela, Aaron remains aloof from the onstage re-enactment of rape and revenge, sharing with the audience his delight in the carnage Ovid has prescribed. He thus updates the contradictory stance of early modern mythographers like Giovanni Boccaccio and Natale Conti, who had recapitulated Ovid's myths of lustful gods and hapless nymphs, while ridiculing the metamorphic terms in which such myths originated. These scholars and their heirs had insisted on the moral or even typological content of pagan mythology, and Aaron's Roman victims have learned this incorporeal brand of exegesis all too well. Even as they invoke or indeed consult the text of the *Metamorphoses*, the Andronici and their foes alike operate under the assumption that its metamorphic precedents are irretrievably fictional, and Aaron gleefully manipulates the shortfall between the universal mythological source and the imitative postures of those around him. A peculiarly cynical proxy for the Ovidian playwright – that is, for Shakespeare himself, but also presumably for Christopher Marlowe, Thomas Kyd, and other contemporaries – Aaron sends Lavinia scrambling to become the consummate Ovidian player, and mocks her inevitable failure.

I am most concerned, then, not with the originality of Aaron's ironic and subversive attitude towards "Roman letters" (5.1.139), but with his cohabitation of the same stage and the same Rome as Lavinia, who embodies that more direct, more earnest and even desperate application of the *Metamorphoses*. From their onstage mutuality, I develop this book's claim that apparently antagonistic Ovidian postures were continuous with superficially positive or direct imitations, as young poets like Chapman and Donne capitalized on readerly impressions that Ovidianism would prove a passing fad. Incorporating this sense of ephemerality into their poetry, such anti-Ovidian postures often had the paradoxical effect of augmenting Ovid's cultural authority in real time. After all, Ovid's signature styles and characteristic mythological content indeed remained indispensable to the early productions of Chapman, Ben Jonson, and others, however loudly their satires castigated professional rivals for immorality and affectation, or chided readers and audiences for the tame acceptance of an outdated product. As the unpublished outlier at the end of the Ovidian vogue, however, Donne most resembles Shakespeare's Aaron, ironically dismissing standard tastes even as he positions himself as the successor to Ovid's persona of the *praeceptor Amoris* – the "teacher" or "master" of Cupid, and by extension of erotic elegy – through the turn of the seventeenth century.[5]

Like the young Shakespeare, then, the young Donne adopted an imitative posture testifying to Ovid's tenacious hold on late Elizabethan literary culture at large. That vogue had originated in the wide availability of printed texts of Ovid's poems, their inclusion in school curricula, and the popularity of pagan mythological figures in university and court entertainments.[6] The burgeoning fashion for poetic imitation, in particular, was continuous with a spate of English translations published in the preceding decades – chief among them Arthur Golding's 1567 *Metamorphoses* – which were generally accompanied by the moralizing commentary characteristic of continental editions of Ovid's Latin texts.[7] Alongside Marlowe's *Hero and Leander*, scholars often identify Thomas Lodge's *Scillaes Metamorphosis* (published 1589) as the Ovidian vogue's gateway text, and similar works continued to be published through the 1590s.[8] Often targeting male aristocratic audiences and patrons, many of these poets experimented with Ovid's elegiac voice and reproduced the erotic play of the *Metamorphoses*, developing along the way some of the most brutally misogynistic and homophobic verse of the Renaissance, as well as some of the tenderest and least inhibited. Certain Ovidian myths, including those of Actaeon, Arachne, and Niobe, were already popular in medieval and Tudor commentaries and allegories, and remained central to Elizabethan depictions of political subversion and its due punishment. The nightingale Philomela and the floral Narcissus, meanwhile, continued to offer themselves to poets as vehicles for complaint, satire, and self-critique. Ovid's popularity extended to the drama-obsessed royal court and to England's rising public theatres, as first John Lyly and George Peele, and then Shakespeare and his contemporaries adapted classical myths to the stage, threading allusions to the *Metamorphoses* and precepts from the *Ars amatoria* and *Amores* through the speeches of comic and tragic characters alike.

The new Ovidians did not so much imitate Ovid indiscriminately as isolate and exploit particular elements in his corpus, including not only the erotic verse, but also the ventriloquized feminine voices of the *Heroides*, the complaints of the *Tristia* and *Epistulae ex Ponto*, the civic aetiologies of the unfinished *Fasti*, and of course the *Metamorphoses*. By the 1590s, Ovid's masterpiece had accumulated many times its weight in more or less esoteric commentary – a vast index of moralized and allegorized interpretation – as numerous critics, beginning with Seneca and Quintilian, took it upon themselves alternately to censure Ovid for his licentious verse and applaud him for his wit.[9] While some, like the libertine Marlowe, chose to ignore the received ethical valences of certain myths, most Elizabethan poets approached such commentaries as further extensions of Ovid's original corpus.[10] To these literary remains could be added the subversive Roman poet's notoriety as an exile, relegated by Augustus Caesar to Tomis on the inhospitable Black Sea as punishment for his licentious publications and a still-mysterious political indiscretion.[11] By the time Shakespeare was writing *Titus*, then, there was an Ovid for virtually any poetic occasion; indeed, when the theatres closed in the plague year of 1593, Shakespeare refocused on a different myth from the *Metamorphoses* for his narrative *Venus and Adonis*, and soon shifted his attention again, adapting a portion of the *Fasti* for the *Rape of Lucrece*.[12]

The onstage postures of Lavinia and Aaron, in other words, are only the earliest examples of one poet's evolving approach to imitation, but these tragic figures are all the more revealing for their forerunner status, and in the following pages, I will look to them for guidance into the midst of the Ovidian vogue. Some of my critical criteria and methodology should become clear as this initial reading develops, but in general, this study attempts to bridge the critical gap between overly expansive and narrowly focused existing scholarship. Although I trace the origins of my critical concerns to Leonard Barkan's landmark 1986 study, *The Gods Made Flesh*, I have exchanged some of Barkan's generous transhistorical scope for more rigorous scrutiny of the 1590s, taking into account New Historicism's recovery of the immediate political and social stakes of cultural production in that pivotal decade. At the same time, I present a more capacious map of Ovidianism than such single-author studies as Jonathan Bate's *Shakespeare and Ovid* (1993), Syrithe Pugh's *Spenser and Ovid* (2005), and M.L. Stapleton's *Spenser's Ovidian Poetics* (2009) in an effort to construct a broadly applicable, comprehensive model of cultural fashion and artistic response. Although I discuss poems in diverse genres, from pornography and beast fable to pastoral and epic, each reading is anchored in the ubiquitous fact of Ovid's celebrity. Interpreting these texts not as isolated instances of emulation or parody but as the evolving set of poetic responses to the 1590s' fashionable superstyle, I consider the various imitative postures critics have long acknowledged as Ovidian alongside a corresponding range of oppositional attitudes usually excluded from such accounts.

This study's methodological copiousness likewise reflects the diversity of contemporary responses to Ovid's central role in late Elizabethan literary culture, as now-classic philological, New Critical, and New Historicist readings serve as my respective departure points for the chapters on Chapman, Drayton, and Spenser. More generally, I seek to build upon pioneering work by Richard Helgerson, Patrick Cheney, and David Lee Miller on the early modern poetic career, and to apply intertextual close readings extrapolated from studies of classical allusion by Stephen Hinds, Alessandro Barchiesi, and Denis Feeney, among others. That intertextual content, however, cannot be considered outside the social and material culture in which such Ovidian poems were composed, published, and read. Hence I scrutinize not only the poems themselves, but their material context, from the bowdlerized manuscripts of Nashe's *Choice of Valentines* to the unstable texts of Donne's posthumous printed anthologies. In short, *The Ovidian Vogue* is meant to provide metamorphic criticism in the protean manner of Ovid himself.

Ovidianism at Centre Stage

Beyond simply confirming Ovid's new hegemony in the humanist library, Lavinia presents her concentric audiences – her family onstage and the playgoers in the theatre – with a crash course in applied Ovidianism: the judicious selection and imitation of a single, specific element from a vast and ever-expanding corpus. Struggling against her family's tendency to reduce her to a static emblem for paralytic grief, Lavinia recognizes that even her identification with Philomela, if too broadly conceived, will not suffice to catalyse the desired revenge. Her uncle Marcus, after all, has already observed the congruity, without drawing any useful conclusions. Upon discovering her raped and mutilated, he had lamented helplessly:

> Fair Philomela, why she but lost her tongue,
> And in a tedious sampler sewed her mind;
> But, lovely niece, that mean is cut from thee.
> A craftier Tereus, cousin, hast thou met,
> And he hath cut those pretty fingers off,
> That could have better sewed than Philomel. (2.4.38–43)[13]

Counteracting the stasis inherent in such poetry of complaint, Lavinia identifies herself not only with Ovid (as opposed to, say, Virgil or

Seneca), and not only with Philomela (as opposed to, say, Ovid's incestuous Myrrha or suicidal Thisbe), but with Philomela at the pivotal moment in Ovid's myth, when she transmutes the silence and paralysis of the victim into the furious activity of the avenger. Ovid's heroine, after an intolerable period of captivity, had woven a tapestry depicting her plight: *stamina barbarica suspendit callida tela / purpureasque notas filis intexuit albis, / indicium sceleris* (*Met.* 6.576–8; "She hangs a Thracian web on her loom, and skillfully weaving purple signs on a white background, she thus tells the story of her wrongs"). Contriving to send it to her sister Procne, the latter in turn "hurries on to confound right and wrong, her whole soul bent on the thought of vengeance" (585–6, *fasque nefasque / confusura ruit poenaeque in imagine tota est*). Citing this moment in the *Metamorphoses*, Lavinia provokes an equally dynamic reaction from her hitherto sympathetic but aimless family.[14] Not only is Ovidian allusion current on this stage, but Lavinia's focused and applied version of its practice proves contagious.

By casting herself as Philomela, Lavinia effectively assigns her relatives corresponding roles in the dramatic re-enactment of her own tragedy, adapting Ovid's script to the contemporary stage. Titus, in particular, takes the part of Procne, adopting a guise of madness to deceive his foes, as Procne had rescued Philomela from prison under the pretext of celebrating Bacchanalian rites. Lavinia's text, moreover, provides her father with a model for their joint vengeance; according to the Ovidian script, Philomela helps her sister cut the throat of Itys (Procne's son with Tereus), roast his flesh, and feed him to his father. Later in the play, before slaughtering Chiron and Demetrius, Titus reaffirms the symbiosis between himself as Procne and Lavinia as Philomela: "For worse than Philomel you used my daughter, / And worse than Procne I will be revenged" (5.2.194–5). In a sense, then, Lavinia's central allusion to the Philomela myth recruits and recasts even her enemies, for Chiron and Demetrius had jointly assumed the part of Ovid's Tereus when they raped and mutilated her, hence they take the unhappy part of Itys when Titus and Lavinia "make two pasties of [their] shameful heads" to feed to their mother Tamora, who thus takes the part of Tereus in turn (2.1.129–32; 5.2.189). Like his daughter before him, Titus cites his precedent in the *Metamorphoses*, such that his victims' final recognition will be of their complicity in the allusive re-enactment, and of their warranting not just any punishment, but the one Ovid prescribes.

Of course, Lavinia no more "chooses" to play the part of Philomela than Chiron and Demetrius voluntarily provide the main ingredients for their mother's dinner. Ultimately, she constitutes only the more obvious half of Shakespeare's judicious appraisal of contemporary Ovidianism as a compulsory and self-consuming mode, as well as an appealing and fashionable one. Lavinia, we might say, has perfected Ovidianism as a means, but not necessarily to any sufficient end. Paradoxically, one of her signal successes during the central scene may help to define the limits of her newfound agency as Philomela, as she infects those around her – even Marcus, slowest of the Andronici – with the same mania for the *Metamorphoses*. Barkan describes Marcus's contribution to the general anagnorisis:

> Yet [Ovid's] book has to be translated. The name Tereus, for instance, has to be translated into Demetrius and Chiron. How can that be done by a heroine who cannot speak, write, draw, or sing? She must struggle for a new medium of communication, one that marries the book and the picture. So her uncle teaches her to write with a stick in the sand. In fact, that system of communicating comes from the same book. That is how Ovid's Io, transformed by the gods into a heifer, managed to identify herself, by scratching a line and a circle in the earth.[15]

Marcus's introduction of his own Ovidian allusion is a logical response to his niece's quotation of Philomela's text, and in one sense it is the tragedy's most hopeful moment, as we imagine Lavinia, like Io, regaining her original voice and human form. While the playwright and his characters here triumph momentarily over an intertextual impasse, however, the dramatic effect remains cruelly farcical: Lavinia identifies her rapists in the posture of fellatio, and is pointedly denied both the comic recuperation of Io and the cathartic metamorphosis of Philomela into the plaintive nightingale.[16] To the average observer, then – and Titus, Marcus, and the rest of her family are decidedly average – Lavinia advertises the sudden relevance and far-reaching utility of Ovidian imitation, as an apt and enabling response to contemporary fashion, a cultural asset yielding immediate, compounding returns. By the end of the tragedy, however, the communal role play of the Andronici and their foes will be subsumed under Aaron's cynical version of Ovidianism, a Shakespearean paradigm for the intertextual shortfall that must ultimately doom the vogue itself.

Ovid behind the Scenes

Lavinia's assumption of Philomela's identity reflects the vitality, urgency, and contemporary relevance of Ovidian allusion, in contradistinction to the growing exhaustion of competing models for imitation. As the central figure in a notoriously hyperbolic play, of course, Lavinia renders absolute and immediate what was in reality a broad, constantly evolving cultural trend. Only a few years earlier, in the "Letter to Ralegh" appended to the first published edition of *The Faerie Queene*, Spenser had reaffirmed his debts to Homer, Virgil, Ariosto, and Tasso, while notably omitting Ovid.[17] Spenser's celebrity, moreover, encouraged younger aspirants to his laurels, such as Drayton and Chapman, to bypass Ovid in favour of safer authorities, at least for their debut publications. By 1591, however, Spenser himself had turned noticeably towards Ovidian models with the publication of the *Daphnaïda* and the *Muiopotmos*, both experimental preliminaries for his wholesale crossbreeding of Ovidian paradigms with allegorical epic in the 1596 *Faerie Queene*.[18] Following Spenser's example, Chapman and Drayton likewise reconsidered their initial disdain for Ovidian imitation in their ensuing publications, pivoting to relate their work to the ongoing vogue.

Though most of these professional about-faces would come later, in *Titus Andronicus* Shakespeare captures this cultural dynamic of Virgilians, Neoplatonists, and Petrarchans – the heirs of Renaissance humanism – striking Ovidian postures, but falling short of wielding the Roman poet's full authority and influence. Aspects of Lavinia's story indeed come close to a parody of Ovid's accelerated cultural ascendence: the sudden superimposition of her body over Philomela's; her convenient, unmediated access to the text of the *Metamorphoses*; her onstage audience's prompt grasp of her vengeful meaning; the rapid unfolding of her prescribed plot. In reality, poets from Petrarch and Chaucer through Sidney and Spenser had long adapted Ovidian paradigms to particular occasions, but for all Lavinia's parodic overdetermination, Shakespeare's dramatization of Ovidianism as a radical new mode, different in kind as well as in degree from prior imitations, possesses its own analytical rigour and perspicacity.

Aaron projects the exuberance of this new Ovidianism, even as he focuses Shakespeare's critique of its practitioners. As the play's chief villain, he takes proactive advantage of the sudden relevance and dramatic potential of the Ovidian corpus, compelling everyone else in the play, including Lavinia, to react to his original allusive "policy and stratagem" (2.1.105). From the scaffold, Aaron boasts of having re-educated Chiron and Demetrius, whom he had first encountered vying absurdly for Lavinia's favour via the ostentatious "languishment" of Petrarchan lovers, but whom he had soon redirected to "serve [their] lust" like Ovid's Tereus, in the woods Titus would later recognize as "patterned" by the *Metamorphoses* (5.1.98; 2.1.111, 130–1).[19] At this originary moment of Ovidian imitation in the play, we can detect Aaron's own aptitude for exactly the kind of applied allusion Lavinia later performs. As he describes the "many unfrequented plots" in the "wide and spacious" forest where the lustful brothers are to commit their crime, he puns on the word "plot," at once connoting a stratagem, a geographic location, and an intertextual passage (115–16).[20] After all, while Philomela had for centuries frequented poetic *sylvae*, she had done so as the nightingale, a metonym for the genre of amorous complaint; her Ovidian myth of origin, meanwhile, as Malcolm Bull reports, "had little impact" on the vast illustrative and iconographical traditions of the *Metamorphoses*.[21] Recognizable without being intuitive, Aaron's planting of the Philomela "plot" on the stage of *Titus* corresponds to his creator's peculiarly searching approach to the Ovidian corpus in that it reflects the myth's uneven dissemination through humanist culture. Shakespeare and his arch-villain exploit the fact that for all the *Metamorphoses*' status as "the Bible of a tradition," certain Ovidian paradigms could still prove more compelling, incisive, and infectious than others.[22] This differential allusive effect recurs in the following scene. When Tamora proposes that she and Aaron re-enact the tryst of Virgil's Dido and Aeneas, he corrects her error with the same judicious allusion: "Philomel must lose her tongue today, / Thy sons make pillage of her chastity" (2.3.43–4). Like the unafflicted carrier of an intertextual plague, Aaron inspires Ovidianism in others, who pass it along in turn, until the entire cast is involved in the original "plot."

Where Virgilian imitation at best breaks even, with one Pius Titus succeeding one Pius Aeneas or with Tamora's prospect of one quick role play in the woods, Aaron's brand of Ovidianism ostensibly yields better returns. As Barkan observes, "What is horrible in Ovid's Tereus story Shakespeare makes twice as horrible in *Titus Andronicus*. Not one rapist but two, not one murdered child but five, not one or two mutilated organs but six, not a one-course meal but a two."[23] Such amplification, however, soon converts to diminution. Even as Titus follows Procne's awful recipe, Lavinia's passive role in the kitchen – merely holding the bowl while her father does the slaughtering, grinding, and baking – testifies ironically to her unbridgeable distance from Philomela, whose participation in Itys's murder had required an agency literally out of Lavinia's reach: *iugulum ferro Philomela resolvit* (*Met.* 6.643, "Philomela cut the throat also").[24] Later, as Titus himself runs out of Ovidian capital, he kills Lavinia in front of his guests at the play's final banquet, abandoning the part of Procne and invoking instead the "pattern, precedent, and lively warrant" of "rash Virginius," who murdered his daughter in exemplary stoic fashion upon discovering that she had been raped (5.3.35–51).[25] Wrenched from her own Ovidian dynamic back into one of her father's static emblems, thus recalling the opening scene's unavailing invocations of Rome's civic paragons, Lavinia falls fatally short of Philomela's revenge:

> sicut erat sparsis furiali caede capillis,
> prosiluit Ityosque caput Philomela cruentum
> misit in ora patris nec tempore maluit ullo
> posse loqui et meritis testari gaudia dictis. (*Met.* 6.657–60)

> Just as she was, with streaming hair, and all stained with her mad deed of blood, Philomela springs forward and hurls the gory head of Itys straight into his father's face; nor was there ever any time when she longed more to be able to speak, and to express her joy in fitting words.

Crude as it seems to measure Lavinia's degree of enabling resemblance to Philomela in such blunt, corporeal terms – two hands short of headhurling – her incapacity to re-enact the final scene of her archetype's revenge proves especially ironic on this stage, where imitation heads and hands have been tossed about by everybody else. Just as earlier in the play her final spoken line, "Confusion fall – " (2.3.184), was cut short of pentameter as she lost her tongue, so in Lavinia herself Philomela's text is left unfinished. Without her tongue, she can tell neither whether she has foreseen this consequence nor whether she approves of her father's performance as Procne, but Shakespeare gives us ample reason to believe that Aaron has indeed foreseen what Ovid has foretold.

Of course, Ovid's myth of Philomela does not end with "her mad deed of blood," but with the metamorphoses of everyone concerned into birds. Tereus becomes the sword-billed hoopoe (*upapa*), forever pursuing Procne and Philomela:

> corpora Cecropidum pennis pendere putares:
> pendebant pennis. quarum petit altera silvas,

altera tecta subit, neque adhuc de pectore caedis
excessere notae, signataque sanguine pluma est. (*Met.* 6.667–70)

As they fly from him you would think that the bodies of the two Athe-
nians were poised on wings: they were poised on wings! One flies to the
woods, the other rises to the roof. And even now their breasts have not lost
the marks of their murderous deed, their feathers are stained with blood.

In his accustomed aetiological mode, Ovid inscribes his version of the
myth indelibly onto the natural world, his characters flying off into our
forests and houses: "even now you would think ... they were poised
on wings!" – but this is precisely what a theatre audience would never
think (even now). Again, it seems too obvious for criticism to point out
that an actor cannot sprout wings onstage, but all along this very in-
accessibility of physical transformation has functioned crucially in the
play's calculus of revenge.[26] Early in the play, for instance, the furious
Tamora, frustrated by the irretrievability of Ovid's exemplary myths
of vengeance, reflects upon her incapacity to metamorphose the im-
pudent Bassianus: "Had I the power that some say Dian had, / Thy
temples should be planted presently / With horns, as was Acteon's,
and the hounds / Should drive upon thy new-transformèd limbs"
(2.3.61–4). Urging his mistress to participate in the Philomela plot instead, which at least yields the dismemberment of bodies, if not their
change, Aaron transforms Tamora's deedless verbiage into mutually
destructive Ovidian action. For the cynical and opportunistic "plot-
ter," this universal recognition that metamorphosis occurs only in ancient myths constitutes the upshot of a practical joke on the aspiring
classicists around him, whose founding poets never reckoned with a
learned Moor. Shakespeare, of course, did not invent Aaron's sardonic
attitude towards metamorphosis. Jonathan Bate identifies a literary genealogy at least a century long of "implicit internalizing, which reads
metamorphosis as psychological and metaphorical instead of physical
and literal."[27] In this regard, too, Aaron complements Lavinia; while
she identifies herself within Ovid's text, as in a mirror she then holds
up to her father, Aaron recuses himself from the "plot" he has retrieved
from that darkest passage of same text. After all, the myth he has chosen for others to imitate yields only victims, unlike Marcus's preferred
myth of Io, and strikingly lacks the familiar pagan divinities who might
otherwise inspire a novice playwright's *deus ex machina*.
Ultimately, however, the issue is not dramaturgical but intertextual; it
is not a function of the stage so much as a reflection of a literary culture

derived from the humanist schoolroom. "I was their tutor to instruct them," Aaron boasts, for like a good pedagogue, he has set his pupils Chiron and Demetrius the task of double translation, to render an exemplary classical text into their own terms, and then to reproduce, as nearly as possible, the original in style as well as substance. Citing John Brinsley's 1612 pedagogy primer *Ludus literarius*, Jeff Dolven describes this ubiquitous practice:

> [Brinsley] wants to see "the very same latine of their Authors," coming back to the same words. The process is like retracing the steps of a journey … In canceling the difference between the exercise and the original by conferring and correcting, the scholar is returned to where he started: he is like a prodigal son, who has ventured out into the vernacular but is now come safe home to a London, or an ancient Rome, that has been waiting, unchanged and immemorial, for his return.[28]

Shakespeare's play, however, depends upon the impossibility of retracing those final steps to an unchanged Rome; "show me Ovid's Philomela," Aaron requires of his pupils, "but without the nightingale's wings, without even the hands to translate Ovid's *pennae* into wings."[29] For Lavinia, Ovidianism is the last stand, but for Aaron, it is everybody else's fall.

I hope in the following pages to encompass the full range of poetic responses to the Ovidian vogue of the English 1590s – that is, to account for the various imitative postures late Elizabethan poets struck in discernible relation to the central fact of Ovid's ever-expanding currency in their literary culture. Some of these poetic postures will recall Lavinia in her resourceful but ultimately hopeless attempt to substitute herself for Philomela. Like Thomas Edwards, John Beaumont, Thomas Cutwode, and other now-forgotten Ovidians, but also like Lodge, Marlowe, and Shakespeare himself under the compulsion of the vogue, Lavinia seeks to approximate as far as possible the ill-fitting myths of a tyrannical "tutor," perhaps knowing the futility of her attempt. The imitative postures of other Elizabethan poets, on the other hand, will more closely resemble Shakespeare's Aaron, as they pursue the starkest possible contrast against the vast contextual backdrop of the Ovidian vogue, rather than seeking vainly to weave themselves into it. Among these latter are Chapman, Donne, and Jonson, but their repeated efforts to signal their independence from the tyranny of fashion could likewise fall short, proving them more obsessed with the imitation of

Ovid even than their peers. After all, Aaron himself is finally consumed by his own script; as the vengeful Lucius orders the Ovidian buried "breast-deep in the earth" and starved (5.3.178), we can imagine the actor descending into the same trapdoor in the stage, which had served first as Titus's Virgilian tomb, and later as the "bloody pit" of Lavinia's incomplete metamorphosis into Philomela. Here, perhaps, the critical appeal of Shakespeare's *Titus Andronicus* as an allegory for literary imitation itself ceases, but Aaron's starvation does not entail the end of the Ovidian vogue in Elizabethan culture at large. If anything, his furiously reductive version of the protean *Metamorphoses* as Philomela's solitary text represents the young Shakespeare's challenge to his fellow poets – and to himself – to invent new Ovids, or else to pass laughably out of fashion.

Such a fate is exemplified by Thomas Nashe, the first poet I discuss in chapter 1, whose prose pamphlets and novels earned him considerable fame, if not wealth, but whose early pornographic imitation of Ovid's *Amores* brought him only notoriety. Nashe's *Choice of Valentines* thus serves as my example of the Ovidian debut, which soon gives way to imitations deemed more respectable or mature. In the second half of chapter 1, by way of contrast to Nashe, I return to Shakespeare, who debuts as an Ovidian poet during the 1593 closure of the theatres with the epyllion *Venus and Adonis*.[30] This highly successful poem, like *Titus*, proclaims the coming eclipse of Ovidianism itself, but serves as the best demonstration that for Shakespeare and for some of his followers, the paradoxical declaration of Ovidianism's obsolescence is itself a key constituent in the practice of imitation.

In chapter 2, I turn to the first of my anti-Ovidians, George Chapman, examining his neglected debut, *The Shadow of Night*, before proceeding to its sequel, *Ovid's Banquet of Sense*, long the subject of critical controversy. I show the latter volume to be a self-corrective recapitulation of the problems and opportunities posed by the Ovidian vogue to young poets in the 1590s. Of course, the clamour surrounding Ovid in this period also drew the attention of the most renowned of England's living poets, Edmund Spenser, who had claimed laureate status with the publication of the first part of *The Faerie Queene* in 1590. In chapter 3, I discuss the bleak "Legend of Justice," at the heart of the epic's 1596 continuation, as Spenser's reinvention of his authorial self through a radically new allusive process. In a decisive departure from the cautious intertextuality of his earlier work, Spenser alludes systematically to the victimized mortals of the *Metamorphoses*, attesting his deep discomfort with imperial policy in Ireland. While Spenser's allusive choreography reaffirms the inexhaustibility of the Ovidian corpus as a poetic resource, by 1596 the very fecundity of the *Metamorphoses* seems as much a menace to the poet as an advantage, as Ovid's reanimated myths invade the formerly Virgilian epic, and overtake the malfunctional mechanisms of symbolic "justice" meant to subjugate or expel them.

This post-metamorphic Ovidian landscape likewise figures prominently in the following chapter, on Michael Drayton's 1595 epyllion, *Endimion and Phoebe*, and his monumental 1597 collection, *Englands Heroicall Epistles*. Like Spenser, Drayton limits his engagement with the Ovidian corpus, gingerly identifying himself as a "partial" imitator of Ovid in the preface to his bestselling volume. But where Spenser constructs an allusive counter-narrative to his own triumphal allegory, Drayton marshals a different set of Ovidian allusions into a sweeping critique of the ineptitude and insouciance of his professional rivals. Only nominally restricted to his epistolary model in Ovid's *Heroides*, he unfolds the full gamut of imitative approaches to the classical tradition, as each ventriloquized "author" compares her or his present plight to the affirmative or admonitory paradigms of the *Metamorphoses*.

The final chapter locates John Donne's apparent antagonism to traditional erotic and mythological models squarely on the spectrum of imitative responses to Ovid's celebrity. Whereas scholars have tended to exclude fashionable Ovidianism from the narrative of Donne's career, or at best have gestured broadly at vague influences on the early elegies, I scrutinize an understudied group of Donne's Elizabethan poems – the epigrams, the revisionist *ars amatoria* "Love's Progress," and the abortive satirical epic *Metempsychosis* – to define his coherent program of poetic self-promotion as Ovid's successor and antithesis. Even after turning away from his hard-won but troublesome status as England's new *praeceptor amoris*, and from secular poetry entirely, the mature Donne does not seek to expunge his own Ovidian record so much as to reorient strategically our sense of his antagonism to bygone literary fashion. *The Ovidian Vogue* concludes with a brief discussion of Ben Jonson's repeated, compulsive, and violent efforts to purge Ovidian influence from his vast body of work across many poetic genres, illustrating ironically Ovid's lingering presence in the cultural memory of the seventeenth century and beyond.

1 Impotence and Stillbirth: Nashe, Shakespeare, and the Ovidian Debut

Francis Meres's famous acclamation of Shakespeare as the poetic repository for "the sweete wittie soule of *Ouid*" arrives in the middle of his "Comparative discourse of our English Poets," and differs little from his praise for other luminaries. Meres does, however, distinguish one contemporary, the satiric pamphleteer Thomas Nashe, with his warmest regard, slipping from third-person adjudication into personal address:

> As *Actæon* was wooried of his owne hounds: so is *Tom Nash* of his *Ile of Dogs*. Dogges were the death of *Euripedes*, but bee not disconsolate young *Iuuenall*, *Linus*, the sonne of *Apollo* died the same death. Yet God forbid that so braue a witte should so basely perish, thine are but paper dogges, neither is thy banishment like *Ouids*, eternally to conuerse with the barbarous *Getes*. Therefore comfort thy selfe sweete *Tom*. with *Ciceros* glorious return to Rome, & with the counsel *Aeneas* giues to his seabeaten soldiors.[1]

For once, the unimaginative Meres varies his accustomed mode of authorial comparison according to genre by pushing Nashe into the familiar frame of Ovid's myth of Actaeon. Meres is tempted to break his rhetorical mould by the accidental similarity between the literal hounds that devoured Actaeon and the titular beasts of Nashe's *Isle of Dogs*, a lost 1597 play so infuriating to the Elizabethan authorities that its co-author Ben Jonson and two fellow actors were imprisoned, while Nashe was forced to flee from London to Yarmouth.[2] Meres seems to sense, however, an unfortunate aspect to his comparison of Nashe's exile to Actaeon's demise, as readers generally interpreted Ovid's myth allegorically as a moral counsel – Actaeon's hounds corresponding to his lustful thoughts or acquisitive nature – which in this case would imply that Nashe is justly "wooried" by his own satirical creation.[3] The ensuing biographical comparisons accordingly distance Nashe's "paper dogges" from Actaeon's lethal hounds, and Meres further dissociates Nashe's temporary self-exile among the Yarmouth fishermen from Ovid's "eternal" banishment among the "barbarous" Getes.

Meres protests too much, however, as Nashe's pamphlets could not be further from Ciceronian elegance or Virgilian elevation, while compelling affinities between Nashe and Ovid persist.[4] Indeed, as Meres was writing his "Discourse," Nashe was producing his *Lenten Stuffe* in Yarmouth, which includes a prominent mock-Ovidian aetiology for the red herring, adapted from the myth of Hero and Leander. Though Nashe accredits the myth to Musaeus and Marlowe, his elaborate yet jocular treatment testifies not only to the Elizabethan absorption of Ovidian mythographic style, but to the contemporary perception of aetiology and metamorphosis as comically overblown, old-fashioned literary tropes.[5] The alternative Ovidian type of the exilic poet, on the other hand, held a more poignant, less mutable significance for the Elizabethans; hence Meres's anxious effort to "comfort" his "sweete *Tom*" by dissociating his temporary trouble from Ovid's permanent fate, and hence too Nashe's own prominent allusion to the *Tristia*, "I may iustly complaine, with *Ouid, Anchora iam nostram non tenet ulla ratem*" (*Lenten Stuff*, 156, quoting *Tr.* 5.2, "No anchor now holds my bark").

The chagrin of *Lenten Stuff* may only be a passing, "dishumored" reflection on the unfortunate circumstances of 1597, but as recently as 1593, Nashe had earned notoriety by declaring his Ovidian status unmistakably in his obscene poem *The Choice of Valentines*, sometimes called by its alternate title, "Thomas Nashe his Dildo."[6] The two titles trace the dubious progress of the poem's antiheroic persona, the diminutively eponymous Thomalin, as he pursues his beloved Francis, an androgynous prostitute, from a festive English country green to a Bankside whorehouse.[7] Though the poem opens on a Chaucerian landscape reminiscent of the *Parlement of Foules* and its free-love Valentine's Day, we quickly find Nashe's workaday characters stifled by legal and moral repression and economic constriction.[8] Francis has been "scar'd" from the provinces to London's red-light district by "Good Iustice Dudgeinhaft, and crab-tree face," whose punitive "bills and staues" replace the kissing "bills" of Chaucer's lovebirds (19–24).[9] This dispiriting pattern recurs through the poem; although Thomalin quickly locates Francis and purchases her services, he ejaculates prematurely during sex and loses his erection, and after watching his beloved pleasure herself with the titular dildo, he departs penniless and disgraced.

Alongside this downshift from Valentine's Day in the country to whoring in the city, Nashe traces a corresponding literary devolution, from the nostalgic (and no longer habitable) Chaucerian green-world to an urban space recognizable as contemporary London, but allusively superimposed over the notoriously decadent Rome of Ovid's erotic elegies. Hence, Nashe's poem presents a frenetic revision of *Amores* 3.7 (numbered 3.6 in early modern editions), the infamous elegy in which Ovid's oversexed persona laments his own sudden impotence. Thomalin's impotent fury at the dildo – "God giue thee shame, thow blinde mischapen owle … / I reade thee beardles blab, beware of stripes … / Thow wilt be whipt with nettles for this geare" (288, 291, 293) – ironically resembles Ovid's comic recrimination of his own uncooperative penis, whom he addresses in the second person as a "shamefaced creature," or as Nashe's contemporary and rival Marlowe translates the lines in *All Ovids Elegies*:

> quae nunc, ecce, vigent intempestiva valentque,
> nunc opus exposcunt militiamque suam.
> quin istic pudibunda iaces, pars pessima nostri?
> sic sum pollicitis captus et ante tuis.
>
> Now when he should not jette, he boults upright,
> And craves his taske, and seekes to be at fight.
> Lie downe with shame, and see thou stirre no more,
> Seeing thou wouldst deceive me as before. (*AOE* 3.6.67–70)[10]

As Nashe admits frankly in an apologetic sonnet he appends to his poem, Ovid "is the fountaine whence my streames doe flowe."

The irony that "streames" of poetic influence "doe flowe" even when other streams do not is at the heart of Nashe's intricately allusive and challenging poem, and in the first portion of this opening chapter I discuss the *Choice* as a provocative paradigm for the early phase of the Ovidian vogue of the 1590s. Contemporaneous with Shakespeare's popular *Titus Andronicus*, Nashe's understudied poem presents another side of the vogue; that is, the new viability of Ovidian imitations tailored to the tastes of private patrons and coterie audiences. Having begun as a hack, producing satirical prose pamphlets for the Elizabethan court's propaganda war against the clandestine publication of the

Marprelate tracts in the late 1580s, with the *Choice* Nashe reintroduces himself as the most explicit, most outrageous of London's Ovidians. Angling for patronage from the same nobleman – Ferdinando Stanley, aptly titled Lord Strange – who had already leant his favour to Marlowe and other Ovidian poets and playwrights, Nashe was nevertheless taking a risk by submitting so objectionable a work even to private readers, and indeed twenty years later John Davies would recall "goodmens hate" tearing the "dampned *Dildo*" to shreds.[11] Such a reception raises a number of questions: if the *Choice* in its time was Nashe's calculated bid for recognition as a fashionable Ovidian poet, what were the stakes and potential rewards of his gambit? By what means and to what extent did he hedge the venture, or could he expect such a poem to define him irrevocably as an Ovidian? How does the relationship this first-time poet traces between literary imitation and sexual impotence bear upon our sense of the vogue's advent and its long-term prospects in late Elizabethan culture?

However we answer these questions, the *Choice* must remain a gateway text for the study of Ovidian poetry in the 1590s, if only because beyond the rhymed couplets of the *Choice* and the blank-verse of *Summers Last Will and Testament* (1592), Nashe barely qualifies as a poet, preferring satirical prose to erotic elegy for the rest of his career.[12] He is not therefore representative of English Ovidianism as it developed over the course of Elizabeth's final decade, nor could his youthful adaptation of one of the *Amores'* sleaziest passages find a wide enough audience to drive its own imitation – the cultural mechanism by which literary traditions compound and vogues evolve. This honour, of course, goes to a pair of mythological poems written within a few years of the *Choice*: Shakespeare's *Venus and Adonis* and Marlowe's *Hero and Leander*. While the latter better resembles Nashe's poem in that it too seems to have been produced initially for a private patron and coterie circulation, Shakespeare once again best illustrates both the deepening intricacy of Ovid's influence and the growing appeal of Ovidian verse. As the vogue's greatest commercial success, the many printed editions of *Venus and Adonis* present the polished, mass-produced counterpart to the inconsistently transmitted manuscripts of Nashe's rough and uneven exercise in pornography.[13]

Accordingly, in the second half of this chapter, I turn from the experimental *Choice* to Shakespeare's searching and prescient debut as an Ovidian poet, exploring in particular his radical approach to the classic Ovidian tropes of metamorphosis and aetiology in the tragic final portion of *Venus and Adonis*. In short, I argue that, while Shakespeare reproduces the floral metamorphosis of Ovid's Adonis with delicate precision, his disconsolate Venus's impulse to uproot the intertextual flower short-circuits the aetiological relation between the Adonis myth and the natural world it once described. No longer a metaphor for springtime rebirth, Shakespeare's Adonis figures metamorphosis – a synecdoche for Ovidian imitation itself – as stillbirth, with far-reaching consequences for how we interpret one of the 1590s' literary touchstones. Having traced between the *Choice of Valentines* and *Venus and Adonis* – the most salacious and most popular Ovidian poems of the English Renaissance, respectively – a miniature history of Ovid's rise to cultural hegemony, the chapter concludes with a brief survey of later poets' efforts to navigate the vogue's implications.

Imitative Choice and Ovidian Compulsion

For smut, Nashe's *Choice of Valentines* proves a surprisingly sophisticated work of literature. The very survival of such an obviously unpublishable poem may derive from its author's astute appraisal of contemporary manuscript culture, as the portion of the poem most objectionable to early modern readers – the hundred lines detailing Francis's employment of the dildo to compensate for Thomalin's erectile dysfunction – is easily cut from the rest of the narrative. Of the poem's six extant manuscripts, three include the passage with the dildo, while three exclude it, making the *Choice* at once the naughtiest and second-naughtiest narrative poem of the English Renaissance, for even in the abridged version, Nashe's pornographic indulgence eclipses the more obliquely erotic passages of the contemporary blue poems of professional rivals – *Hero and Leander* and *Venus and Adonis* most notably.[14] Where Shakespeare displaces his poem's most explicit sex onto a stallion's pursuit of a mare, and Marlowe leaves much of his characters' unruly sexuality to the reader's imagination, Nashe flings open the bedroom door:

> He rubd', and prickt, and pierst hir to the bones,
> Digging as farre as eath he might for stones.
> Now high, now lowe, now stryking short and thick;
> Now dyuing deepe he toucht hir to the quick. (145–8)

Specially censored to provide a more straightforward stimulating reading experience, the shortened version of the *Choice* arrives at its telling extreme in one partly enciphered seventeenth-century manuscript –

held in the Victoria and Albert Museum's Dyce Collection – whose compositor has not only eliminated the dildo sequence, but also the parodic Petrarchan and Neoplatonic interludes that distract the over-imaginative Thomalin from his libidinous purpose in the poem's fuller versions.[15]

After all, following his initial disappointment in the countryside and some fifty lines of bargaining with Francis's bawd, there remain no apparent obstacles to consummation, and Thomalin exclaims:

> Oh, who is able to abstaine so long?
> I com, I com …
> First bare hir leggs, then creepe up to hir kneese.
> From thence ascend unto hir mannely thigh.
> (A pox on lingring when I am so nighe)
> Smock climbe a-pace, that I maie see my ioyes. (98–9, 102–5)

Thomalin's narrative "ascent" from "leggs" to "kneese" to "thigh" inverts the blazon's usual progress from the beloved's hair downward, but even before we register this error the almost inadvertent "I com, I com" comes far too early. Indeed, as he pursues his sexual goal with an efficiency that mocks the interminability of contemporary sonnet-sequences, Thomalin finds himself too stimulated to describe his partner's body in detail; his sole adjective, "mannely," reminds us of Francis's androgyny. Once he beholds Francis's vagina, however, he pauses foolishly for rhapsodic foreplay:

> Oh heauen, and paradize are all but toyes,
> Compar'd with this sight …
> A prettie rysing wombe without a weame,
> That shone as bright as anie siluer streame;
> And bare out lyke the bending of an hill,
> At whose decline a fountaine dwelleth still,
> That hath his mouth besett with uglie bryers
> Resembling much a duskie nett of wyres. (106–7, 109–14)

This description reduces the familiar gendered landscape of Renaissance romance – the hills and streams of Spenser's Garden of Adonis – to a prone and vulnerable corporeal topography, and by implication elevates Thomalin momentarily to the omnipotence of a sky god. As in the opening scene's abrupt removal from the Chaucerian *locus amœnus* to the brothel, however, the description loses itself precipitously in the "uglie bryers" of Francis's genitalia. It is not Sartrean disgust so much as a sudden loss of *enargeia*: a rhetorical failure prefiguring and contributing to Thomalin's sexual malfunction. Ejaculating prematurely during a playful spanking, he barely registers the fact as narrator:

> A loftie buttock barred with azure veine's,
> Whose comelie swelling, when my hand distreine's,
> Or wanton checketh with a harmeless stype,
> It makes the fruites of loue eftsoone be rype;
> And pleasure pluckt too tymelie from the stemme
> To dye ere it hath seene Ierusalem.
> Oh Gods, that euer any thing so sweete
> So suddenlie should fade awaie and fleete. (115–22)

Nashe marks this emergency with the most explicit allusion in the entire *Choice*, as Thomalin laments, "Hir arme's are spread, and I am all unarm'd. / Lyke one with Ouids cursed hemlock charm'd, / So are my limm's unwieldie for the fight" (123–5). While the first line's equation of *amor* with *arma* is commonplace, it resonates with Ovid's well-known sentence from the first book of the *Amores*, *Militat omnis amans, et habet sua castra Cupido* (*Am.* 1.9.1, "Every lover is a soldier, and Cupid has a camp of his own"), which may prompt the allusive hemlock in the following line, as Thomalin likens himself to the impotent persona of the *Amores*:

> At non formosa est, at non bene culta puella,
> at, puto, non votis saepe petita meis!
> hanc tamen in nullos tenui male languidus usus,
> sed iacui pigro crimen onusque toro …
> et mihi blanditias dixit dominumque vocavit,
> et quae praeterea publica verba iuvant.
> tacta tamen veluti gelida mea membra cicuta
> segnia propositum destituere meum …
>
> Either she was foule, or her attire was bad,
> Or she was not the wench I wisht t'have had.
> Idly I lay with her, as if I lov'd not,
> And like a burthen griev'd the bed that mov'd not …
> Yea, and she soothd me up, and calld me sir,

> And usde all speech that might provoke, and stirre.
> Yet like as if cold Hemlock I had drunke,
> It mocked me, hung downe the head, and sunke. (*AOE* 3.6.1–4, 11–14)

By transposing the Latin text's *veluti* (a comparative element, here translated "as if") to the beginning of Thomalin's simile – "Lyke one with Ouids cursed hemlock charm'd" – Nashe quietly literalizes the original, as if Ovid had not only drunk the poisonous hemlock (*cicuta*), but had taken possession of it, even dispensed it to others. Where Marlowe's contemporary translation amplifies and to some extent justifies the Ovidian persona's comical suspicion that his sudden impotence is due to witchcraft, Nashe's "charm'd" reassigns the witchcraft to Ovid himself.

In a sense, of course, Thomalin's premature ejaculation is precisely the inverse of Ovid's impotence, but in forestalling consummation the two opposed sexual malfunctions amount to the same catastrophe, at least for Francis, who finds herself in the same sad situation as Ovid's *puella*, crying, "Vnhappie me … and wilt' not stand? / Com, lett me rubb and chafe it with my hand" (131–2). Ovid relates, *Hanc etiam non est mea dedignata puella / mollitur admota sollicitare manu / sed … nullas consurgere posse per artes …* (*AOE* 3.6.73–5, "Nay more the wench did not disdaine a whit, / To take it in her hand, and play with it. / But … she sawe it would by no meanes stand"). So absolute is the Ovidian persona's impotence that it resists all encouragement from the *puella*, in a sense rendering her impotent as well, nor is this contagious aspect of impotence limited to the *Amores*, but spreads intertextually to the hapless couples of subsequent imitations. Hence, M.L. Stapleton has identified Francis's lament over Thomalin's flaccidity with the fifth elegy of the late Latin poet Maximianus (commonly identified in the Renaissance with the Gallus to whom Virgil addressed his *Eclogues* and whom Ovid identified as a direct influence). The courtesan of Maximianus's poem proves no more successful than Ovid's frustrated *puella* at revivifying the impotent *senex* who narrates the elegy, and in the second half of the poem she embarks on a furious, parodically apocalyptic complaint against penises everywhere.[16] If Nashe's Thomalin fears the taste of "Ouids cursed hemlock," Francis echoes the lament of an intervening poet's *puella*, who has suffered the poison's effects at one remove. The protagonists of the *Choice* seem on the verge of joining this intertextual community of frustrated lovers, whose unhappy members likewise include Marlowe's translated persona and his dissatisfied partner.

Fortunately for Thomalin, Francis succeeds where her predecessors failed:

> She tooke and rould it on hir thigh,
> And when she lookt' on't, she would weepe and sighe,
> And dandled it, and dance't it up and doune,
> Not ceasing, till she rais'd it from his swoune.
> And then he flue on hir as he were wood,
> And on hir breeche did thack, and foyne a-good …
> Plaie while him list; and thrust he neare so hard,
> Poore pacient Grisill lyeth at hir warde,
> And giue's, and take's as blythe and free as Maye,
> And ere-more meete's him in the midle waye. (139–44, 151–4)

As the sex is so good for Thomalin, so directly opposed to the Ovidian impasse of impotence and frustration, the narrative returns to the Chaucerian register of the poem's opening lines: "Poore pacient Grisill" sexualizes the grotesquely demure heroine of Chaucer's misogynistic *Clerk's Tale*, while "blythe and free as Maye" recalls the adulterous wife of the *Merchant's Tale*. Here, as throughout the *Choice*, the clearest Chaucerian allusions correspond to the persona's virility, his capacity to perform sexually as a proper Englishman.

From this momentary triumph, Thomalin proceeds – with startling rhetorical dissonance, but at the same time with the erotic author's appreciation for the alternating abandon and sublimity of sexual encounter – to an overwrought Neoplatonic vision that in context must be parody, but could easily be extracted and inserted verbatim into any legitimate Renaissance love poem:

> On him hir eyes continualy were fixt,
> With hir eye-beames his melting looke's were mixt,
> Which lyke the Sunne, that twixt tuo glasses plaies
> From one to th'other cast's rebounding rayes.
> He lyke a starre, that to reguild his beames
> Sucks-in the influence of Phebus streames … (155–60)

Thomalin's enthusiasm barrels onward for a dozen more lines before Francis interrupts, "Oh not so fast, … / Leaste my content, that on thy life relyes / Be brought too-soone from his delightfull seate, / And me unwares of hoped bliss defeate" (179–82). Despite this plea for orgasmic mutuality, Thomalin ejaculates again, this time likening the act to Jove's impregnation of Danaë, "Hould wyde thy lap, my louelie Danae, / And entertaine the golden shoure so free, / That trilling falles into thy treasurie" (193–5). At this climactic moment (and only here), the poem's Ovidian and Chaucerian registers converge, as Francis at last achieves her own orgasm, "With Oh, and Oh, she itching moues her hipps, / And to and fro, full lightlie starts and skips. / She ierks hir leggs, and sprauleth with hir heeles, / No tongue maie tell the solace that she feeles" (199–202). While one manuscript replaces "solace" with mere "pleasures," the other compositors prefer the Chaucerian archaism – the sexual "solace" of the *Canterbury Tales'* fabliaux. This is enough Valentine's Day poetry for the impatient compositor of the Dyce manuscript, however, who skips ahead to the poem's final lines, "What can be added more to my renowne? / She lyeth breathlesse, I am taken doune, / The waues doe swell, the tydes climbe or'e the banks, / Iudge gentlemen if I deserue not thanks" (311–14).[17]

Were all the manuscript copies of Nashe's poem as straightforward as the radical Dyce abridgment, the *Choice* would deserve the dismissal (or at best, relegation) it has received from scholars until recently. But in its longer versions, Francis desires further satisfaction, while Thomalin can no longer perform, at which point the poem transforms from the *Choice of Valentines* into *Thomas Nashe his Dildo*. Indeed, the climactic passage provides a veritable instruction manual for the assembly and use of a dildo, couched ironically in anatomical terms:

> He is a youth almost tuo handfulls highe,
> Streight, round, and plumb, yett hauing but one eye ...
> Attired in white veluet or in silk,
> And nourisht with whott water or with milk ...
> Vpon a charriot of fiue wheeles he rydes,
> The which an arme strong driuer stedfast guide's,
> And often alters pace, as wayes growe deepe ...
> In clammie waies he treaddeth by and by,
> And plasheth and sprayeth all that be him nye. (269–70, 273–4,
> 277–9, 283–4)

Thomalin's bitter description is effectively a "Wanted" poster for the dildo: "If anie wight a cruell mistris serue's ... / Curse Eunuke dilldo, senceless, conterfet, / Who sooth maie fill, but neuer can begett" (261,

263–4). Especially in the longer version of the *Choice*, then, Nashe exposes the lingering sexual anxieties of early modern England's patriarchal culture, for the dildo enables Francis to dispense with Thomalin entirely – "she lyeth breathlesse, I am taken doune," takes on a very different meaning – yet he pays the brothel's madam "scott and lott at moste," and leaves looking "as leane and lank as anie ghoste" (312, 309–10), bearing his Chaucer and his Petrarch with him.[18] Francis, meanwhile, has achieved a sexual satisfaction unrelated to any of Thomalin's poetic precedents, remaining emphatically independent of the elegaic community of impotence he is obliged to join. The only "choice" in the *Choice of Valentines* is Francis's preference of her own dildo to the same old impotence.

As a prosthesis, the dildo serves as more than merely an erotic aide to Francis (or to Nashe's voyeuristic readers); it also presents a metaphoric commentary on the manufacture and reception of imitative poetry. For Thomalin, the imperative throughout the poem's first half is to overcome Ovid's "cursed hemlock," and to achieve instead the sexual ideal (and idyll) of giving and receiving "solace" in the native Chaucerian tradition. Doing so requires he avoid his predilection to apostrophize sex in the overwrought and artificial manner of contemporary amorous verse – Neoplatonic and Petrarchan, above all – for each such stylistic distraction leads to his literal loss of turgidity. Construing Thomalin thus as an initial proxy for Nashe as the imitative poet, guided by his own confused sense of competing literary fashions, Francis becomes a corresponding proxy for the reader of the *Choice*, for a coterie audience craving salacious verse. What kind of verse, exactly? Surely not Chaucerian, for Francis never evinces the nostalgia for the countryside Thomalin apparently feels, and she seems happy enough, well paid, and self-satisfied in the London whorehouse. Francis wants something new, something more than what little Thomalin (or the johns before him) can offer. The readerly impulses and appetites thus embodied in Francis guide the poet's hand in turn, as Nashe abandons his own persona to the quagmire of elegiac precedents, preferring the unprecedented titillation of the dildo sequence. Francis's "choice" could not be more final: "Adiew unconstant loue, to thy disporte ... / Henceforth no more will I implore thine ayde, / Or thee, or men of cowardize upbrayde. / My little dilldo shall suplye their kinde" (233, 237–9).

Francis may fare better than Ovid's *puella*, but we should nevertheless consider the concessions Nashe has made to the overwhelming elegaic tradition. In the *Amores*, after all, Ovid testifies repeatedly to his persona's sexual prowess, nowhere more so than in the notorious impotence elegy, with its protests of bygone virility:

> at nuper bis flava Chlide, ter candida Pitho,
> ter Libas officio continuata meo est;
> exigere a nobis angusta nocte Corinnam
> me memini numeros sustinuisse novem. (*Am.* 3.7.23–6)

> Yet boorded I the golden *Chie* twise,
> And *Libas*, and the white cheekt *Pitho* thrice.
> *Corinna* crav'd it in a summers night,
> And nine sweete bowts we had before day-light (*AOE* 3.6.23–6)

Of course, we can hardly trust the Ovidian persona's grandiose memory of his many conquests in the midst of defeat, but even if we doubt his boast (or the very existence of his mistresses), sexual mutuality remains theoretically possible throughout the *Amores*. The persona ironically regains his erection after the *puella* leaves unsatisfied, revealing that he has endured such failures before, presumably followed by a return to form. In contrast, Nashe forecloses all hope of mutuality in the narrower confines of Francis's brothel. Although Thomalin proves resilient to an extent, regaining his erection long enough to satisfy himself, to Francis's disappointment there is no chance of the satisfaction bestowed upon Chlide, Pitho, Libas, and above all Corinna. Penniless, superseded, and dismissed, Thomalin not only fails to provide what Francis wants, but surrenders the very idea of such virility as the stuff of myth: "I am not as was Hercules the stout, / That to the seauenth iournie could hould out" (301–2).

By cutting the deadwood Thomalin loose and replacing him with Francis's inexhaustible dildo, Nashe would seem to free his poem from the constraints of the impotence tradition, but there is a further and heavier price to be paid for this liberty: namely, a rootless, branchless sterility. The Ovidian persona's self-flattering boasts of a once-and-future potency had seemed far-fetched, but the imprecations of Nashe's vindictive "ghost" are manifestly true. Francis has indeed preferred the "Eunuke dilldo" to the man, an epitome of eros to eros itself. As readers, we may approve her "choice," like the seventeenth-century readers who transcribed the poem in full, but we should not expect this poet to offer any further choices. After all, what more can he provide, beyond the foreplay, eroticism, autoeroticism, voyeurism, shame, and satire with which he has filled his poetic debut? To expect an *Amores* or an *All Ovids Elegies* from Nashe after the *Choice* is like imagining Francis bearing children to "Eunuke dilldo."

Having spent his utmost prematurely, Nashe as poet is threatened with an ironic dismissal to his persona's impotent place, until there is no distance between the two in the poem's final passage:

> I pennd this storie onelie for my self,
> Who giuing suck unto a childish Elfe,
> And ["Am"?] quite discourag'd in my nurserie,
> Since all my store seemes to hir, penurie.
> I am not as was Hercules the stout,
> That to the seauenth iournie could hould out.
> I want those hearbe's and rootes of Indian soile,
> That strengthen wearie members in their toile ...
> Sufficeth, all I haue, I yeald hir hole,
> Which for a poore man is a princelie dole. (297–304, 307–8)

Nashe's persona fantasizes a self-fulfilment in ridiculous emulation of the happy Francis – a kind of penis-envy with gender roles reversed – though this soon gives way to a confession of total emasculation in the ensuing metaphor of having nursed the "childish Elfe" (i.e., the *Dildo*), until it no longer required nourishment and could operate independently. Indeed, this final complaint of exclusion ruefully recalls the over-exuberant heterosexuality of the poem's first half, as a "want" of aphrodisiacs replaces the need to counteract "Ouids cursed hemlock," and as Thomalin's triumphant self-image as Jove hovering over Danaë gives way to that of an effeminate Hercules subjugated by Omphale. Nashe's final puns cut in every conceivable way; "all I haue" (his money, his semen, his poetry), he admits, "I yeald hir hole" (her purse, her vagina, the reader's desire for more). Meanwhile, the "princelie dole" (great expense, great pain, great remorse) suggests a full community of male impotence, from "poore man" to prince or from Thomalin to Hercules. Indeed, by this point even the dullest of Nashe's male coterie readers, "watching" a sexual gratification beyond his capacity, must recognize the satirical price to be paid for the marginal increase of voyeuristic titillation offered by the *Choice*.

John Davies, whose 1611 "Papers Complaint" gives voice to the reams of paper abused by the poets of the 1590s, registers this anxiety over the emasculating effects of reading the *Choice* when he recalls that "good-mens hate did me in peeces teare"; a private vandalism for self-defence, as much as a public act of moral censure.[19] At the same time, Davies's retrospective "Complaint," which includes equally anxious images of female readers masturbating to Shakespeare's *Venus and Adonis* in "venerian speculation" (i.e., in the mirror, or with the poem as mirror), implies a mixed audience for Nashe's *Choice* and poems like it. Thomalin's parting injunction, "Regarde not Dames, what Cupids Poete writes" (296), is tongue-in-cheek, ironically and exclusively addressing female readers who have just finished reading of Francis's masturbation (Nashe thus annexes Ovid's traditional title of "Cupids Poete" for himself). The *Choice*'s potential to attract these female readers doubles the threat it poses to male readers, who must now prevent their wives or mistresses from playing Mistress Francis – that is, from preferring the "Dildo" to a penis – while defending themselves against emasculation.[20] Whether exasperated to the point of violent censorship or aroused to climax, Davies's depiction of the consumers of "such bawdy Geare," however dubious as an account of actual reading practice, helpfully conveys a sense of readerly compulsion, a telling lack of interpretive "choice." In its most objectionable aspect, the poem figures its censors as prudes, its readers as whores, and the poet himself as a bawd.

Perhaps in flight from this last identity, Nashe effectively retracts his poem in the apologetic sonnet to Stanley, appended to the longer versions of the *Choice* manuscripts. Strikingly, he disowns the poem by making Ovid his "fall guy":

> Thus hath my penne presum'd to please my friend;
> Oh mightst thow lykewise please Apollo's eye.
> No: Honor brooke's no such impietie;
> Yett Ouids wanton Muse did not offend.
> He is the fountaine whence my streames doe flowe.
> Forgiue me if I speake as I was taught,
> A lyke to women, utter all I knowe,
> As longing to unlade so bad a fraught.
> My mynde once purg'd of such lasciuious witt,
> With purifide word's, and hallowed verse
> Thy praises in large volumes shall rehearce,
> That better maie thy grauer view befitt.
> Meanewhile yett rests, yow smile at what I write,
> Or for attempting, banish me your sight.

By portraying himself as Ovid's pupil, Nashe concedes poetic authority to the original *praeceptor amoris*, as the Roman poet grandiloquently titles himself in his *Ars amatoria* (1.17). Nashe's contention that "Ouids wanton Muse did not offend" is all but unaccountable, unless in the sense that the Muse did not offend the *praeceptor* himself, for in the *Tristia* the forlorn Ovid cites his own *Ars* as the youthful indiscretion partly responsible for his exile from Rome to the empire's bleakest frontier (*Tr.* 2.2.207). Hence the anxiety of the sonnet's closing couplet, in which Nashe figures his patron as the all-powerful Augustus, and himself as risking Ovid's fate. In an apparent effort to forestall this "banishment," Nashe excuses his *Choice* as a purgative preliminary to the "hallowed verse" of poetic maturity, the "large volumes" – presumably epic poems – he will write to honour his aristocratic patron.

That Stanley died within a year of the composition of the *Choice* may have little to do with Nashe's failure to make good on his sonnet's promise of an epic sequel. In the immediate context of 1592, Nashe's sonnet would likely be interpreted as a joke at the general expense of poets with epic pretentions, and at the particular expense of Spenser, whose 1590 *Faerie Queene* had earned some financial remuneration from Queen Elizabeth, but little lasting favour at court. Gesturing towards "Ouids wanton Muse," Nashe further undercuts his promise by echoing Ovid's own disingenuous expression of remorse for having failed to compensate for his *lascivia Musa* with poetry on the theme of *immania Caesaris acta* (*Tr.* 2.313, 335, "Caesar's mighty deeds"). But however hollow Nashe's assurances of epic progress, the apologetic sonnet, like the *Choice* itself, should be read in relation to the wider Ovidian vogue; the poem capitalizes on Ovid's burgeoning celebrity, while the sonnet disowns his age-old notoriety.[21] Although the closing couplet appears to leave to the patron the ultimate "choice" between Augustus's imperial rigour and a lighter, more merciful response, both options flatter Stanley: in the one case, he becomes the new Augustus, in the other he improves upon Augustus.[22] The image of the bifronted patron is familiar enough from any number of authorial dedications, but in this case the possibility of disapproval is underwritten by the historical fact of Ovid's exile, and the final line of Nashe's sonnet exposes the trepidation with which he has assumed the Ovidian voice.

As the detachable appendage to the *Choice*, after all, the sonnet resembles *Thomas Nashe his Dildo* itself, and recapitulates the poem's dizzying sexual ambiguities ironically in miniature. By identifying Ovid directly with the dildo ("He is the fountaine whence my streames doe flowe"), Nashe implies his own effeminacy, and the sonnet's ensuing puns toy with this notion that the male poet, having once seized on the "lasciuious witt" of his precursor, must play the woman's part (i.e., the part of Francis in the poem) until he may "unlade so bad a fraught." By "unlading" the Ovidian dildo and "purging" it of "such lasciuious witt," Nashe will reclaim his masculinity, though only in the punning, negative sense of "unlad[y]-ing." Until that false orgasmic moment, however, he remains "A lyke to women," and this central pun – that the poet of the *Choice* is like women but is also liked by them – threatens to emasculate Nashe's male reader even further. Having read this far, he has presumably enjoyed the poem about a woman enjoying her dildo, perhaps even masturbating to its pornographic content (and rendering himself as "soft" as the poem's Thomalin in the process). The sonnet's reader, then, is left with one last "choice": put the dildo-poem down to resume a masculinity striving towards the "hallowed verse" and "large volumes" of epic, or pick the poem up again for renewed stimulation and remain "lyke to women," akin to the androgynous Francis refilling the spent dildo with fresh fluid.

For poet, patron, and reader alike, there is only one way forward: disowning Ovidian verse (at least the erotic variety). Despite Nashe's intertextual promiscuity – the dreamy Chaucer, the self-defeating Petrarchism, the plaintive Maximianus – the *Choice of Valentines* remains fundamentally an Ovidian poem. "Forgiue me if I speake as I was taught," Nashe writes in the sonnet, with the understanding that the patron (and the readers he represents) will forgive him only on the condition that he renounce his dubious status as *praeceptor amoris*. Indeed, the brief postscript included in at least one manuscript edition of the *Choice – Claudito [sic. Claudite] iam riuos Priape, sat prata biberunt. Tho: Nash.* ("Shut off the springs now, Priapus, the meadows have drunk enough") – refers us not to Ovid's *Amores*, but to Virgil's *Eclogues* (3.110–11). Originally addressed to a pair of young shepherds (*pueri*) to signal the end of a pastoral singing contest, Nashe (or perhaps the manuscript's compositor) perversely readdresses the imperative to the phallic god. The postscript no longer signals the end of a pastoral poem, but rather the silencing of the elegaic voice. If Ovid "is the fountaine whence [Nashe's] streames doe flowe," then closing off the *rivos* not only renders Priapus himself ironically impotent, but neutralizes Ovid's influence on Nashe, disconnecting the "fountaine" of influence from the "streames" of imitation.

This is not to say that Nashe abandoned Ovid as a congenial, even inspirational source, but he did abandon the imitation of Ovid – whether the strict, slavish pursuit of style and form mocked by Erasmus or the extensive latitude granted to imitators by Roger Ascham and Philip Sidney.[23] *Pierce Pennilesse, The Unfortunate Traveller,* and all of Nashe's pamphlets are peppered with Ovidian allusions, heralding the pointed asides and broad parodies of *Lenten Stuff,* but Nashe avoids any more sustained or systematic engagement with this most fashionable of classical models after the *Choice,* perhaps even to the point of abandoning verse itself. Of course, what I call "abandonment" may only reflect the patron's untimely death or Nashe's writerly disposition – after all, Drayton recalls him as a "Proser" (though in the midst of a catalogue of laurel-crowned poets) – but conversely there is never any sense even in the *Choice* that Nashe considers Ovidianism a promising model for the development of a literary career. For Nashe, erotic elegy is like Francis's dildo: an outrageous bid for attention, appealing to certain types of readers and perfect for rereading and transcription, but sterile and puerile – "Eunuke dilldo … a youth almost tuo handfulls highe."

Ultimately, disseminating the *Choice of Valentines,* if only in manuscript, may not have been worth the notoriety, as the Ovidian label proved difficult for Nashe to shake. While Meres was sympathetic enough not to press too heavily on his own association of the *Isle of Dogs* with the fate of Actaeon, Nashe's inveterate foe Gabriel Harvey gleefully exploited the stigma in his *Pierce's Supererogation:* "One Ouid was too-much for Roome, and one [Robert] Greene too-much for London: but one Nashe more intolerable then both; not bicause his witt is anye thinge comparable, but bicause his will is more outragious."[24] If the *Choice* had advertised Nashe's facility at *aemulatio* – what G.W. Pigman identifies as the imitator's eristic "surpassing" of the model – Harvey's indictment made a vice of that virtue: Ovid only more so. Nashe's rejoinder was a curious equivocation:

> I should haue forgot to haue answerd for the *baudie rymes* he threapes vpon me. Are they *rymes*? and are they *baudie*? and are they *mine*? Well, it may be so that it is not so; or if it be, men in their youth (as in their sleep) manie times doo something that might have been better done, & they do not wel remember.[25]

Without confessing to the *Choice's* authorship, Nashe nevertheless conditionally retracts the poem as youthful folly, best forgotten. The safety mechanism built into the sonnet to Stanley – the "longing to unlade so bad a fraught" – seems to have failed. Harvey is no fair judge of Nashe, but he testifies to the vulnerability of at least one of the Ovidian postures available to the poets of the 1590s.

There were other Ovids to imitate, of course, beyond the impotent complainer of the *Amores*, and many of Nashe's contemporaries turned to these alternative models in the following years. Like Nashe, some of these poets – the brothers John and Francis Beaumont, for example – seem to have considered Ovidianism a youthful posture, appropriate only for a poetic apprenticeship or first publication; others, like Spenser and Shakespeare, revisited Ovid time and again. These greater poets demonstrated, as Nashe could not, that by the 1590s an evolving Ovidian style could signal professional self-awareness, even a laureate maturity.[26] At the same time, Nashe's *Choice* helps to clarify several of the more important and distinctive aspects of the Ovidian vogue: namely, that the poet's turn to Ovid always entailed a wager of present fashionability against perennial notoriety; that the poet addressed and responded pre-emptively to an audience specially attuned to Ovidian models; and that poet and audience alike considered Ovidianism a passing fad, an inherently ephemeral cultural phenomenon. Whether by calculation or compulsion, Nashe gave way before this last, most dynamic aspect of literary fashion, but in any case his concession may not have registered much beyond Harvey's condescension. By 1593 Shakespeare had integrated the perceived ephemerality of the Ovidian vogue so fully and so significantly into his own *Venus and Adonis*, that ever since Nashe's *Choice of Valentines* has been read as nothing but a blue footnote to literary history.

Deflowering Adonis

Flowers carpet Ovid's *Metamorphoses*: Narcissus, Ajax, Hyacinthus, Clytie, Pyramus and Thisbe (whose blood stains the mulberry purple), throwaways like Crocus and Smilax.[27] It is in the *Fasti*, however, that Ovid effectively declares himself the florist-in-chief of classical mythology, in the boast of Flora, the goddess of flowers herself:

> prima per immensas sparsi nova semina gentes:
> unius tellus ante coloris erat.
> prima Therapnaeo feci de sanguine florem,
> et manet in folio scripta querella suo.
> tu quoque nomen habes cultos, Narcisse, per hortos,
> infelix, quod non alter et alter eras.
> quid Crocon aut Attin referam Cinyraque creatum,
> de quorum per me volnere surgit honor? (*Fasti* 5.221–8)

I was the first to scatter new seeds among the countless peoples; till then the earth had been of but one colour. I was the first to make a flower out of Therapnaean blood [i.e., from the blood of Hyacinthus], and on its petals the lament remains inscribed. Thou, too, Narcissus, hast a name in the trim gardens, unhappy thou in that thou hadst not a double of thyself. What need to tell of Crocus, and Attis, and the son of Cinyras [i.e., Adonis], from whose wounds by my art doth beauty spring?

The poet is here commemorating the Roman festival of the Floralia, and the goddess's claims are accordingly grandiloquent (she proceeds to boast of her flower-induced delivery of Mars from the womb of Juno), but if Flora cannot justifiably take credit for these mythographic flowers, Ovid may indeed take credit for them, for every one has roots in the *Metamorphoses*. Through Flora, not only does Ovid gather the flowers of his own epic into the full-scale catalogue of the *Fasti* – a light, elegiac variation on Orpheus's assembly of trees in Book 10 of the *Metamorphoses* – but he also ascribes to himself the universal principle of mythographic horticulture, an aetiological function by which all conceivable flowers spring from his own endlessly fertile text.[28] If Flora appears to be a thief of pre-existing myths – or a divine fence for Ovid's intertextual thefts – it is because her loot consists of the *loci amoeni* of prior poets like Bion, Theocritus, and above all Virgil, whose second eclogue features the most famous of all classical flower catalogues. On the other hand, to gather literary flowers is of course the poet's prerogative and responsibility, as the swarm of apian metaphors from Seneca through the Renaissance attests.[29] Ovid is merely the most industrious bee in the literary hive.

Against this colourful backdrop of the Ovidian Floralia, the treatment Shakespeare accords the titular myth of his immensely popular 1593 epyllion, *Venus and Adonis*, at once appears extreme, nor is the distinction merely a question of scope. The movement from the *Metamorphoses* to *Venus and Adonis* is not a step down from epic's macrocosmic elaboration to the microscopic investigation of the epyllion, but a radical reduction of all mythology to a single myth, all metamorphoses into one. In the midst of a culture given over to eclectic imitation, where real gardens like Bomarzo and Nonsuch teemed with effigies of Ovid's nymphs and monsters, Shakespeare's solitary flower must appear extraordinary, indeed unique.[30] Beyond his singular presence, Shakespeare's Adonis proves exceptional in his metamorphic fate – that is, in Venus's peremptory decision to "crop" the flower he becomes, as if uprooting the last of all the myths that once filled those Ovidian gardens. It is a symbolic act as catastrophic, in its microcosmic way, as the epic hero Sir Guyon's destruction of the lush, romantic Bower of Bliss in a single stanza of Spenser's 1590 *Faerie Queene* (2.12.83).[31]

Of course, the startlingly abrupt conclusion of *Venus and Adonis* may not strike readers as the poem's salient feature, for as Clark Hulse notes, "The most remarkable thing about Shakespeare's treatment of the myth of Venus and Adonis is his elimination of its central erotic action."[32] The ostentatious elimination of eros, however, is not independent of Adonis's metamorphosis and demise, but serves instead as the prelude to that irreversibly destructive and indeed apocalyptic moment. If the springing and cropping of the Adonis flower has produced surprisingly little critical comment, perhaps it is because Shakespeare devotes so little space to the decisive act; a mere two stanzas, in contrast to the hundreds devoted to Venus's failed seduction and passionate complaint:

> By this the boy that by her side lay killed
> Was melted like a vapour from her sight,
> And in his blood that on the ground lay spilled
> A purple flower sprung up, chequered with white,
> Resembling well his pale cheeks, and the blood
> Which in round drops upon their whiteness stood.
>
> She bows her head the new-sprung flower to smell,
> Comparing it to her Adonis' breath,
> And says within her bosom it shall dwell,
> Since he himself is reft from her by death.
> She crops the stalk, and in the breach appears
> Green-dropping sap, which she compares to tears. (1165–76)[33]

The violence of the notorious boar and the fatal wound he inflicts upon Adonis – the principal action in an overwhelmingly rhetorical poem – is distilled in these two stanzas to the microcosmic level of the flower. The cropping of the posy thus serves as a synecdoche for the uprooting of "poesy" itself. There is, however, a wholly new element at the end of Shakespeare's brief description: the "Green-dropping sap, which [Venus] compares to tears." The anomaly is marked by the poet's technical mastery, especially in the second stanza, as metrical regularity gives way to the medial caesura in the penultimate line, which corresponds to the "breach" itself, while the spondaic "Green-dropping sap" fills the final line's first two feet, pending Venus's replacement of the sap with "tears." The prosodic subtleties of these stanzas, however, merely complement the larger poem's striking chromatic choreography, as an intricate yet familiar dance of red and white, which here gives way at last to the unheralded and ephemeral green.

The first recorded reader of Shakespeare's *Venus and Adonis*, the mentally unstable William Reynolds, remarked upon the poem's "much ado with redde & whyte," and early commentators, imitators, and parodists were equally alive to what Colin Burrow calls the poem's "persistent play of colour … its continual minglings of crimson and pale."[34] Reynolds's undiscriminating "much ado" notwithstanding, Shakespeare clearly differentiates between the vitality of redness and the mortality of whiteness, meticulously orchestrating their admixture into relative degrees of "rose" (e.g., Adonis's cheeks) and "purple" (e.g., Adonis's blood). At key junctures, however, Shakespeare allows his hydraulics of blush and pallor to spill over their ordinary rhetorical domains as Petrarchan tropes for female chastity and beauty, respectively. Hence the corporeal is rendered cosmic, as in the strange eclipse of the sun's "purple-coloured face" in the first line of the poem, or the "empty [i.e., white] skies" into which Venus ascends in the final stanza. In a poetic landscape defined by the complementarity of white and red, we grow hyperattuned to those moments when the two are out of balance, as when Venus calls Adonis a "Stain to all nymphs," or when the poem's universe bleaches to an ominous achromaticism in the closing stanza (9, 1191).

After a thousand lines in this dichromatic landscape – or, more immediately, after the preceding stanza's surfeit of blood, "pale cheeks," and the "purple flower … chequ'*red* with white" – a spot of green appears singular indeed, marking Adonis's metamorphosis as vividly as with a red flag in another context. While the word "green" does appear earlier in the poem – Venus, comparing herself to a fairy, claims she will "trip upon the green," and Adonis employs both the noun and adjective to characterize his youthful inexperience (146, 527, 806) – it is difficult to ignore Shakespeare's association of greenness with life's brevity, as a colour that vanishes as soon as it is introduced.[35] Indeed, Venus scarcely tolerates the chromatic novelty, translating her beloved's sudden verdure into the clarity of "tears," and soon burying the superlatively delicate flower itself, already cropped, within the "snowy" whiteness of her breast.

Despite its ephemerality, however, the "green-dropping sap" of the Adonis flower proves the most radical element of the poem's pervasive chromaticism, and serves as a far-reaching intertextual critique as well as a metaphoric dissonance within the text. The flower's momentary green pushes through the poem's garish *topoi* of red and white into richer allusive territory, and dissociates Shakespeare's peculiar treatment of the Adonis myth from its ultimate source in the *Metamorphoses* and, simultaneously, from the rival Ovidian imitations of the early 1590s.[36] Shakespeare's Adonis, after all, is no mere transplant from an isolated moment in Ovid's poem, but a site of confluence for numerous metamorphic figures, beginning with the equally beautiful, equally doomed boys Cyparissus, Hyacinthus, and Narcissus. Jonathan Bate accounts not only for the "smoking guns" among Shakespeare's allusions – Venus reminding Adonis of Narcissus's fate, for example (161–2) – but also for his less explicit but no less integral adaptations of Ovidian myths of sexual deviance, including the ever-popular Hermaphroditus.[37] Bate focuses principally, however, on Adonis's incestuous mother and half-sister Myrrha:

> When Shakespeare read Book Ten of the *Metamorphoses*, the first thing he was told about Adonis was that he was the "misbegotten chyld" of the union between Myrrha and her father, Cinyras (Golding, x. 577). At the same time, he would have learnt that the lovely boy was born not from his mother's womb, but by the splitting open through Lucina's agency of the tree into which his mother had been metamorphosed. Incest and a kind of posthumous caesarean section ... initiate the reader into a world of unorthodox swervings of gender and generation.[38]

Both of Bate's principal claims – that Shakespeare's treatment depends upon the story of Myrrha's incest, and that most (if not all) of Ovid's tragic lovers merge in the peerless body of Adonis – are just, but together these allusions do not imply merely "unorthodox swervings of gender and generation," but rather the end of mythographic generation altogether. Adonis's incestuous genealogy portends his sterility, and as Venus crops the *Metamorphoses*' only remaining flower, Adonis's mythological brothers die with him. It is as if Arcadia itself has shrunk to half a line, or the entire green world been transfused into a single stalk, which is then broken. Adonis's blood, moreover, works as a universal defoliant: "No flower was nigh, no grass, herb, leaf or weed / But stole his blood, and seemed with him to bleed" (1055–6). Beyond the fictional landscape of Shakespeare's own epyllion, these newly bloodstained weeds and flowers correspond to the teeming ekphrastic gardens and catalogues of his poetic predecessors and contemporaries.

This intertextual catastrophe is easiest to perceive against the poem's most immediate backdrop: Spenser's Garden of Adonis, the generative centre of the 1590 *Faerie Queene*, where Venus miraculously preserves Ovid's once-tragic figure from the boar's rage:

> And sooth it seemes they say: for he may not
> For euer dye, and euer buried bee
> In balefull night, where all thinges are forgot;
> All be he subiect to mortalitie,
> Yet is eterne in mutabilitie,
> And by succession made perpetuall,
> Transformed oft, and chaunged diuerslie:
> For him the Father of all formes they call,
> Therefore needs mote he liue, that liuing giues to all. (*FQ* 3.6.47)

In 1590, only three years before the publication of Shakespeare's epyllion, Spenser depicts his Adonis siring the innumerable forms of *The Faerie Queene*'s third, most Ovidian book. This generation, "by succession made perpetuall," functions as an infinite, protean extension of the boy's original metamorphosis, hence Spenser places the newly immortal Adonis fittingly atop an Ovidian floral catalogue: "And all about grew euery sort of flowre, / To which sad louers were transformde of yore" (45.1–2). Adonis's own flower, of course, is absent from the commemorative catalogue, as he survives "eterne in mutabilitie."[39]

To be sure, Spenser's Venus and Adonis are not unambiguously positive figures, but neither are they doomed, inept, unsatisfied, nor unsatisfying, as in Shakespeare's treatment.[40] Effectively, the younger poet reverts to Ovid's dead Adonis, aborting the "Father of all formes" described by Spenser, and robbing his Venus both of her "sweet pleasure" and her accustomed fecundity (46.3). At the same time, Shakespeare uproots the numinous flowerbed on which Spenser's Adonis lies, removing the myth from the epic context of the catalogue, and further rendering Adonis's metamorphosis both anomalous and terminal. However often the "wanton boy" has been reborn throughout the classical tradition and the early modern poetry derived from it, his intertextual rebirth is here rewritten as a stillbirth.

Of course, Shakespeare's reader is free to cut the allegorical Adonis down to a more convenient size. Beneath his universality, the doomed youth still represents the fleeting springtime (as mythographers like Boccaccio and Conti read him), or represents the unattainable Petrarchan mistress, or represents Shakespeare's patron – the self-involved Earl of Southampton – under royal pressure to marry the ward of England's Lord Treasurer, and so on down the topical slide (the crazed Reynolds even assumed the poem was about his imagined personal relationship with Queen Elizabeth).[41] But whatever allegorical content Shakespeare's reader bestows upon the Adonis flower, the phenomenon itself is defined by its singularity and terminality. It is the *last* of everything: the last springtime; the last May game; one last glimpse of Arcadia or Faerieland; Southampton's last chance to sire a suitable heir. However boldly comprehensive or narrowly topical our readings, in an Ovidian context – that is, in the context of late Elizabethan literary fashion – Shakespeare's Adonis undergoes the last metamorphosis.

At the same time, Venus's parting imprecation imposes the last of all aetiologies: "Since thou art dead, lo, here I prophesy, / Sorrow on love hereafter shall attend" (1135–6). Although she does not preclude generation altogether, her curse on love reduces all future relations to mere lust, for even as she continues to call the thing she curses "love," the two impulses merge in her vengeful speech:

> It [i.e., "love"] shall be fickle, false, and full of fraud,
> Bud and be blasted in a breathing-while;
> The bottom poison, and the top o'erstrawed
> With sweets, that shall the truest sight beguile. (1141–4)

The beneficiaries of this revolution from love to lust include "the fool … the staring ruffian … the coward," but "They that love best their loves shall not enjoy" (1145–58, 1164).[42] Of course, such disappointment in love is at the centre of the poetic tradition, nowhere more so than in the *Metamorphoses*, where countless figures who "love best" (or at least those who love most ardently) never "enjoy" any consummation, as exemplified by Narcissus, whose floral metamorphosis prefigures that of Adonis, and Orpheus, who narrates the Venus and Adonis myth.

Disappointment, however, is by no means universal in Ovid's poem, and Venus and Adonis themselves provide one of mythology's readiest examples of erotic mutuality: *pressitque et gramen et ipsum / inque sinu iuvenis posita cervice reclinis / … ac mediis interserit oscula verbis* (*Met.*

10.557–9, "she reclined upon the ground and on him … pillowing her head against his breast and mingling kisses with her words"). Far from cursing love and reducing it to lust, Ovid's Venus memorializes her beloved in death:

> questaque cum fatis "at non tamen omnia vestri
> iurus erunt," dixit. "luctus monimenta manebunt
> semper, Adoni, mei, repetitaque mortis imago
> annua plangoris peraget simulamina nostri;
> at cruor in florem mutabitur." (*Met.* 10.724–8)

> Reproaching fate, she said: "But all shall not be in your power. My grief, Adonis, shall have an enduring monument, and each passing year in memory of your death shall give an imitation of my grief. But your blood shall be changed to a flower."

Early modern mythographers duly extrapolated the Adonis story onto the cosmos, allegorizing its aspects of death and resurrection in the same breath. Conti's interpretation is typical:

> When the Sun is in one of the six southern constellations as it proceeds through the zodiac, the days are short and the nights long. Then Adonis is supposed to reside with the dead. But when the northern constellations have made the days longer, he's in Venus's company, and she's the one who brings back all the lost beauty and brightness of the fields (*Myth.* 5.16).

When Shakespeare eliminates any potential for the Adonis flower's annual renewal, then, he short-circuits this traditional application of the myth as a universal cycle of life, death, and rebirth. In the most extensive sense, he not only uproots Ovid's authoritative version, but undoes the humanist interpretations growing for centuries around that version.

Venus's departure at the end of the poem provides a final, spatial correlative to the aetiological abortion she has performed on the floral Adonis:

> Thus weary of the world, away she hies,
> And yokes her silver doves, by whose swift aid
> Their mistress, mounted through the empty skies

> In her light chariot, quickly is conveyed,
> Holding their course to Paphos, where their queen
> Means to immure herself and not be seen. (1189–94)

Of the events the poet recounts directly, only the murderous boar's momentary intrusion into the poem (900–4) occupies less narrative space than Venus's flight from "the world," while both Adonis's metamorphosis and the goddess's act of cropping his flower likewise occupy a stanza each. The final stanza's three enjambments complement the immediacy of Venus's catastrophic departure, as do the words "hies," "swift," "empty," "light," "quickly," and "conveyed," which speed past or fly over the ornamental description otherwise characteristic of the poem's Ovidian style. The lone rhetorical embellishment of the doves' "silver" colouration seems downright puritanical, especially when we recall the seventeen separate adjectives Shakespeare has devoted to the description of Adonis's stallion in a single earlier stanza (295–300). The skies' emptiness, meanwhile, provides a disturbing contrast to the populous skies of the *Metamorphoses* in particular and of love poetry in general. As Venus's chariot disappears from the narrator's sight, the emptiness remains; the blank skies reflect the blank landscape, robbed of its only flower and deserted by the poem's creatures – not only the goddess and her beloved, but the stallion and his mare, Adonis's wounded hounds, even the fatal boar. Venus "means … not to be seen," so there is nothing at all left to see here, justifying the narrator's abrupt conclusion.

Shakespeare's readers may well have desired more narrative – *Venus and Adonis* proved immensely popular, after all, and brevity was never the soul of its wit – but the concluding stanza provides no hint that Venus will ever return. To the contrary, by "holding [her] course," Venus does what characters in Ovidian poetry almost never do: she travels from the point of departure to her destination without wandering into a neighbouring myth. Ordinarily, the digressions and accidental aetiologies of mythographic verse interrupt any progress so straightforward, much as errancy delays and diverts the questing knights of chivalric romance. Indeed, throughout the poem, Venus's judgments, actions, and rhetorical paradoxes have been defined by and consumed in wayward vacillation; rolling eyes, wandering feet, and self-contradictory tongue. Fittingly, then, a loud shift in colour marks this wavering character's sudden transformation into an unrecognizably grim and decisive goddess; as she discovers Adonis's body, "she falleth in the place she stood, / And stains her face with his congealèd blood" (1121–2). Now permanently identified with the poem's angrier hue, Venus performs her remaining acts with purpose and in quick succession: cursing love, cropping the flower, and flying directly home to "immure herself" like a medieval anchorite.

In a narrative literally sexless, transgression is figured allusively, and the poem's vanishing point on Paphos refers us one final time to Ovid's account of Myrrha's incest and the birth of Adonis in the *Metamorphoses*.[43] Venus's resolve to "immure herself" on Paphos reflects a perverse effort on Shakespeare's part, as an Ovidian poet, to rebury his imitation of the *Metamorphoses* in its own textual source. According to Ovid, after all, Paphos is not only the geographic site of Venus's temple, but the scene of Adonis's criminal conception and the root of his entire self-involved family tree. Cradling the already fading flower in her breast, Shakespeare's Venus merges with the incestuous Myrrha in the word-play on "immure," recalling Ovid's *murra* ("myrrh"): *"stillataque cortice murra / nomen erile tenet nulloque tacebitur aevo."* (*Met.* 10.501–2, "and the myrrh which distils from the bark preserves the name of its mistress and will be remembered through all the ages"). But whereas Ovid's Myrrha had given birth to Adonis despite her metamorphosis into a tree, Shakespeare's vengeful goddess imposes her own stony infertility on the unkind landscape of *Venus and Adonis*. Her disappearance sews up the rupture in the tree from which Adonis was born.

"My lyfe shall everlastingly bee lengthened still by fame"

The myth of Venus and Adonis is the last song Ovid's Orpheus sings before the raging Maenads tear him to pieces, yet the prototypical poet does not fall silent completely. Instead, as the sympathetic trees and rivers of the *Metamorphoses* mourn his sudden death, the poem turns miraculous: *membra iacent diversa locis, caput, Hebre, lyramque / excipis: et (mirum!) medio dum labitur amne, / flebile nescio quid queritur lyra, flebile lingua / murmurat exanimis, respondent flebile ripae* (*Met.* 11.50–3, "The poet's limbs lay scattered all around; but his head and lyre, O Hebrus, thou didst receive, and (a marvel!) while they floated in mid-stream the lyre gave forth some mournful notes, mournfully the lifeless tongue murmured, mournfully the banks replied"). There remain difficulties in reading the passage as an allegory for the continuity of the poetic tradition (an unaccountable snake immediately attacks the head, for example), but in any case as Ovid resumes his primary narrative voice and as his epic enters a new phase, the tragic song of Orpheus can hardly be construed as the poet's last word. By extension, it is no more valid to declare the end of the Ovidian vogue of the 1590s, nor of Shakespeare's eager participation in it, simply because the uncompromising catastrophe of *Venus and Adonis* signals the ephemerality and indeed sterility of poetic imitation. As she silences the Ovidian song instead of commemorating Adonis in perpetuity, Shakespeare's Venus indeed resembles the murderous Maenads more than she does her gentle namesake in the *Metamorphoses*. The poets themselves, however, remain free to sing new songs, whatever havoc their characters have wrought on the landscapes of past fictions.

To be sure, Shakespeare resets that freedom in critical tension with the startling array of apocalyptic figurations he imposes on Ovid's myth: the stillbirth of Adonis, the cropping and withering of the last flower, the bloodstained wasteland, Venus's self-entombment, the silencing of rhetoric, and the cutting of the intertextual thread back to the *Metamorphoses*. We are left with something like the final massacre of *Titus Andronicus*: the committed Ovidians dead or silenced, without any counteractive rejuvenation of alternative precedents for action (imperial Virgilian models least of all). On the bleak stage of *Titus*, the condemned Aaron, chief instigator of the plot to imitate and amplify the Philomela myth, had vowed never to speak again, while Lucius's empty declaration of Rome's renewal had been contradicted by everyone and everything onstage, from the corpse of the degenerate caesar to the barbarian army occupying the forum. *Venus and Adonis* presents a different aspect of the same catastrophe, as in both cases Shakespeare depicts a global compulsion to imitate an Ovidian myth to the point of re-enactment, only to insist upon the futility and sterility of that imitation.

But however much *Venus and Adonis* recalls *Titus*, there is no straightforward cause-and-effect relationship between these two early Shakespearean imitations of Ovid; no blood seeps from stage onto page. The texts remain distinct from one another – composed in different genres, performed through different media, addressing different audiences, adapting different myths – yet both present a fundamentally similar response to the Ovidian vogue of the early 1590s, according to which the imitation of Ovid proves compulsory in the present, but appears to yield nothing for the future. Such a posture is hardly unique to Shakespeare, of course, as a glance at any one of his Ovidian texts will show. The dedication of *Venus and Adonis* to Southampton, for example, with its attitude of relinquishing Ovidianism as the "barren" poetry of youth, at once resembles the apologetic sonnet of Nashe's *Choice*. With a typical hedge, Shakespeare assures patron and readers that, "if the first heir of my invention prove deformed I shall be sorry it had so noble a godfather, and never after ear so barren a land, for fear it yield me still so bad a harvest."[44] The very coexistence of multiple Shakespearean engagements with Ovid, however – his repeated overemphasis on the vogue's approaching end – evinces an imitative posture fundamentally different from that of Nashe and other Ovidian debutants of the 1590s. Shakespeare has not merely been captivated by the *Metamorphoses*, but identifies and exploits the opportunity implicit in the structure of any imitative vogue: the imitated poet's authority inheres in his cultural prominence – in Ovid's case verging on celebrity – which outlasts any individual imitator's portrayal of his passage from the literary scene. Venus cannot take Ovid with her into exile, any more than Ovid can be buried with Aaron; each of these instances (or Nashe's sonnet, for that matter) declares a momentary, largely pyrrhic victory over Ovidian influence, but Shakespeare has the prescience to recognize in such local triumphs a long-term, renewable resource. The Southampton dedication's promise of "some graver labour" in the future can be held out again and again to all classes of readers and audiences, so long as Ovid remains in vogue. When the vogue ends in fact, as it does so often in his fiction, Shakespeare will prove the prophet as well as the product of his culture.

In the meantime, of course, *Venus and Adonis*, did not "prove deformed," but quickly became a bestseller, fostering its own imitations and establishing Shakespeare as a major poet of a distinctly Ovidian pedigree.[45] Not only did the debut's success excuse the new poet from his self-imposed condition "never after to ear so barren a land," but it seems to have encouraged him to return to Ovid almost immediately, adapting elements of the *Fasti* for *The Rape of Lucrece*.[46] Nor was Ovid's appeal generically bound to what would prove after all a quite limited corpus of narrative poetry; in his plays, too, Shakespeare stages at least a partial recovery from the early Ovidian massacres of *Titus* and *Venus and Adonis*. *The Taming of the Shrew*, for instance, demonstrates the continued efficacy of Ovidian precepts, while *As You Like It* replants lavishly the green world laid waste at the end of *Venus and Adonis*.[47] *A Midsummer Night's Dream*, of course, comes closest to a full recovery from the apocalypticism of *Venus and Adonis*, as Shakespeare repopulates the numinous forest, permits the aetiological fantasy of love-in-idleness (the aphrodisiac flower so similar in colour to Adonis), and even reinstitutes enough of a metamorphic principle to change Bottom's head temporarily into an "ass's nole" (*Dream*, 3.2.17). Of course, Bottom and company also reduce Ovid's myth of Pyramus and Thisbe to foolishness; as amateurs, they prove unable to revitalize Ovid even as they adapt his myths to suit the present occasion of providing entertainment for the royal wedding. From this perspective, the parodic excesses of the mechanicals' "tedious brief scene" (5.1.39) – Quince's blundering versification as playwright, Bottom's histrionics and inadvertent sexual puns, Flute's transparent cross-dressing as Thisbe, even Snout's effort to metamorphose into a wall (i.e., to "immure himself") – correspond not only to the antics of an inexperienced theatre troupe, but to the sins of hacks and opportunists trying and failing to publish imitations of Ovid. More urgently, if less directly, the mechanicals mock would-be imitators of Shakespeare the Ovidian poet.

The mechanicals of the Elizabethan literary scene included Thomas Heywood, whose plagiaristic *Œnone and Paris* (the earliest known imitation of *Venus and Adonis*) was published within a year of Shakespeare's bestseller. The "tedious brief scene" likewise targets Thomas Edwards, whose *Cephalus and Procris* (1595) is rendered "Shaphalus and Procrus" in Bottom's mouth. Of course, the *Dream*'s ultimate satire cuts not only against the inept imitations of contemporary rivals (and the aging verse of Golding, on which they are based), but likewise against Shakespeare's own earlier testimonies as to the limitations of popular Ovidian mythology as a poet's first recourse. Even our sense that Shakespeare has played this trick of proclaiming the end of Ovidianism too many times becomes part of the show, culminating in Bottom's onstage suicide as Pyramus, with his overemphatic cry, "Now die, die, die, die, die!" (5.1.295). The final "mechanism" of Ovidian imitation, the *Dream* implies, is the sense that imitation itself is about to end, end, end, end, end. That it never does – at least not through the turn of the seventeenth century – testifies as much to the currency of Shakespeare's *Venus and Adonis* as to the enduring appeal of Ovid's *Metamorphoses*. As always, self-parody is tantamount to self-validation, and when Bottom pops back up from so much dying, he affirms once more that resurrecting Ovid is never enough for Shakespeare. The point is to resurrect him, then kill him, then resurrect him again.

2 Shadow and Corpus: The Shifting Figure of Ovid in Chapman's Early Poetry

Unsurprisingly, the authors of commendatory sonnets – those ubiquitous squares prefacing early modern publications – cultivated hyperbole rather than ambiguity, and projected enthusiastic conviction far more often than critical poise. The first three sonnets introducing George Chapman's 1595 volume, *Ovid's Banquet of Sense*, accordingly applaud the commended poet's superlative genius, as distinguished from the inferior productions of contemporary rivals peddling popular and derivative Ovidian imitations, the late Marlowe and the newly successful Shakespeare most prominently. Richard Stapleton opens the *Banquet* volume with a characteristic commendation, "*Phoebus* hath giuen thee both his bow, and Muse; / With one thou slayst the Artizans of thunder ... / The other decks her with her golden wings," and Thomas Williams follows with two sonnets of his own, testifying to Chapman's triumph "(like *Ioue*)" over "that bastard traine / Whose ... iudgments, formeles still remaine." Both sonneteers resolve Chapman's divinity in contrast to the nullity of his competitors in the literary marketplace.[1]

The final two commendatory sonnets by the epigrammatist John Davies, however, present a subtle dissonance, both from the preceding standard fare, and between themselves. The first not only elevates Chapman over his contemporaries, but identifies him with Ovid as the *praeceptor amoris*, love's original schoolmaster:

Betweene these hallowed leaues *Cupid* dooth keepe
The golden lesson of his second Artist,
For loue, till now, hath still a Maister mist
Since *Ouids* eyes were closd with iron sleepe;
But now his waking soule in *Chapman* liues ...

> And doth more Prophet-like loues art enroule:
> For Ouids soule, now growne more old and wise,
> Poures foorth it selfe in deeper misteries.[2]

For Davies, Chapman enjoys Cupid's patronage (something short of the preceding sonnets' predictable apotheoses), but the new poet's chief claim to our attention lies in his descent from Ovid himself. The Roman poet's soul is imagined inhabiting Chapman – an instance of Pythagorean metempsychosis adapted from the final book of the *Metamorphoses* – but that soul has also "growne more old and wise," matured to "deeper misteries," and left behind "loues art" as originally promulgated by Ovid.

Davies's second sonnet is more fun:

> Since *Ouid* (loues first gentle Maister) dyed
> He hath a most notorious trueant beene,
> And hath not once in thrice fiue ages seene
> That same sweete Muse that was his first sweet guide;
> But since *Apollo* who was gratified
> Once with a kisse, hunting on *Cynthus* greene,
> By loues fayre Mother tender Beauties Queene,
> This fauor vnto her hath not enuied,
> That into whome she will, she may infuse
> For the instruction of her tender sonne,
> The gentle *Ouids* easie supple Muse,
> Which vnto thee (sweet *Chapman*) she hath doone:
> Shee makes (in thee) the spirit of *Ouid* moue,
> And calles thee second Maister of her loue.

Davies here celebrates the "infusion" or reinspiration of "Ouids easie supple Muse" in Chapman himself. This poetic genealogy is not cultivated through arduous, mysterious learning, but given freely and ready-to-order by a personified Venus. The charmingly ephemeral myth of Apollo's kiss, invented by Davies to explain Venus's preference for Chapman, replaces the high metempsychosis of the first poem, and recalls instead the brief, interstitial aetiologies of Ovidian verse. Here Ovid is reborn in Chapman, whereas in the previous sonnet Ovid was reformed by Chapman.

Unlike his fellow sonneteers, Davies captures an ambivalence at the heart of *Ovid's Banquet of Sense*, regarding Chapman's intertextual engagement from two subtly distinct angles. His attitude seems appropriate to the anamorphic, paradoxical status of the poem's central image of the weeping statue of Niobe, which "more neerely viewed, / Nor weeping, heavy, nor a woman shewed."[3] Indeed, the sanguine, one-dimensional jingoism of Stapleton and Williams seems almost inexplicable when applied to the self-divided *Banquet*, and far more in keeping with the hypersatirical tone of Chapman's debut performance, *The Shadow of Night*, published a year earlier with extensive (though specious) annotations testifying to the new poet's learned humanist credentials. In the *Shadow*, Chapman had fulminated against the vulgar eroticism and stylistic excess of professional peers and rivals, positioning himself in diametrical opposition to the unapologetically Ovidian verse then in fashion.

In the following pages, I argue that we cannot account for Chapman's ambivalent attitude in *Ovid's Banquet of Sense* – the simultaneously reformed and reborn Ovid Davies identifies with the poet himself – without first setting that famously perplexing poem against its much less competent and less studied predecessor. The furious allegorical satire of the *Shadow* presents Chapman's initial posture of anti-Ovidian polemicism; a garish backdrop against which the canny poet reintroduces himself as the sensitive and culturally informed author of the *Banquet*. Though he had pointedly excluded Ovid from the *Shadow*'s annotations, Chapman boldly resuscitates the Roman libertine as the misguided protagonist of the *Banquet*, essentially convening the trial that the historical Ovid – summarily exiled by the emperor Augustus in 8 CE – never received. While Chapman's Ovid ultimately condemns himself, the poem's refreshingly liberal narrative voice and newly multivalent allusive texture finally constitute a surprising testimony to the continuing relevance of a responsible and considered engagement with Ovid. In effect, the *Banquet* grants Ovid a reprieve, as Chapman seeks to recreate a traditional Italian humanist attitude of ambivalence towards the Roman libertine, updated and amplified for an Elizabethan literary culture awash in what he saw as second-rate Ovidian eroticism.

This is not to claim that by the English 1590s Ovid was synonymous with the *praeceptor amoris*, nor that Ovidianism stood monolithically for eroticism. On the contrary, I argue that the judicious ambivalence of Chapman's sophomore poem corrects for the *Shadow*'s shrill insistence that contemporary Ovidianism's rich and protean mixture of eroticism, mythology, materialism, aetiology, and allegory could be reduced to a single corporate villain and hunted out of culture in a few hundred fustian lines. Still in the golden age of the epyllion and erotic elegy, Chapman's satirical *Shadow* – published five years before the bishops of London and Canterbury would order all satires burned in the streets – proved premature, giving way to the *Banquet*'s elaborate compromise with literary fashion. The calculated visibility of Chapman's rapid poetic maturation to contemporaries (or at least to Davies) thus reflects more than the continued marketability of Ovidian imitations. Returning to the *Banquet* via the *Shadow* reveals a poet at once typical of his literary milieu and surprisingly self-analytical, whose Ovid flickers between familiarity and novelty, between the poles of reformation and rebirth.

Banishing the Ovidian Corpus from the *Shadow of Night*

Both Ovid's *Metamorphoses* and Chapman's *Shadow of Night* begin with chaos, pending renovation by divine fiat. While such a cosmogony is hardly unique to these two works, Chapman presumably derives his improbable adjective "indigest" (*HN* 30, 59) – which he applies both to the cosmic formlessness preceding the world's creation, and to the corrupted state of contemporary civilization – directly from Ovid's *rudis indigestaque moles*, the "rough, unordered mass" of the *Metamorphoses'* opening lines (*Met.* 1.8). The debt, however, would seem to end with this indigestion, for Chapman's resolution of the chaos of the *Metamorphoses* into Neoplatonic order requires nothing less than the repudiation of Ovidian style and substance: specifically, the remainder of the *Shadow* presents the new poet's rejection or subversion of metamorphic myths, the castigation of a licentious poetics identified in the Elizabethan period with Ovid's erotic elegies, and the telling exclusion of Ovidian reference from the volume's elaborate (and spurious) citations.

This decidedly anti-Ovidian stance, however, most directly opposes not the Roman poet himself, but his Elizabethan descendants – Lodge, Marlowe, Shakespeare, even Spenser – riding the crest of the contemporary vogue for Ovidian imitations. Pointedly ironizing the Ovidian epigraph to Shakespeare's immensely popular *Venus and Adonis*, published the year before, Chapman converts his rival's self-congratulation to an admonishment against poetic license: "Presume not then ye flesh confounded soules, / That cannot beare the full Castalian bowles, / Which seuer mounting spirits from the sences, / To looke in this deepe fount for thy pretenses" (*HC* 162–5).[4] Already espousing the Neoplatonic division between "mounting spirit" and "confounded flesh" – the constant theme of his oeuvre – Chapman castigates all who succumb to the "lawlesse flames of Cupids Godhead," while celebrating "Wise Poetes" who "properlie" portray the chastity of his Cynthia (484, 501). Alongside this distinction, Chapman endorses an old-fashioned allusive adjudication: those myths in accord with Christian ethics are to be preferred, adapted, and imitated; the "flesh confounded" elements of classical literature, on the other hand, are to be rejected – the Ovidian most of all.

Yet even as he establishes Ovid as anathema, Chapman refers his reader repeatedly and explicitly to the myths he denigrates. Thus he impugns versions of the Endymion story that portray Cynthia as an adulteress:

> Those Poetes did most highly fault,
> That fainde thee fiftie children by Endimion,
> And they that write thou hadst but three alone,
> Thou neuer any hadst, but didst affect
> Endimion for his studious intellect. (490–4)

The inclusion here, not only of the most licentious portrayal of Cynthia as the mother of fifty bastards, but also of an intermediate version of the myth, in which she bears "but three," reveals Chapman's tendency to draw attention to the kind of poetry he would be seen to avoid. Again, proposing to purge unsalvageably wicked myths from Diana's temple, Chapman ironically ushers them into his poem:

> Thy virgin chamber then that sacred is,
> No more let hold, an idle Salmacis,
> Nor let more sleights, Cydippe iniurie [i.e., "injure"]:
> Nor let blacke Ioue possest in Scicilie,
> Rauish more maids … (509–13)

As the *Shadow* draws to its close, this itemization of proscribed myths underscores the paradoxical element in Chapman's allusive practice; Salmacis, Cydippe, and the rapacious Pluto – called "blacke Ioue" as Jupiter's diabolical manifestation – are all of Ovidian provenance (*Met.* 4.285–388 and 5.346–571, *Her.* 20–1).

Chapman's paradoxical reliance on Ovidian content, moreover, corresponds to an opportunistically Ovidian style throughout the *Shadow*, most emphatically during the poem's longest narrative digression, in which the divine Cynthia spends an afternoon hunting down the sensual passions, figured as a hapless mob of rubes and dogs. In keeping with Neoplatonic doctrine – according to which the divine One differentiates itself into an infinite series of lower manifestations, increasingly subject to our human comprehension – Chapman depicts his goddess's descent from her diffuse heavenly sphere to a mythic landscape more amenable to narration.[5] As Cynthia steps into the anthropomorphic dimensions of Ovid's vindictive Diana, Chapman's allegory likewise descends from a hymnic exposition of Neoplatonic mysteries to an incisive satire of the contemporary literary scene. Subverting one of the most widely imitated of Ovid's myths – Diana's transformation of Actaeon into a stag, to be devoured by his own hounds (*Met.* 3.138–255) – Chapman "confounds" his rivals with their own material.[6]

At the same time, Chapman takes great care to keep his Cynthia chastely aloof from satire and sensuality. Having crafted a nymph she dubs Euthymia from pure ether, the goddess proceeds to summon a vociferous rabble of hunters and hounds out of the lower elements – from "the flowrs, the shadowes and the mists, / (Fit matter for most pliant humorists)" (*HC* 221–2) – and sends them in pursuit of her simulacrum, transforming the latter into a panther for bait. Once she confounds the hunting party, we last see Euthymia "turnd a Bore / More huge then that th'Ætolians plagud so sore" (378–9) – that is, larger than the beast described most fully by Ovid in the eighth book of the *Metamorphoses.* While the narrative thus verges on incoherence, the digression's satirical gist remains clear enough: both earthly monarch and universal principle, Cynthia commissions Euthymia – Chapman's own "shadow," endowed with stoic imperturbability – to turn the tables on the sensual, semi-bestial Ovidians of the 1590s.

Yet even as Chapman pursues an allegory simultaneously lampooning the contemporary literary scene and illustrating his own initiative to reform it, he reproduces and exaggerates the allusive and rhetorical tropes characteristic of early modern Ovidianism itself. Hence, his Actaeons proliferate; his Calydonian Boar balloons; his Cynthia begets an Ovidian Diana, whose metamorphic familiar bags more Ovidian game than ever. To be sure, Chapman eliminates the eroticism of Ovidian elegy, for now rejecting the unsavoury role of *praeceptor amoris*, but everything else we might expect of Ovidian verse is here: the episodic and digressive narration, the recombination of mythic materials, the corrective moralization, the aetiological retrofitting of form to character, and a half-virtuosic, half-parodic epic catalogue modelled on Ovid's enumeration of Actaeon's dogs. As he shows himself transcending the febrile sensuality of his own milieu, the new poet deploys his rivals' low mythological means to his own higher philosophical ends, regenerating the Ovidian landscape in order to re-enact its dissolution. As a chaste answer to Shakespeare's voluble Venus, Chapman's Cynthia reflects her opposite, and the new satirist's fustian ultimately echoes the complaint he derides. The cacophony of confounded hounds and hunters, likened to a whirlwind and an earthquake, drowns out commonplace morality, until the poet must banish his own unruly myths with an arbitrary nightfall:

> But dayes arme (tir'd to hold her torch to them)
> Now let it fall within the Ocean streame,
> The Goddesse blew retraite, and with her blast,
> Her morns creation did like vapours wast [i.e., "waste"] … (HC 390–3)

It is meant, perhaps, as sprezzatura – venery and the venereal dispelled within a line – but it reads with notable effort: both the parenthetical "(tir'd to hold her torch to them)" and Cynthia's "retraite" confess the exhaustion of a poet unable to cope and quiet the elements that after all make up his matter. On its own, this anticlimactic fiat cannot erase what is manifest in the preceding digression: as much as his contemporaries, Chapman identifies himself in relation to the literary fashion for Ovidian verse.

Perhaps because the imitative and adaptive aspects of the *Shadow*'s constituent hymns invite readerly misidentifications of the poet with undesirable models like Ovid, Chapman appends an elaborate self-critical apparatus advertising his debt to a select group of preferred classical authors. Yet the volume's forty-one endnotes are also a blacklist, the exclusions – especially of Ovidian texts – as pointed as the inclusions. In these notes, Chapman develops a subgeneric play space, in which each precursor's influence corresponds to his place among competing citations.[7] Here, the poet exercises a more direct control over his own allusive register, presenting his scholarly credentials, while simultaneously testifying to the unimpeachable mores of the authors inspiring his *furor poeticus*. The notes thus re-cast the *Shadow* as it was meant to be, correcting for the ambiguities of mythographic poetry as conventionally practiced, and shoring up the new poet's uncompromising anti-Ovidian posture.

However classically oriented the *Shadow*'s notes, only two of which refer to early modern authors, scholars have long noted the precedent of Spenser's *Shepheardes Calender* (published anonymously in 1579) and the copious commentary appended to it by the mysterious "E.K." Elaborating the resemblance between the *Shadow* and the *Calender*, Gerald Snare distinguishes "Chapman the glossarial interpreter" from "Chapman the poet," and argues that the "glosser articulates in another voice the precise preoccupations of the material invention itself, a voice made to be somewhat distant from the obsessions of poetic artifice and the voice invented to articulate them."[8] Less bold than Spenser's "E.K.," Chapman permits his scholarly third-person voice to break down in the final, unnumbered note to the "Hymnus in Noctem," as he dismisses ignorant readers in the first person: "for the rest, God help them, I can not (do as others), make day seeme a lighter woman then she is, by painting her." The "other voice" of the *Shadow*'s glosses merges with the voice of the *Shadow* poet at the exact point where Chapman admits his "preoccupation" with the vulgarity he would be seen to forgo. The visual metaphor seems more appropriate than the vocal one, for the note arrives at the centre of the volume, preceding the "Hymnus in Cynthiam" as the last word of the "Hymnus in Noctem" – a prominent authorial interjection in the midst of scholarly posturing, and one that reflects Chapman's approach to Ovidian material in the hymns themselves.

Of course, scholars have long regarded the *Shadow*'s notes as imposture, ever since Franck Schoell exposed Chapman's wholesale exploitation of Natale Conti's popular *Mythologiae*.[9] Chapman adapts virtually all of the lore compacted in the hymns themselves from Conti's encyclopedic work, while the learning on display in his notes is even more directly "extracted" from the same source – paraphrased, translated, or simply transcribed.[10] As John Mulryan and Steven Brown have demonstrated, many early modern English authors quoted or paraphrased extensively from the *Mythologiae*, often without attribution, but Chapman actively dissembles the nature and degree of his borrowing, citing Conti only once in a minor note (*HN* 204n).[11] The initial notes to each hymn give the further impression that Chapman has obliged his readers by translating recondite his Greek "sources" into familiar Latin (though never into vulgar English), when he has merely transferred both the Greek texts and Conti's Latin translations from the *Mythologiae*.[12]

Given the ubiquity of Conti's influence in the period, it seems unlikely that Chapman expected to deceive his well-educated readers, among them the aristocrats and potential patrons whose names he dropped in his dedicatory epistle. By opening the dedication – and literally beginning his poetic career – with a paraphrase of Conti's discussion of the Medusa myth as an elaborate allegory for scholarly endeavour, Chapman was presenting himself as one of a select intellectual community, who knew exactly where to find and how to apply the best available interpretations of classical literature. Chapman's application of Conti thus entailed a twofold authorial strategy: even as he displayed his deep classical learning to the general reader, he sought to impress his more knowledgeable readers with his judicious selection and deft distribution of overabundant mythological material. To this latter end, he produced a significantly partial epitome of the *Mythologiae*, straining whatever seemed vulgar out of that universal source.

Above all, this meant presenting a mythology cleansed of the Ovidianism of the moment, which indeed amounted to a revision of Conti, for while the preface to the *Mythologiae* culminates in a pointed dismissal of the *Metamorphoses*, Conti nevertheless cites Ovid more than 150 times, ranging across the entire Ovidian corpus, referring even to the fragmentary *Medicamina faciei* and the forgettable *Consolatio ad Liviam*.[13] When Chapman mines the *Mythologiae* for his *Shadow*, however, he discards all references to Ovid, even as he ventriloquizes the rest of the classical tradition. Judging from his self-critical apparatus, Chapman appears to rely on Aratus, Hesiod, Plato, Homer, Lycophron, Orpheus, Pherecydes, Callimachus, Catullus, Menander, Pausanias, Plutarch, Apollonius, Strabo, Nicander, Euripides, and Cicero, as well as on Giraldi and on Conti himself, but never on Ovid, whose exclusion is all the more conspicuous for the inclusion of the equally salacious Catullus.

Hence, while he lifts the material for at least seven of his notes from Conti's discussion of the goddess Diana in a single chapter of the *Mythologiae*, Chapman avoids any reference to the extensive quotations from Ovid's *Metamorphoses* at the heart of that same chapter.[14] And though Conti cites both Euripides and Ovid as authorities on the Iphigenia myth, his Elizabethan beneficiary eliminates the latter reference from his notes, while pointedly retaining the former (*HC* 422n., following *Myth.* 3.18). Extensively adapting Conti's accounts of the tragedies of Actaeon and Meleager, Chapman moreover obscures the *Metamorphoses* as the chief source for these myths.[15] Wherever Conti had anchored his research in Ovid's accounts, Chapman has systematically erased the vestiges of that influence from the mythographic record, banishing the

Ovidian corpus from the phantom library of the *Shadow* as Augustus had once banished Ovid's body from Rome itself.

I do not mean to suggest that Chapman appended such an extensive self-critical apparatus to his debut volume merely to eliminate all traces of Ovidian influence, any more than I claim that the *Shadow*'s allegorical content is limited to its satire of Ovidian sensuality. Whether explicit or implicit, anti-Ovidianism presents only one aspect of the late Elizabethan poet's necessarily complex negotiation among a multiplicity of past and present cultural authorities and literary models. Hence, even as he excludes Ovid from his notes, Chapman likewise suppresses any reference to Virgil, despite the prominence of both Augustan poets in Conti's *Mythologiae*. In effect, Chapman's exclusion of Virgil is even more pronounced than his exclusion of Ovid, insofar as the former had been defended and promoted, often at Ovid's expense, by many generations of humanists, from Boccaccio and Erasmus to Ascham and Sidney. Conti, too, had noticeably exploited the differential between the poets' reputations, generally quoting them in reverse order and allowing the elder laureate's authority to correct the misprision of the exiled libertine.[16] Yet the very recognizability of Virgilian *exempla* – taught in grammar schools, quoted in courtesy books, imitated by poets everywhere, used up over the course of the Renaissance – prompts Chapman's ostensible preference for more arcane and original learning. However superior his ethical claims to imitation, Virgil's traditional eminence renders him as unsuitable for Chapman's purposes as the increasingly vulgar or popular Ovid. More than ever, the precursor's reputation drives the Elizabethan poet's allusive choices and imitative postures, even when the result is the collapse of any effective distinction between fame and notoriety. In order to simulate an allusive investment in the remoter lore of classical antiquity, Chapman dismisses contemporary poetry's most familiar precedents – Virgil as well as Ovid.

These counter-allusive gestures of exclusion, however, were only apparently commensurate. By the mid-1590s, the Ovidian authorial posture had grown increasingly viable, finding receptive audiences among patrons, readers, and playgoers. At the same time, the prestige of a traditional Virgilian persona proved all but unavailable to a new generation of poets writing in the shadow of the 1590 *Faerie Queene*. For even as he had simultaneously invoked and exploited the ideological dependability of Virgilian imitation, Spenser had pushed such obvious laurels beyond the reach of rivals and successors; indeed, he too responded to his own effectual laureate status with a recognizable turn towards Ovidianism in the second half of his career.[17] While Marlowe, Shakespeare, and others were happy to follow the fashion, Chapman sought to present an alternative set of allusive credentials, triangulating his own intellectual primacy by identifying himself increasingly with Greek sources.[18] In practical terms, while this intertextual self-centring entailed a simple avoidance of Virgilian precedent – Chapman all but ignored the Augustan laureate throughout his career – the Ovidianism against which the new poet sought to define himself presented a far more urgent and formidable challenge.[19] The desultory satire and selective annotations of *The Shadow of Night* were hardly adequate for that challenge, and within a year Chapman would publish the obsessional *Ovid's Banquet of Sense*.

Ovid's Banquet of Sense as Retrial and Mistrial

For an Elizabethan writing self-consciously in the tradition of *quattrocento* Italian humanism, the correct attitude towards Ovid, as he was perceived through his extant works and legendary biography, was not the polemical rejection of *The Shadow of Night*, but a politic reservation of judgment. To most neo-Latin stylists, Ovid's verse was admirable but frequently overwrought, an attitude underwritten by Quintilian's classic assertion that Ovid was "unduly enamoured of his own gifts" (*nimium amator ingenii sui*).[20] The poet's rumoured affair with Augustus's daughter Julia – generally identified with the "Corynna" who obsesses the lascivious persona of Ovid's early elegies – lent this appraisal a moral valence, and many commentators regretted that the *praeceptor amoris* had apparently taught himself too well. Angelo Poliziano illustrates the temperate critical standard in his *Nutricia*, a hyperlearned digest of ancient authors composed in 1486:

> Sed Tiberim, dominum rerum mundique potentem,
> ambigitur riguine tener Sulmonis alumnus
> nobilitet magis an vero tibi, Roma, pudori
> sit potius, Getica sic semisepultus harena
> (proh dolor!) exsul, inops, nimium quia forsan amico
> lumine Caesareae spectaverit ora puellae.

> It is uncertain whether the dear scion of well-watered Sulmona [i.e., Ovid] lends more nobility to the Tiber, master and ruler of the world, or whether he is rather a source of shame to you, Rome, half-buried as he was on the

Getan shore, alas! an impoverished exile, perhaps because he cast too fond a glance at Caesar's young daughter.[21]

The grammatically passive, impersonal verb *ambigitur* marks this noncommittal response as received wisdom, though the verb also distinguishes Ovid from the more objectionable authors Poliziano unequivocally condemns.[22] Commenting almost 150 years later, George Sandys commits more firmly to Ovid's exoneration:

> The cause of this his so cruell and deplored exile, is rather coniectured then certainely knowne. Most agree that it was for his too much familiarity with Iulia the daughter of Augustus, masked vnder the name of Corinna. Others that hee had vnfortunately seene the incest of Cæsar: which may be insinuated, in that he complaines of his error, and compares himselfe to Actæon. But the pretended occasion was for his composing of the Art of Loue, as intollerably lasciuious and corrupting good manners. A pretence I may call it, since vnlikely it is, that hee should banish him in his age for what hee writ when hardly a man, and after so long a conniuance.[23]

The anti-Ovidian acrobatics of the 1594 *Shadow*, then, seem retrograde in relation to a broad historical trend towards Ovid's recuperation, locating Chapman at a potentially undesirable cultural extreme.

To be sure, disowning Ovid entirely could differentiate a young poet (and his patrons) from the unbridled eroticism of rivals like Marlowe and Nashe, who took evident delight in adapting salacious Ovidian models.[24] In the midst of the Elizabethan vogue for Ovidian *imitatio*, however, the utterly reactionary attitude espoused in the *Shadow* might well have struck many readers as obsolete, redolent of an earlier generation's efforts to discredit poetry in general, exemplified by Stephen Gosson's 1579 *Schoole of Abuse*. Gosson had been especially shrill in his rejection of Ovid, and had specifically condemned "that trumpet of Baudrie, the Craft of loue" – the *Ars amatoria*. In his famous riposte to Gosson, the *Defence of Poesy*, Sir Philip Sidney quotes and translates a harmless line from the *Ars*, and resorts periodically to Ovidian allusions.[25] At the same time, several of Sidney's allusions retain the studied ambivalence of Poliziano, and his elegant, diplomatic Ovidianism exposes the truculence of Gosson, whose diatribe – derivative even in 1579 – was hardly current in 1595 when Chapman published his *Banquet of Sense*.[26]

Chapman's sophomore poem corrects for the stale polemicism of the previous year's *Shadow*, reclaiming the traditional attitude of ambivalence towards the Ovidian corpus as a model for imitation.[27] Indeed, the *Banquet*'s long, bifurcated critical legacy – identifying the poem alternately as sardonically anti-Ovidian or as recuperating even the *praeceptor amoris* through an appeal to Ficinian Neoplatonism – has followed naturally from this fundamental ambivalence.[28] In the *Banquet*, Chapman neither emulates Ovid's style nor parodies it, but rather stages a trial of the poet himself, resuscitating the *praeceptor amoris* and his beloved Corynna as characters, in order to investigate the origins of Ovidian eroticism and adjudicate the ethos at its core. The *Banquet*'s ambivalence, I argue, resides not in Chapman's treatment of the resuscitated Ovid, who is in any case prejudicially condemned – his physical corpus destined for banishment, his subversive literary corpus to be left in the hands of unscrupulous imitators – but rather in Chapman's metaphorical deferral of that sentence's execution, in his ambiguous presentation of a mediating narrator, and in his deployment of a multivalent allusive texture altogether opposed to the specious Contian annotations of the *Shadow*. Chapman's *Banquet*, unlike Sandys's apologetic preface decades later, is not meant to exonerate Ovid, whose cold case the unabashed sensuality of Elizabethan admirers had undermined anew. Instead, Chapman presents the mature poet's response to the cultural phenomenon of Ovidianism, facing poetic fashion – however regrettable, however ephemeral – as a present fact. In the process, whether by design or by accident, he develops one of the most complex portraits of Ovid to emerge from the Renaissance.

Chapman begins by shuffling the "facts" of Ovid's biography, engendering a more problematic, self-ironizing figure. According to his own apology in the late *Tristia*, Ovid's banishment had resulted from *carmen et error*, a poem and a political misstep (*Tr.* 2.207–8). As Sandys notes, Ovid himself identified the former as the *Ars amatoria* – the infamous erotic primer Chapman's character promises to compose towards the *Banquet*'s conclusion – but the *error* remained unspecified and was therefore open to later biographical embellishment. At least for the purposes of his *Banquet*, Chapman subscribes to the "conjecture" of Ovid's "familiarity" with Julia/Corynna (herself later banished by her father for sexual licence), but he also reverses the order of the Roman poet's supposed transgressions: rather than interpreting the furor over the long-notorious *carmen* as an official cover-up for the mysterious *error*, Chapman reimagines the *error* as the inspiration for the *carmen*.[29]

By rearranging this conveniently dubious biography, Chapman clears space for the presentation of an Ovid we do not quite recognize: the classical poet portrayed before the composition of his poetry, a pre-influential Ovid. This fictionalized persona proves a peculiar, composite character, at once the classical lover and the early modern Neoplatonist, reckless in his actions but paralytically deliberative in his thought, capable of shaping his poetry to his desire, but driven by desire to the distortion of his poetry. By prioritizing Ovid's *error* over his *carmen* and trying the erratic poet where others had summarily condemned his erotic art, Chapman implicitly indicts not licentious texts but the fallen natures of the poets who produce them, not the written corpora of his contemporaries but their fleshly corpora.

On its face, it seems semantic to differentiate in this way between Ovid's summary "disappearance" from the *Shadow* and the textual habeas corpus of the *Banquet*, for even in the latter poem there is finally no question of Ovid's culpability, and by extension that of the Ovidians descended from him. Indeed, one might claim that the *Banquet*'s recapitulation of the Roman poet's *error* is rather meant to justify Chapman's prior animus towards Ovidians than to temper it, for while the Elizabethan poet now permits Ovid an unprecedented licence to speak and act anew, the unscrupulous libertine only damns himself once more, betrayed by his own turpitude. Upon encountering the nude Corynna bathing in Caesar's private garden, wooing her, feasting each of his senses in turn, and approaching (though never achieving) sexual consummation, Chapman's Ovid declares, "For thy sake will I write the Art of loue" (*OBS* 113.5). Deliberate in the *Banquet* where he had been peremptory before, Chapman depicts the genesis of the very poem Gosson had dismissed out of hand: the *Ars amatoria*, the archetype for early modern erotic elegy.

Chapman thus ironizes the characteristic aetiological aspect of the Ovidian mythographic mode, identifying Ovid at the site of poetry's original sin, for in the *Banquet*, Caesar's garden is an Edenic space, Corynna an enciphered Eve, and Ovid superimposed over Adam. In this secular recapitulation of the Fall, Ovid willfully chooses his role of *praeceptor amoris*, elects to instruct his descendants in his "Art," and is fittingly cast out of the garden in the *Banquet*'s penultimate stanza:

> Heere *Ouid* interrupted with the view
> Of other Dames, who then the Garden painted,
> Shrowded himselfe, and did as death eschew

All note by which his loues fame might be tainted:
And as when mighty *Macedon* had wun
The Monarchie of Earth, yet when hee fainted,
Grieu'd that no greater action could be doone,
And that there were no more worlds to subdue,
So loues defects, loues Conqueror did rue. (116)

Like the villain of a Chaucerian fabliau, Ovid dives into the bushes to conceal his illicit dalliance, yet he cannot escape the tragic implications of "shrowd[ing] himselfe … as death." Though compared to Alexander the Great in his moment of global triumph, Chapman's Ovid simultaneously evokes the quintessential conqueror's ironically limited worldly vision, mortal weakness ("when hee fainted"), and premature death; the "Monarchie of Earth" merges with the grave. The stanza's final word, from the Latin *ruere* ("to fall") likewise puns on Ovid's status as a secular Adam.[30]

This fictional, Adamic Ovid seems oddly dissociated from the real Ovid's textual corpus. Whenever the Roman poet's extant erotic or mythological verse would naturally seem most relevant to his long monologues, Chapman's resuscitated corpus/corpse of Ovid speaks paradoxically only with other voices, of generally anachronistic provenance: Petrarchan conceits, Neoplatonic commonplaces from Ficino, and snapshots from Spenser's Bower of Bliss. This allusive cacophony accompanies a malfunctioning rhetoric, as the unwitting anti-hero punningly foredooms himself whenever he opens his mouth. Declaring his ears "sette on fire / With an immortall ardor" (17.1–2), the hapless poet pronounces himself hellbound in a threefold sense: paronomastically ("sette" can also mean "bound"), etymologically ("ardor" derives from the Latin *ardere*, "to burn"), and metaleptically (insofar as "immortall" can evoke the flames of hell as readily as the music of heaven, more so as the adjective modifies "ardor").[31] His ears burning, and desiring "that every tuch may make such Musick" (19.9), Ovid moreover confounds himself through synaesthesia, the trope of sensory unity cultivated by Chapman's professional rivals as a mark of rhetorical virtuosity. In the process, he forecasts his precipitous descent down the ladder of the senses even as he presumes to climb it.[32]

There is more to the *Banquet*, however, than Ovid's self-incriminating speeches, and we should not imagine that Chapman reserves his poem's rhetorical fireworks only for his faulty protagonist. On the contrary, the synaesthetic tropes characterizing Ovid's hypersensitive and self-involved monologues equally inform the poem's purely narrative sections, and indeed precede Ovid himself into Corynna's garden. The puns that so bedevil Ovid's speeches spread to every corner of the poem, and render Chapman's most sententious pronouncements ironic, as in the case of a pivotal stanza often read unironically as legitimizing the poet's Neoplatonic credentials:

> This beauties fayre is an enchantment made
> By natures witchcraft, tempting men to buy
> With endles showes, what endlessly will fade,
> Yet promise chapmen all eternitie:
> But like to goods ill got a fame it hath,
> Brings men enricht therewith to beggerie
> Vnlesse th'enricher be as rich in fayth,
> Enamourd (like good self-loue) with her owne,
> Seene in another, then tis heauen alone. (51)

The couplet's emphasis on "good self-loue … / Seene in another" obviously reflects Ficino's account of Platonic love,[33] but the initial pun on "fayre" threatens the entire stanza's moral rectitude, by suggesting that feminine "beauty" is constantly for sale as an artificial commodity, however "natural" its "witchcraft." This dangerous corporeal beauty seems to attract "men" in general rather than Ovid in particular, nor are these "men" identified in any way as vulgar sensualists like those castigated in the *Shadow*; on the contrary, the repetition of the unspecified indirect object lends a new universality to Chapman's social critique. The most fully individuated presence in this central stanza, in any case, is not Ovid, momentarily stunned into uncharacteristic silence by his first glimpse of Corynna, but Chapman, who puns unmistakably on his own name, referring to the "chapmen" who buy and sell "beauties fayre" at "beauty's fair." Hence, while the stanza seems to climb to "heauen alone" (with or without Ovid in tow), the poet undermines any claim to philosophical seriousness by depicting himself as a huckster of "all eternitie," as someone who would sell that "heauen" to any customer. The noun "chapmen," moreover, can refer as readily to those who buy as to those who sell, and the personal pun thus implicates Chapman on both sides of an unsavoury commercial transaction.[34] *Ovid's Banquet* itself is "beauties fayre": the poet promises "heauen" to those who will buy its "endles showes," and is himself promised eternity – presumably in the form of fame or wealth – by its sale.

Chapman's ironic intervention at this pivotal moment is a pointed instance of the poem's narratological complexity, which is everywhere mediated by a narrator-persona so well defined as to constitute a third ghostly presence in Corynna's garden. Sympathetic to Ovid and clearly in love with Corynna, this narrator, rather than the character Ovid himself, vocalizes the poet's ambivalence.[35] He is the repository of Chapman's ironic self-awareness as an anti-Ovidian resuscitating Ovid, and thus provides the chief interface between the poet, his subject, and his reader.

"Her Voyces Vitall Sounde": Allusive Rejuvenation in *Ovid's Banquet of Sense*

At the centre of Corynna's garden, Chapman presents an *ekphrasis* of the myth of Niobe, whose fourteen children were massacred by Apollo and Diana after the hapless mother had boasted of her own fertility, while foolishly mocking the divine Latona for having borne only one set of twins. Chapman's figure is as much a portent as a tomb:

> Stone *Niobe*, whose statue to this Fountaine,
> In great *Augustus Caesars* grace was brought
> From *Sypilus*, the steepe *Mygdonian* Mountaine:
> That statue tis, still weepes for former thought
> Into thys spring *Corynnas* bathing place;
> So cunningly to optick reason wrought,
> That a farre of, it shewd a womans face,
> Heauie, and weeping; but more neerely viewed,
> Nor weeping, heauy, nor a woman shewed. (*OBS* 3)

This is no mere effigy, but the petrified Niobe herself, encircled by the contorted forms of her dying children, carved out of Ovid's *Metamorphoses* and imported to imperial Rome (and by extension into Elizabethan culture). As the *ekphrasis* spills into the following stanza, we discover that the gloomy emperor has even devised a mechanism by which the execution of the children may be reproduced on a daily basis, erecting twin prismatic obelisks representing Apollo and Diana, through which blood-coloured sunbeams are shot in fusillade at the dying statues (6.1–7). Any sunny day fit for bathing finds the heedless Corynna washing herself in proud Niobe's tears, surrounded by the concentric punishment of the guiltless children; like the statues all around her, Corynna too is transfixed by the gods' punitive, prismatic arrows, in a sense becoming the latest Niobid. Corynna's garden is thus an allusive graveyard, a *memento mori*.[36]

But it is also an Edenic playground, custom-built for a sexual encounter. Chapman emphasizes the anamorphic nature of Niobe's statue; indeed, the more we stare, the less the fountain resolves itself into a monitory allusion, until it no longer appears to weep at all.[37] Fifty lines before Ovid enters his own *Banquet*, Chapman's narrator treats the reader to a sneak preview of Corynna's bath in this very fountain:

> In a loose robe of Tynsell foorth she came,
> Nothing but it betwixt her nakednes
> And enuious light. The downward-burning flame,
> Of her rich hayre did threaten new accesse,
> Of ventrous *Phaeton* to scorch the fields:
> And thus to bathing came our Poets Goddesse,
> Her handmaides bearing all things pleasure yeelds
> To such a seruice; Odors most delighted,
> And purest linnen which her lookes had whited. (7)

There is plenty here to uphold negative readings of the *Banquet*. The "threat" of Phaethon's catastrophic descent, for example, overcompensates for the titillation of the stanza's opening image, as if the narrator is hoping to forestall or correct the reader's arousal, or his own.[38] As Darryl Gless notes, the allusion assigns Corynna a moral vector askew from her straightforward progress into the garden:

> She is associated ... with Phaeton, whose Niobe-like presumption destroyed his own life and scorched large expanses of the world beside. The fine image of her hair, a "downward-burning flame," not only adumbrates Ovid's descent from higher to lower senses; it also extends the admonitory symbolism of the setting, for such flames conventionally symbolize death – and in Roman funerary symbolism, Amor himself often leans against the inverted torch.[39]

Seemingly in league with Augustus, then, the narrator's allusion "extends the admonitory symbolism of the setting," but the intended beneficiaries of these extensive warnings remain unclear. Whom, exactly, does Corynna's hair threaten: Ovid, who has yet to be introduced; Corynna, whose bath was meant to be private; or the narrator, who just now gawked at her nearly naked body? That "such flames conventionally symbolize death" may be less instrumental to the interpretation of these lines than our recognition that the narrator has arrived prematurely at his allusive image for global mortality, for the "funerary symbolism" could easily have waited until after our peep into the princess's boudoir. Phaethon aside, the narrator seems to be enjoying himself – the reader too, perhaps – as he anticipates those tantalizing "Odors most delighted," and indulges in the Petrarchan conceit of the "purest linnen … whited" by Corynna's superlative beauty.

We lose sight of that linen in the following stanza, however, as Corynna disrobes:

> Then cast she off her robe, and stood vpright,
> As lightning breakes out of a laboring cloude;
> Or as the Morning heauen casts off the Night,
> Or as that heauen cast off it selfe, and showde
> Heauens vpper light, to which the brightest day
> Is but a black and melancholy shroude:
> Or as when *Venus* striu'd for soueraine sway
> Of charmfull beautie, in yong Troyes desire,
> So stood *Corynna* vanishing her tire. (8)

Chapman's manic narrator patterns forth with repeated similes the meteoric ascent of the Neoplatonic lover, only to diagram allusively his precipitous fall to an earth subjugated by sensuality. The first line is literal narration, and immediately provocative, but the next sublimates the image to the clouds; the lightning that felled Phaethon no longer punishes presumption, but now figures more-than-earthly beauty. The next line climbs even higher – not to the beauty of the terrestrial atmosphere, but to the beauty of light itself, first creation of heaven. Yet the following line takes us past our sensual eye to the prime heaven beyond the light we perceive every day, at which point a disastrous enjambment – "to which the brightest day is but a black and melancholy shroude" – plunges us into the negative side of the simile, swats us out of the sky like Phaethon. The brooding narrator finally relates Corynna to the Venus of Paris's Judgment, the origin of Troy's fall. From the flight to heaven's heaven we are thrown down to an earth as desolate as Phaethon left it. But the final line, "So stood *Corynna* vanishing her tire," bounces us right back into the poem's *locus amœnus*, reverting from epic simile to high-brow pornography so as to capture Corynna once again *en déshabillé*. The line evokes both the body and the ghost, the "purest linnen" and the "vanishing tire."

Neither stanza, then, traces any simple rising/falling motion of sensual indulgence ending in remorse. On the contrary, both stanzas begin with indulgence, interrupted in each case by a transitory spell of remorse – delivered via mythological (indeed Ovidian) allusions – but both then emblematize a *return* to the original sensuality. In other words, the *Banquet* is erotic not because it features Ovid's individual progression up or down the ladder of the senses, but because the reader may shoot up and down that ladder repeatedly, even before Ovid appears, guided and encouraged by a narrator attuned to the rhythms of desire. Hence, as the following stanzas introduce the familiar catalogue of flowers, which "cling about this Natures naked Iem [i.e., Corynna], / To taste her sweetes, as Bees doe swarme on them" (10.8–9), an entire community of voyeuristic readers is figured metaleptically at one remove from Corynna herself – we are like the bees swarming on the flowers, which cling to her body to "taste her sweetes." As if to correct for this unauthorized foretaste – after all, this is to be *Ovid's* banquet – the narrator returns his gaze to Caesar's stone Niobe and her massacred children, but by now Corynna's erotic presence has rendered the sensual inextricable from the monitory:

> And now shee vsde the Founte, where *Niobe*,
> Toomb'd in her selfe, pourde her lost soule in teares,
> Vpon the bosome of this Romaine *Phoebe*;
> Who; bathd and Odord; her bright lyms she rears,
> And drying her on that disparent grounde;
> Her Lute she takes t'enamoure heuenly eares,
> And try if with her voyces vitall sounde,
> She could warme life through those cold statues spread,
> And cheere the Dame that wept when she was dead. (11)

Bathing her breasts in Niobe's tears, Corynna completes her necrophiliac striptease, yet the *Banquet* has only just begun; her bath produces, literally and immediately, a poem-within-a-poem promising the regeneration of the garden around her – the inset "Song of CORYNNA," which will also invite and ignite Ovid, sense-by-sense.[40] Corynna's conceit, that her own voice's "vitall sounde" might reinstill life and joy to the petrified and lachrymose Niobe, epitomizes the central conceit of *Ovid's Banquet of Sense*: that "dead" forms may be reanimated, and "lost soules" rehabilitated through an allusive poetry at once monitory and sensual.

Corynna's song, of course, cannot "cheer" Niobe, however much it charms Ovid, and insofar as "her voyces vitall sounde" falls on stony ears, the *Banquet*'s opening sequence once again presupposes the failure of any quixotic effort on Chapman's part to reform or redeem the *praeceptor amoris* and his petrified myths. Yet the poet has been performing just such a revitalization throughout this intricately allusive passage, employing an intertextual technique far more sophisticated than his surreptitious consultation of Conti for the previous year's *Shadow of Night*. Hence, much as Corynna's unlikely agnomen of "Romaine Phoebe" momentarily transforms history's lascivious Julia, daughter of Augustus, into the Petrarchan equivalent of chaste Diana/Cynthia, so Chapman's introduction of the flower catalogue as "A soft enflowered banck ... / Of *Chloris* ensignes" (9.1–2) rejuvenates the Roman goddess Flora by referring us to her innocent, vernal manifestation. The name Chloris, after all, unequivocally evokes the virginal nymph, whose apotheosis into the goddess of flowers occurred only after her rape by Zephyrus, the west wind.[41] Best known from Botticelli's allegorical depiction in the *Primavera*, Chloris's story is recounted most evocatively by Ovid in the *Fasti*, where Flora, recalling her original identity, declares, "*Chloris eram, quae Flora vocor ... / Chloris eram, nymphe campi felicis*" (*Fasti*, 5.195, 197, "I who now am called Flora was formerly Chloris ... Chloris I was, a nymph of the happy fields ...").[42] Hence, Ovid literally underwrites Chapman's reassuring, retroactive transition from the ruins of Troy to a virginal springtime, for the otherwise dependable Conti nowhere discusses Flora's Greek alter ego.[43]

Conti does, however, refer to another Chloris: one of only three children of Niobe to survive the massacre, according to the Greek geographer Pausanias's alternative version of the myth.[44] To some extent, Chapman can here be observed reproducing the illusory learning of the *Shadow*'s annotations and slighting Ovid, as he plucks the name of the obscure survivor from a passage of the *Mythologiae* otherwise deeply indebted to Ovid's more famous and less merciful account of the Niobids' demise. But Augustus's tableau presents an allusive paradox: namely, that it only serves its monitory purpose insofar as it refers exclusively to *Ovid*'s version of the myth, for as Conti notes, "Ovid insists that fourteen children were killed," whereas Chapman's recondite Greek source here offers an escape route from the massacre. That the draconic Augustus should thus invoke an Ovidian myth, even as he castigates the moral errancy it signifies, again recalls the *Shadow*'s convolutions (specifically, the invocation of excluded myths in the "Hymnus in Cynthiam"), but the key distinction lies in the unprecedented intertextual options now left to the *Banquet*'s readers: we may condemn the lovers by authorizing Ovid's own myth, or we may call Conti's Pausanias to witness and permit Corynna at least an appeal. Crucially, this intertextual tangle cannot be blamed on Chapman's reconstituted Ovid, who has yet to enter the poem's endlessly resonant garden.

Such local allusive gestures as Flora's nominal rejuvenation into Chloris can hardly redeem the ghosts of the *Banquet* fully or permanently, any more than an appeal to the narrator's most prudent or sententious pronouncements can exempt Chapman and his readers from voyeuristic complicity in the poem's erotic vision.[45] Yet precisely because Chapman neglects or refuses to specify the provenance of the vast majority of the *Banquet*'s allusions, in stark contrast to his pointed annotations to *The Shadow of Night*, he allows for the critical accumulation of mediating intertexts. As he departs from the illusory encyclopedic range of the *Shadow*, and demonstrably imbricates his sources in the *Banquet*, Chapman liberates his readers from the earlier poem's reductively anti-Ovidian stance.

By incorporating Ovid without fully embracing the Roman poet's elegiac or mythographic personae, Chapman moreover signals his own maturation, aligning himself with the established, authoritative figures of Elizabethan literary culture. He emulates Sidney, who had allowed Ovid an audience while reserving judgment in the *Defence*, as well as Spenser, who had maintained a meticulous balance between Christian, Virgilian, and Ovidian intertexts in the 1590 *Faerie Queene*. Simultaneously, Chapman implies a corresponding distance between his own verse and that of rival upstarts like Marlowe or Shakespeare, who would rebrand Ovidian *imitatio* unscrupulously, exploiting and encouraging the growing ignorance of common readers and patrons.

Chapman, however, was not yet finished with the Ovidian vogue, despite Davies's testimony to his immediate success at reforming and reinvigorating Ovid himself in the *Shadow* and *Banquet*. Even as he found his niche as the translator of Homer, Chapman returned to the question of Ovidianism – still vibrant and controversial – with his completion of Marlowe's *Hero and Leander*, published in 1598. Despite its promised finality, the poem's closing passage, describing the doomed couple's metamorphosis into a pair of goldfinches, reconstituted once again the *Banquet*'s ambivalence in a self-divided blaze of colour:

Their wings, blew, red and yellow mixt appeare,
Colours, that as we construe colours paint
Their states to life; the yellow shewes their saint,
The deuill *Venus* left them; blew their truth,
The red and black, ensignes of death and ruth.[46]

With regard to Chapman's career, then, the *Banquet* proved a work in progress – neither a condemnation nor an exoneration of Ovid, but rather a deferral of judgment.[47] In the larger literary-historical context of early modern Ovidianism, however, the *Banquet of Sense*, as a corrective revision of the *Shadow of Night*, presents us with the opportunity to observe the evolution of Ovid's celebrity status beyond the immediate influence of his textual corpus, and equally beyond the flat, satirical rejection of his erotic and mythographic styles. Half-disgusted, half-enraptured by Ovid, Chapman's early poems reflect the complexity of imitative fashion itself.

3 Ovid in the Godless Poem: Allusive Rebellion in Edmund Spenser's Legend of Justice

Over the past few decades, Spenser scholarship has progressed from general inquiries as to whether or to what degree *The Faerie Queene* qualifies as an imitation of the *Metamorphoses*, towards a more confident scrutiny of the timing and shape of Spenser's intertextual engagement with the broader Ovidian corpus. Initial claims that "the *Metamorphoses* provide a groundwork for something Spenser absolutely requires: a self-reflexive theory of his own poetic process" – as Angus Fletcher rationalizes his sense of *The Faerie Queene*'s "Ovidian matrix" – encouraged increasingly close readings, like Colin Burrow's line-by-line analysis of the hermaphroditic aetiology for the "Well of Idleness" in the first book of Spenser's epic (*FQ* 1.7.4–5), or Raphael Lyne's demonstration that some of Spenser's "most carefully signalled intertextualities [are] with Ovid, but not with the *Metamorphoses*."[1] Recently and in due course, scholars of Spenser's Ovidianism have broadened their field of inquiry once again, but now more generously, to encompass the constituent elements of the Spenserian corpus as a reflection on the entire Ovidian corpus, at the same time grounding the poet's intertextual engagement more firmly in the context of Tudor and Elizabethan translations, commentaries, and imitations.[2] As such intertextual approaches have proliferated, some Spenser scholars have called for a new restraint, or as David Wilson-Okamura has urged, "The point here is not to dismiss the Ovidian parallels, but to be cautious in finding patterns."[3]

At the risk, then, of an excessive critical zeal, this chapter begins with my broad agreement that most of "the Ovidian parallels" in Spenser's works would have been clear to his readers, from the early *Shepheardes Calender* through the *Prothalamion*, the last poem published before Spenser's death in 1599. Indeed, I take as my premise the sense that by the time Spenser published the second instalment of his *Faerie Queene* in 1596, certain patterns of Ovidian allusion – to the erotic postures of the *praeceptor amoris*, for example, or to the myths of Diana agreeable both to the court of the Virgin Queen and to its satirists – were already common and obvious enough to elicit recognition from most readers. This cultural phenomenon, fundamental to the Ovidian vogue of the 1590s, in turn enabled England's most established poet to signal his adjustments to his own professional attitude precisely through the careful application of a new and surprising network of allusions to the *Metamorphoses*. In the terms laid out in my introduction, I hope to show Spenser in a fresh imitative posture, but one which, unlike Chapman's *Shadow of Night*, corrects not so much for the misprisions and excesses of professional rivals, as for the poet's own previous postures.[4] In other words, Spenser is quintessentially Ovidian not merely because he alludes to Ovid throughout his career, but because he self-revises through his choreography of such allusions into shifting patterns, which his own earlier imitations have already trained his readers to recognize.[5]

After all, when Spenser imitates and adapts Ovid, he also reprises the earliest Ovidianism, for the Roman poet's own imitative mode is always self-referential, self-critical, self-corrective. In addition to his allusive reinterpretation and redistribution of the prior traditions of the classical world – Greek, Roman, Egyptian, epic, elegiac, dramatic, aetiological – at a comprehensive level and with an uncompromising sense of innovation, Ovid echoes, revises, and even repudiates himself throughout his corpus, both between poems and within them. The overall effect is an apparent proliferation of Ovids, relations between them sometimes parasitic, sometimes symbiotic, and on occasion mutually exclusive. Ovid's most skillful imitators emphasize this hyperactive tendency towards self-revision. Chapman's *Banquet of Sense*, for instance, depends upon the reader's prior awareness that in his late elegies, Ovid seeks to disown his youthful *Ars amatoria*, the *carmen* which, along with some unspecified *error*, served as Augustus's rationale for his banishment (*Tr.* 2.209).[6] But the very first lines of Ovid's earliest extant poem, the *Amores*, testify to the same self-revisionism, reporting that the poet has abbreviated his lost five-book original into three books; indeed, Marlowe would whimsically retain this prologue at the beginning of *All Ovids Elegies*, precisely because it refers his reader back to an Ovid who cannot be translated because he can never be found.

These intertextual testimonials at the beginning and end of Ovid's career are the macrocorporeal extensions of the self-allusivity at its centre, in the *Metamorphoses*, where swirling, iterated tensions compete for authority. On the poem's broadest thematic level, Ovid's constant polarizations of his own poetic voice – into Arachne/Minerva, Achelous/Hercules, Ajax/Ulysses, Demiurge/Pythagoras, and so forth – resolve into an overall confrontation between two general categories of myth: the productive, regenerative, open-ended, aetiological myths of metamorphosis on the one hand, and the reductive, entropic, end-stopped, non-aetiological myths of fragmentation on the other.[7] The former movement sows the botanical garden and breeds the menagerie we have come to recognize as fundamentally Ovidian – whence the laurel, the hyacinth, the woodpecker, and so forth. The latter category tends in a retrograde manner to reduce the poem's local varieties into an undifferentiated chaos, as forms are cancelled through the dismemberment or obliteration of the characters themselves. It is easier to speak of the *nova … corpora* (*Met.*1.1–2, "new forms") of Ovid's poem – of the wolves running through the world or the fountains springing out of it – than it is to recall, say, Phaethon's *ossa … condita* (2.337, "buried bones") or the nothingness that is left of Erysichthon once he is finished eating himself, but the latter examples are no less Ovidian for their self-annihilation.

At the beginning of the 1590s, Spenser's approach to imitation had been carefully balanced in a similar fashion, as his significant revisions to the weaving contest between Ovid's Arachne and Minerva in the *Muiopotmos* demonstrate. Published among the juvenilia and occasional pieces of the 1591 *Complaints* volume, Spenser's pivotal but understudied insect fable is an exercise in circumspection, for by reweaving the contest so as to soften the politically subversive aspects of Ovid's original treatment of the Arachne myth, Spenser renders any topical applications of the *Muiopotmos*'s allegory irrecoverably obscure. Far clearer, however, is the little poem's recapitulation of the large-scale allusive tensions of the 1590 *Faerie Queene*, which in Book 3's Legend of Chastity had culminated in competing imitations of Virgil and Ovid, as embodied in the hermaphroditic Britomart and as depicted in the Arachnean tapestries of the villainous enchanter Busirane. The Ovidian aspect of the *Muiopotmos*, like that of its epic prefiguration, is at once numinous, metamorphic, aetiological, and generative, as Spenser reincorporates the Roman pantheon, recounts the metamorphic origins of his insects and their dispositions, and weaves new myths of his own from disparate threads in Ovid's original text. The *Muiopotmos* thus presents itself as Spenser's retrospective on his own allusive technique, but not (or at least not obviously) as a radical revision of his prior approach to Ovidian mythology.[8]

By 1596, however, Spenser has developed a decided preference for Ovid's myths of fragmentation, and in Book 5's Legend of Justice, he mounts the most comprehensive and sustained effort in Elizabethan literature to imitate this element of the Ovidian poetics, to the exclusion of the metamorphic. He begins by banishing the gods and goddesses familiar from the middle books of *The Faerie Queene*, and proceeds to redirect our readerly attention away from the aetiological and generative myths of the *Metamorphoses*, towards Ovid's myths of form's annihilation, until the *Muiopotmos* and its filigree metamorphoses fade to distant memories. Almost immediately, however, Spenser's castigation of his own protean tendencies proves exaggerated and self-defeating, as he pursues an allegorical purity that the 1590 *Faerie Queene* has already shown to be beyond any poet's capabilities. Hysterical from the beginning of the Legend of Justice, the violent suppression of any and all metamorphosis grows into an intertextual tyranny by the climax of Book 5, which consistently and uncomfortably recalls the bloodshed generated by the wars of the Reformation and by Elizabeth's own imperial policies. In Ireland, of course, Spenser had participated eagerly in that brutal history, and as a poet he gilds it often in *The Faerie Queene*, but through the troublesome Ovidian allusions of Book 5, he offers us a new and painful sensibility of its personal, national, and human cost.

Outlasting Proteus

Book 5's narrative continuity with the preceding books of *The Faerie Queene* is clear: the Legend of Justice concludes the adventures of Florimell and Marinell, continues the courtship between Britomart and Artegall, and even reveals the whereabouts of Guyon's horse. As an Ovidian text, however, *The Faerie Queene* as a whole shifts decisively not at the start of Book 5, but slightly earlier, on the fulcrum of the tiny canto at the end of the fourth book's Legend of Friendship, in which Spenser clears his poem of the meddlesome gods of the *Metamorphoses*. It is a somewhat delayed purge, to be sure; the Olympians' haphazard, mostly benign presence in the 1590 poem, exemplified by Venus's and Diana's foster care of Amoret and Belphoebe in 3.6, has already proven vulnerable to Busirane's slanderous depictions of the metamorphic throes of passion. As Britomart has happily repudiated the enchanter by the end of Book 3, however, the whimsical immortals enjoy an extended life in the Legend of Friendship. Thus, Scudamour's retrospective description of Venus's temple places the goddess of love on one final pedestal, and in the eleventh canto's pageantry for the Marriage of the Thames and Medway Rivers, Spenser throws a glorious retirement party for a host of natural deities who never return to the poem. Beyond these festivities, however, it is Proteus's relinquishment of the captive Florimell back into the romance in the twelfth canto that most clearly signals Spenser's self-revisionary approach to Ovid for the purposes of the poem's 1596 continuation, as the poet wipes his allusive slate clean in preparation for the Legend of Justice.

In his metamorphic efforts to seduce or ravish Florimell, Proteus in Book 3 had embodied the threat depicted in Busirane's tapestries and dramatized in the wicked enchanter's Masque of Cupid.[9] The surrender of the god of change himself thus emphatically punctuates Spenser's engagement with Ovid in the central books of *The Faerie Queene*, but Proteus's tyranny over the poem – and by extension Ovid's commanding role in its intertextual construction – has in any case grown tenuous by the end of the Legend of Friendship. In its simultaneous status as epilogue to the numinous Faerieland of 1590 and prologue to the desolate landscape of Book 5, the heroless fourth book recirculates the characters, allegories, and energies of the poem into new channels, according to a process of intratextual admixture whose greatest figure remains the marriage of rivers. Within this process, the activity of Ovidian imitation proves difficult to trace, as Spenser retracts the most obvious allusive signposts of Book 3: in particular, Busirane's tapestries, clearly modelled on those of Arachne in the *Metamorphoses*, and his idol of the triumphant Cupid, recalling the beginning of the *Amores*.[10] The Legend of Friendship, at least at first, presents its imitations as subtler and its intertexts as more intricate. Even as the opening cantos' enmities and platonic friendships duly give way to amorous pursuits, the cynical strategies and oversexed motivations of Ovid's *Ars amatoria* and *Amores* remain largely concealed under the decorous conventions of chivalric love and Petrarchan rhetoric.[11]

This vitiation of Ovidianism carries over to the smiling, androgynous Venus described by the momentarily heroic Scudamour as he recalls winning his beloved Amoret (4.10.41.6–9). The Venus of Book 3 kept one foot in the *Metamorphoses* – seducing the sleeping Adonis in the tapestries adorning Malacasta's castle, for instance, or searching high and low for the wandering Cupid and bickering with the chaste Diana in the central canto. By the end of Book 4, however, Spenser's statuesque

Venus has come to embody the strenuous paradoxes of continental Neo-platonism, as elaborated onto the pagan pantheon by Ficino, Poliziano, the poets of the Pléiade, Conti, and Spenser himself in *Colin Clouts Come Home Againe*.[12] The Ovidian cartoon of the 1590 *Faerie Queene* thus gives way to a conglomerate of predigested allegories, and while the marriage of sources embodied by the androgynous Venus perfectly suits a book characterized by shifting tetrads and octets, we are left with the impression that it is more the marriage than the sources that matter to Spenser in this part of the poem.[13] Looking up at the smiling Venus through the untrustworthy eyes of Scudamour, or listening to the rivers stream through the following canto, we may be lulled into forgetting to read for allusions at all, but should we thus disarm ourselves as readers, the pointed allusions of the ensuing Legend of Justice will feel all the more punitive. In his projection of cosmic harmony, however, Spenser promotes just such a Saturnalian attitude, as he closes his Legend of Friendship by chasing off the killjoy Proteus, the last of the 1590 poem's Ovidian impediments.[14]

Late in Book 3, by entrapping Florimell – by then the object of all the desire in Faerieland – the metamorphic Proteus had served as a vanishing point for the proliferating energies of romance narrative.[15] Lurking just off the poem's farthest shore, imprisoning his captive at its most remote and mysterious depth, Proteus had presented the antithesis of his fellow Ovidian Adonis, the benificent "Father of all formes" (3.6.47.8), generating the mutable world from the hidden centre of Book 3. Formless themselves, Adonis and Proteus had represented the positive and negative poles – the good and bad geniuses, respectively – of Ovidian imitation itself.[16] Adonis had sired the poem's forms and sent them forth from his garden (rather like the knights and ladies dispatched from Gloriana's unseen court), whereupon Proteus had vacuumed them into his undersea dungeon. Florimell's fate is representative:

> There did this lucklesse mayd seuen months abide,
> Ne euer euening saw, ne mornings ray,
> Ne euer from the day the night descride,
> But thought it all one night, that did no houres diuide. (4.11.4.6–9)

For six years and sixteen cantos, there had been no escape from this negative space, until the marriage of the Thames and Medway in Proteus's house.

At last, with the festivities about to commence, Spenser reminds us of the prisoner locked in the basement. Nominally a joyous occasion, the Marriage of Rivers is in another sense the tyrannical Proteus's moment of triumph. Spenser recounts by name all the waters of the known world as they flow into this narrative emptiness, until the number of vanishing river-gods and sea-nymphs exceeds even this poet's rhetorical capacity:

> So both [Thames and Medway] agreed, that this their bridale feast
> Should for the Gods in *Proteus* house be made;
> To which they all repayr'd, both most and least,
> Aswell which in the mightie Ocean trade,
> As that in riuers swim, or brookes doe wade.
> All which not if an hundred tongues to tell,
> And hundred mouthes, and voice of brasse I had,
> And endlesse memorie, that mote excell,
> In order as they came, could I recount them well. (4.11.9)[17]

Proteus's house thus functions not only as a narrative black hole, but as a generic one, for as the metamorphic god hosts the marriage of Thames and Medway, the potentially comic aspect of the poem's first marital consummation is itself engulfed by the obscurity of his undersea realm, with Florimell's lost voice at its indescribable centre.

Happily, Proteus's tyranny comes to an abrupt end in Book 4's breezy final canto, as Cymodoce circumvents his authority with an appeal to Neptune himself. Through her diplomacy, the naiad wins Florimell's release for her lovesick son Marinell, at the same time securing her own freedom from the uncomic paralysis induced by Proteus's earlier inhibitive prophecy that Marinell "of a woman ... should haue much ill" (3.4.25.8). Neptune's uncharacteristic liberality is in keeping with the holiday mood of his descendent Thames's marriage, while a very Ovidian Apollo, "King of Leaches" (4.12.25.4), contributes to this tiny canto's weird optimism by successfully diagnosing Marinell's melancholy, which is soon cured.[18] The gods of former books re-enter the poem, make good on their old promises or repent their past sins, and depart, not vanishing inexplicably like Book 1's Aesculapius, but with finality. Indeed, the shapeshifting god's unwilling act of liberating Florimell – "[he] was grieued to restore the pledge, he did possesse. / Yet durst he not the warrant to withstand" (32.9–33.1) – marks the effective end of all divine agency in the 1596 *Faerie Queene*, and as the old metamorphic gods surrender their place in the poem, they make room for the happiest ending of any book of *The Faerie Queene*: no wasted Bower of Bliss; no "halfe enuying" Britomart (3.12.46.6 [1590]); no unfinished business save the happy business of marriage.[19] Proteus not only takes Neptune and Apollo into retirement with him, but likewise the jealous Vulcan of the House of Care, the lustful Venus of Malacasta's tapestries, and all the myriad gods of Busirane's house. The rapacious shapeshifter thus unexpectedly serves the ends of comedy, enabling Spenser to resolve most of the 1590 poem's loose ends; in the third canto of Book 5, the stories of Marinell, Florimell, the false Florimell, Guyon, Braggadochio, and Trompart are all concluded, happily for the heroes, and with ironic and disturbing fitness for the villains. By then, however, the belated justice the poet dispenses to a few veterans from 1590 can hardly compensate for the cosmic injustice of Book 5, which has already desolated Faerieland and overwhelmed its hapless denizens.

Ovid in the Godless Poem

As Harry Berger, Jr observes, "the Marriage of Rivers looks forward toward Book V: toward a frame of reference which sets love in a historical, national, and political context alive with contemporary European problems," and hence we might expect the divine exodus from the poem at the end of Book 4 to mark the end of Spenser's engagement with Ovidian mythology in general and with the *Metamorphoses* in particular.[20] What business could Phaethon's solar chariot, Medea's witchcraft, or Proteus's primordial shapeshifting have in that portion of *The Faerie Queene* closest to the poet's own experience as a functionary of the Elizabethan regime and as a participant in Reformation conflicts over the only God not in the pantheon? But while the gods indeed are fled, the vestiges of myth are everywhere in Book 5, disembodied but reconfigured within the allusive texture of the Legend of Justice. Immediately we find that the proem, the longest in *The Faerie Queene*, has nothing directly to do with current affairs until its final stanza praising Elizabeth; instead, Spenser restarts his poem by backtracking allusively to the chaotic origin myths of the *Metamorphoses*' first book:

> So oft as I with state of present time,
> The image of the antique world compare,
> When as mans age was in his freshest prime,
> And the first blossome of faire vertue bare,
> Such oddes I finde twixt those, and these which are,

As that, through long continuance of his course,
Me seemes the world is runne quite out of square,
From the first point of his appointed sourse,
And being once amisse growes daily wourse and wourse.

For from the golden age, that first was named,
It's now at earst become a stonie one;
And men themselues, the which at first were framed
Of earthly mould, and form'd of flesh and bone,
Are now transformed into hardest stone:
Such as behind their backs (so backward bred)
Were throwne by *Pyrrha* and *Deucalione*:
And if then those may any worse be red,
They into that ere long will be degendered. (5.Pr.1–2)

Spenser signals from the outset that his description of the "state of present time" will derive from the "image of the antique world," but in the second stanza he also indicates the degree to which he is prepared to transform that image itself, by means of a radically revised allusive process. By selecting a new set of more violent myths, and by the violence he is prepared to perform on his own sources even as he imitates them, Spenser will apply this new allusivity to reflect "justly" both the catastrophic disarray of his present world, and the extent of the grotesque transformation of "men themselves."

The proem begins with a return to humanity's origins; not to the Eden of *The Faerie Queene*'s first book, but instead to the four classical ages, which Spenser proceeds to wrench "quite out of square." His principal source is Ovid, who describes the original golden age under Saturn, then two transitory, increasingly unpleasant ages of silver and bronze, and finally the iron one in which all the remaining myths of the *Metamorphoses* transpire, and which proves open ended.[21] Spenser's addition of a "stonie" age is therefore a radical extension of Ovid's degenerating temporal sequence; the introduction of a fifth, worst age follows logically from the traditional account in the *Metamorphoses*, but also produces a new, superlative category unique to Book 5 of *The Faerie Queene* and the world it figures forth. This innovation moreover transfers mythographic authority from Ovid to Spenser, from source to imitation: Ovid's original inability to forecast the "stonie" age leaves only Spenser, with his revisionary hindsight, to describe the world's full degeneration over time. Spenser the Ovidian thus updates, renovates, and completes Ovid's primary but insufficient version of events.

Yet as he does so, paradoxically, he relies more deeply than ever on the aetiologies of the *Metamorphoses*. Ovid's poem proceeds directly from the description of the iron age to the story of the flood, the survival of Pyrrha and Deucalion, and their regeneration of the human race from stones thrown over their shoulders. Spenser follows this basic order of events, but once again distorts the source myth. In Ovid's account and its many Renaissance illustrations, we witness Pyrrha and Deucalion mollifying stones into people, or in Golding's 1567 translation:

> Thus by the mightie powre of God ere lenger time was past,
> The mankinde was restorde by stones, the which a man did cast.
> And likewise also by the stones the which a woman threw,
> The womankinde repayred was and made againe of new.
>
> > (Golding, 1.489–92)[22]

Spenser, however, inverts Ovid's myth, by re-envisioning the original scene as the petrification of "flesh and bone" into the "hardest stone" denizens of his "stonie" age. Startlingly, we are witnessing the story of Deucalion and Pyrrha in rewind, "degendered" human figures sailing back over the progenitors' shoulders and into their hands, that the couple may repetrify the world with stones where once they repopulated it.[23] But by reminding us parenthetically that the human race was "backward bred," Spenser not only signals his inversion of Ovid's account of the human race's regeneration into "degeneration," but also reroutes the original myth's aetiological point. The Latin associates our stony origins with our durability: *Inde genus durum sumus experiensque laborum / et documenta damus qua simus origine nati* (*Met.* 1.414–15, "Hence come the hardness of our race and our endurance of toil; and we give proof from what origin we are sprung"). By moralizing the stoniness of humankind, however, Spenser gestures towards a traditional Christian interpretation of the passage as a type for the biblical Fall. The Puritan Golding's dubious rendering of the lines is indeed representative, clearly alluding to God's imposition of labour on Adam and his descendants prior to the expulsion from Eden (*Gen.* 3:17–19): "Of these [stones] are we the crooked ympes, and stonie race in deede, / Bewraying by our toyling life, from whence we doe proceede" (Golding, 1.493–4).[24]

As he proceeds to his own rendition of Ovid's myth of Deucalion and Pyrrha, however, Spenser diverges from Golding's traditional moralizing, for Book 5's long proem allegorizes not so much humanity's Fall itself, as the lingering consequences of that original disaster. Because those consequences include a nascent human incapacity to recognize the Christian God and his divine prerogative of justice, Spenser turns to pagan mythology in general, and to the early narrative trajectory of the *Metamorphoses* in particular, for material from which to build his allegory of earthly justice. To be sure, the Protestant reader, as directed by the experience of Redcrosse in the first book of *The Faerie Queene*, must still look to heaven for a sufficient grace entirely beyond his or her own power, but whereas that divine grace had revealed itself repeatedly in the 1590 poem's Legend of Holiness, it remains hidden throughout the Legend of Justice. In the epistles prefacing his translation, the dependable Golding had reassured his Protestant readers that the myths of the *Metamorphoses* periodically reflect the truths of Scripture. Spenser, by contrast, eschews any reference to Eden here in the proem to Book 5, and thus refuses to anchor his Legend of Justice to *The Faerie Queene's* ultimate textual authority, relying instead on the manifestly false authority of Ovid. The poet looks to the heavens and, as if automatically, superimposes an Ovidian cosmos onto the sky and its revolutions: "that same golden fleecy Ram ... the Bull, which fayre *Europa* bore ... those two twinnes of *Ioue* ... the great *Nemœan* lions groue" (5.Pr.5.6, 9 and 6.2, 4). Spenser's narrator grows increasingly hysterical as he considers the dire astrological consequences of the zodiac's errancy:

> Right now is wrong, and wrong that was is right,
> As all things else in time are chaunged quight.
> Ne wonder; for the heauens reuolution
> Is wandred farre from where it first was pight,
> And so doe make contrarie constitution
> Of all this lower world, toward his dissolution. (4.4–9)

We cannot even be sure that this final "dissolution" refers to the Christian apocalypse of Revelation; indeed, all indications are that the poet is cursed with a terminally idolatrous vision.[25] Here Spenser personifies "this lower world," as he personifies the sun in the following stanza, while ignoring the Lord, who goes unmentioned until the long proem's final moments; it is the *world's* "creatures" who "from their course astray, / ... arriue at their last ruinous decay" (6.8–9). Comparing the position of the sixteenth-century sun with the original calculations of "learned *Ptolomæe*," and putting a curious "faith" in "those *Ægyptian* wisards old, / Which in Star-read were wont haue best insight," the poet registers his fear that "in time he [the sun] will vs quite forsake" (7.6, 8.1–3, 7.9).

Arriving after Spenser's recapitulation of the *Metamorphoses'* opening flood sequence, this forecast of the world's destruction by an erratic sun reminds us of Phaethon, who also notably sent the constellations spinning out of control early in Ovid's poem. For their part, the *"Aegyptian wisards old"* recall Spenser's own mage Busirane, the ultimate Ovidian villain of the 1590 *Faerie Queene*, who decorated the walls of his castle with tapestries depicting the metamorphic lusts of the gods, including Jupiter's rapes of Helle and Europa, types for the falling sky of Book 5's proem. When the heroic Britomart viewed those bygone tapestries, she was "amazd, / Ne seeing could her wonder satisfie, / But euermore and more vpon it gazd, / The whiles the passing brightnes her fraile sences dazd" (3.11.49.6–9). Six years later, as the Legend of Justice begins, Spenser leaves us wondering whether he too has been dazzled like his own Britomart, or whether as poet he is imitating Busirane by spangling Ovid's myths across the sky of *The Faerie Queene*. In their cosmic waywardness and manifest falsity, the mythologized constellations introduce a narrator suddenly unable or unwilling to judge rightly.

Of course, the proem to the Legend of Justice, like the proems to *The Faerie Queene*'s other five books, ultimately insists on the sanctity of the book's titular virtue, and culminates in an appeal to the authority of Queen Elizabeth herself:

> Dread Souerayne Goddesse, that doest highest sit
> In seate of iudgement, in th'Almighties place,
> And with magnificke might and wondrous wit
> Doest to thy people righteous doome aread,
> That furthest Nations filles with awfull dread,
> Pardon the boldnesse of thy basest thrall,
> That dare discourse of so diuine a read,
> As thy great iustice praysed ouer all:
> The instrument whereof loe here thy *Artegall*. (5.Pr.11)

Of all Spenser's direct addresses to his queen, this is easily the most troubling, not only for the immediate gloom of its language ("doome" and "thrall" bode especially ill), but also in its deterioration from *The Faerie Queene*'s earlier proems, which have ended far more confidently. The proem to Book 1, for instance, closes with an appeal to Elizabeth as the poet's "dearest dread" (1.Pr.4.9) – the superlative love of "dearest" tempering the awe of "dread" – whereas Book 5's address replaces "dearest" with "awfull," echoing the metrically emphatic "Dread Souerayne Goddesse" of the stanza's opening line.[26] The contrast to the proem to the Legend of Friendship, which precedes that of Justice in the 1596 edition, is yet more pointed: in the prior case, the poet addresses not Elizabeth directly, but Cupid, whom he petitions, "From her high spirit [to] chase imperious feare, / And vse of awfull Maiestie remoue." Portraying Cupid (for once) as more inclined to pity than the "dearest dread" of Book 1's original proem, Spenser prefaces Book 4 by asking the god of love to heal whatever damage the poem's "Stoicke censours" may have done between editions:

> In sted thereof with drops of melting loue,
> Deawd with ambrosiall kisses, by thee gotten
> From thy sweete smyling mother from aboue,
> Sprinckle her heart, and haughtie courage soften,
> That she may hearke to loue, and reade this lesson often. (4.Pr.5, 3.9)

In this earlier instance, a chain of heart-softening tears links Venus, Cupid, Elizabeth, and Spenser, and leads to the mutuality of the final couplet, where the "Queene of loue, and Prince of peace from heauen blest" attends to her poet so far as to "reade this lesson often" (4.9).[27] Unfortunately, the mollifying liquid chain evaporates in the proem to Book 5, which begins with the disastrous global metamorphosis of "earthly mould … into hardest stone," and ends with the absolute separation of Spenser as the "basest thrall" from his "Dread Souerayne Goddesse," no longer influenced by love in any of its aspects. Nor does the poet hold out any hope that this new version of the monarch will "reade" his "lesson" at all, never mind "often"; the arbiter of justice will instead "aread" her own "righteous doome" (the adjective is all that separates her "doome" from tyranny) to all her people, including the prostrate poet, in a voice reverberating through the "furthest Nations." In what is perhaps the most alarming malfunction of this forboding stanza, Spenser's dependable rhyme scheme breaks down: Elizabeth's "aread" clangs so metalically against the initial b-rhyme, "in th'Almighties *place,*" as to undermine the ensuing eulogy with ironic dissonance.

This ruinous rhyme is paradigmatic of Book 5's larger allegory for the endlessly imperfect imposition of justice upon fallen subjects by an equally misguided temporal authority. Throughout the Legend, justice functions – or rather malfunctions – according to a process of unjust substitution: stone for gold; vice for virtue (5.Pr.4.1–3); spinning myths for fixed stars; the "Dread Souerayne Goddesse … / in th'Almighties place." From its very opening, then, Spenser's Legend of Justice undermines the central assumption of the monarch's direct derivation of justice from heaven, and the poet further figures this disastrous substitution allusively, as he replaces the imperial and centripetal Virgilian imitations of the 1590 *Faerie Queene* with a systematically subversive, centrifugal Ovidianism. To be sure, as Syrithe Pugh and others have amply demonstrated, the Virgilian core of the poem's first half was never stable, and Ovid was always its most potent troubler, but the stony "transformation" of Book 5's proem heralds a final, decisive break with Virgil, which soon arrives in the first canto. Introducing the superlatively Ovidian figure of Astraea – the classical goddess of justice herself – as Faerieland's original lawgiver, Spenser imposes what amounts to a death sentence on the very possibility of his poem's reconcilement with Virgilian imitation, or indeed with any other allusive network.[28]

Spenser's Astraea, like Ovid's, is defined by her irrevocable absence. The goddess's flight from the archaic world of the *Metamorphoses* into the stars (to become the constellation Virgo) renders the iron age and its characteristic injustice perpetual; in Golding's translation, "All godlynesse lies under foote. And Ladie Astrey, last / Of heavenly vertues, from this earth in slaughter drowned past" (Golding, 1.169–70). More than mere storytelling, Ovid's famous couplet is also an emphatic instance of his signature revisionist approach to the Virgilian canon. Specifically, Astraea's departure inverts the prophetic opening of Virgil's fourth, messianic eclogue, which heralds the goddess's return: *Ultima Cumaei venit iam carminis aetas; / magnus ab integro saeclorum nascitur ordo. / iam redit et Virgo, redeunt Saturnia regna* (*Ecl.* 4.4–6, "Now is come the last age of Cumaean song; the great line of the centuries begins anew. Now the Virgin returns, the reign of Saturn returns").[29] It is a stark distinction; Virgil readmits Astraea to the earth as part of the emperor Augustus's retinue, whereas Ovid continues to mourn the goddess's self-imposed exile. Along the *Metamorphoses'* trajectory, then, and in contrast to Virgil's optimism, Spenser provides no hint that Astraea has returned or will do so to alleviate the "stonie age" of the present.

In an equally uncompromising Ovidian gesture, the first canto of the Legend of Justice – the pivot between the proem's cosmic "dissolution" and the unfortunate adventures of Artegall – opens with dubious nostalgia for this vanished Astraea, reintroduced via flashback to the prehistory of the unjust world. The opposite of a second coming, Spenser's discouraging portrait of the pre-stellified goddess – "Whilest here on earth she liued mortallie" (5.1.5.5) – offers a perverse aetiology for the injustice at the heart of Elizabeth's domestic rule and imperial ventures. In Spenser's rendering, Astraea constitutes an original, degenerative principle of divisiveness and criminality. Hence, her first act is to kidnap the toddler Artegall from Faerieland's playground:

> Whiles through the world she walked in this sort,
> Vpon a day she found this gentle childe,
> Amongst his peres playing his childish sport:
> Whom seeing fit, and with no crime defilde,
> She did allure with gifts and speaches milde,
> To wend with her. So thence him farre she brought
> Into a caue from companie exilde ... (6.1–7)

Spenser proceeds to describe Artegall's education in terms that ironically forecast the demogoguery of the Leveller Giant in the next canto: "There she him taught to weigh both right and wrong / In equall ballance with due recompence." She soon requires her charge to practice his justice on wild beasts "with rigour ... for want there of mankind," until the beasts learn to run away from him (7.5–6, 8). Over time, she makes Artegall's hand "wreakfull," so that he will approach the world with the same "wrathfulnesse" that afflicted the irascible Guyon in the Bower of Bliss, albeit this time without even the pretence of temperance (compare 2.12.83.4). She even arms Artegall with the sword Chrysaor, which she has pilfered from Jove's armoury, so that he may crush human injustice with the same invincible weapon with which the king of the gods once destroyed the titans (5.1.8.8–9). Having refashioned her apprentice in her own image, she abandons earth, leaving him the terrible gift of the robotic policeman and executioner Talus, the ultimate means of power projection without prior self-judgment.

After such havoc, this corrupt Astraea's departure is a relief rather than a disaster, as justice is whitewashed onto the heavens:

> Now when the world with sinne gan to abound,
> *Astræa* loathing lenger here to space
> Mongst wicked men, in whom no truth she found,
> Return'd to heauen, whence she deriu'd her race;
> Where she hath now an euerlasting place,
> Mongst those twelue signes, which nightly we doe see
> The heauens bright-shining baudricke to enchace;
> And is the *Virgin*, sixt in her degree,
> And next her selfe her righteous ballance hanging bee. (5.1.11)

In its apparent stability, Astraea's "euerlasting place" in the sky coun-ters the reeling constellations of Spenser's proem, as together with her balance (the constellation Libra) she is poised at the centre of the sud-denly well-ordered sequence of twelve heavenly signs.[30] At the same time, Virgo's permanent separation from the balance is troubling, for not only does that empty space separate the sky into halves, but it is just as easy to declare that justice has been blazoned onto the heavens di-vided from her scales as it is to insist that the scales lie "next her selfe." Indeed, given his astrological erudition, Spenser would have known that the constellation Libra was itself a late addition to the zodiac, hav-ing first formed the claws (*Chelae*) of Scorpio, its neighbouring constel-lation on the other side. Once again, however, Spenser's "star-read" has less to do with natural philosophy than with an underlying inter-textual ferment. In the opening encomium to Augustus in his *Georgics*, Virgil describes how the presumptively stellified emperor interposes himself between Scorpio and Virgo – assuming the place of justice's balance – whereas Ovid pointedly retains the giant claws as one of the cosmic terrors threatening the Phaethon on his disastrous ride through heaven.[31] At first glance, Spenser's testimony of Astraea's serenity in heaven gratifyingly tips the allusive balance in favour of the Virgilian account of an ordered universe, overseen by an absolutely just author-ity at its centre. Unfortunately, the apotheosis is only momentary: the quintessentially precarious image of Libra/*Chelae* always threatens to tip backward towards the violent chaos of the anarchic Ovidian uni-verse. Against the backdrop of the proem and his account of Astraea's earthly injustice, Spenser's vision of an ordered cosmos reads like a wish-fulfilment: the poet desires to find a just rule in heaven that can be clearly contrasted to worldly injustice, but even as he describes such a concept, his fallen language undermines itself, threatening the heavens with the world's injustice.[32]

Inevitably, the dispassionate inactivity of Spenser's Ovidian Astraea testifies to the persistent malfunctioning of justice in Book 5, rather than to that virtue's renovation. Nor should we forget Astraea's topical iden-tity as an Elizabeth who pales before Spenser's own earlier portrayals of his queen. Richard McCabe explores this self-revisionary shift as part of Book 5's political allegory of Lord Grey and his ill-starred tenure as the queen's lord deputy in Ireland:

> For the purposes of formal Elizabethan panegyric "Eliza" was "Astraea." Spenser's own *Aprill* eclogue is modelled upon Virgil's prediction that As-traea is destined to return to earth and renew the Golden Age ... In *Mother*

> *Hubberds Tale*, by contrast, the keynote for Spenser's vitriolic attack upon
> the state of the nation is struck by Astraea's absence ... Her departure at
> the outset of the "Legend of Justice" signals an unprecedented conver-
> gence of epideictic and satiric modes, and the result not infrequently reads
> like mock-heroic, or even self-parody. Artegall operates in the vacuum cre-
> ated by Astraea's absence, as Grey operated in the absence of royal
> favour.[33]

As the "instrument" of the queen's justice, Artegall himself is only just
by political extension, and his virtue wanes as he wanders further from
its royal source, even assuming the queen's absolute justice as God's
anointed. Spenser explodes the latter assumption from the very opening of Book 5, by broadcasting the "degeneration" of his own prior allegories for Elizabeth.

However unflattering Spenser's portrait of Astraea, the pace of Faerieland's degneration only increases following her departure. In the
latter half of Book 5, in place of the vanished Eliza of *The Shepheardes
Calender* and the elusive Gloriana of the 1590 *Faerie Queene*, Spenser introduces a final allegory for Elizabeth in the person of Mercilla. Despite the positive royal iconography with which she is (over)adorned,
Mercilla's unlikeness to Virgil's returning Astraea could not be more
pronounced, for her very presence depends upon the continued, Ovidian absence of heavenly justice from Faerieland.[34] By introducing this
ultimate, iron-age version of the poem's royal "mirrours more then
one" (3.Pr.5.6), Spenser improves upon his deadbeat Astraea's original decision to leave the very mortal Artegall in her capacity as the
world's enforcer of justice. Indeed, all that is disturbing about Astraea
re-emerges compounded in Mercilla's equivocating presence, in large
part because, like the starry virgin, this further iteration of the Virgin
Queen dispenses agents to execute her will, which more than ever
authorizes a sign or show of justice, in contradistinction to the virtue
itself. In the notorious scene modelled on the trial of Mary Stuart, as everyone but the vestigially noble Prince Arthur clamours for the execution of the suddenly sympathetic villain Duessa, Mercilla "would not
let iust vengeance on her light; / But rather let in stead thereof to fall /
Few perling drops from her faire lampes of light" (5.9.50.5–7). Both instances of the slippery verb "to let" here could be puns, signifying that
Mercilla restrains her tears while allowing "iust vengeance," but even
if we read these verbs as straightforward permissives, the iron virtue
will not change – vengeance is inevitable, sympathy irrelevant; only

four stanzas later Mercilla will shed more tears over Duessa's "wilfull fall" and "wretched corse" (5.10.4.7, 9).[35] Unlike the "softening" tears of the proem to the Legend of Friendship, Mercilla's tears are at best ineffectual, at worst hypocritical, but in any case they distract us from the abysmal lacuna in the midst of her allegorical pomp: despite her throne, scepter, captive lion, attendant cherubs, the "kings and kesars at her feet ... prostrate," her rusty sword – "Yet when as foes enforst, or friends sought ayde, / She could it sternely draw, that all the world dismayde" (9.29.9, 30.8–9) – Mercilla does not hold the scales of justice. Those scales, if they ever existed at all, remain in heaven, where Ovid's Astraea left them.

Killing the Souldan: Allusive Disintegration

Between the departure of Astraea and the appearance of Mercilla, the Legend of Justice develops according to a fitful episodism that is not consistently Ovidian. The Leveller Giant of the second canto, for example, is the product of an entirely different set of allusions than those constituting Astraea or Mercilla, while the central story of Artegall's captivity to Radigund retains at best only a secondary resonance with the Ovid of the love elegies, as Spenser returns to direct imitation of Ariosto. Ovid re-emerges at the centre of the poem's allusive network in the eighth and ninth cantos, however, as Artegall and Arthur diverge from their respective quests to assist Mercilla's herald Samient. The Souldan, Adicia, and Malengin, the foes to which the cunning Samient leads the Faerie knights, are each composed of intricate Ovidian allusions, which trouble and exceed the basic narrative coherence required for allegory to unfold. Each villain presents a distinct challenge to the uncompromising, lethally reductive brand of iron-age justice authorized by Astraea/Mercilla, imposed by Artegall and Arthur, and executed most spectacularly by Talus. Individually, the Ovidian villains of Book 5 have no chance against such an allegorical phalanx, but considered in sequence, their allusive challenge grows insurmountable.

The Souldan rides into the poem on "a charret hye, / With yron wheeles and hookes arm'd dreadfully" (5.8.28.4–5), but by the time Arthur is done with him, "Onely his shield and armour ... there lay, / Though nothing whole, but all to brusd and broken" (44.1–2). Critics have read this episode as Spenser's jingoistic allegory for the destruction of Philip II's Armada, and in an effort to justify the poet's sixteen stanzas of car chase and bloodshed between the Souldan's appearance and his disappearance, several have drawn attention to an allusive triangulation between the tyrant's "cruell steedes" (28.6), Philip II's royal *impresa* of Apollo's chariot, and Spenser's extensive reference to Ovid's myth of Phaethon, who famously lost control of his father's solar horses with cosmically disastrous consequences.[36] Spenser's Souldan, however, is more than simply Phaethon adapted to Elizabethan propaganda; he is an allusive monster, ironically assembled from an elaborate network of references to several myths characterized by mutilation and disintegration. The murderous tyrant overtaking his victims in his chariot may initially remind us of Oenomaus (who treated his daughter Hippodamia's suitors thus), but the Souldan's carnivorous horses – "which he had fed / With flesh of men, whom through fell tyranny / He slaughtred had, and ere they were halfe ded, / Their bodies to his beasts for prouender did spred" (28.6–9) – are modelled on the flesh-eating mares of Diomedes.[37] As it was one of Hercules's labours to steal these beasts (in the process feeding them Diomedes himself), the Souldan's barbarity fittingly opposes Artegall's civilizing identity as Faerieland's Hercules. Spenser draws attention to the parallel:

> Like to the *Thracian* Tyrant, who they say
> Vnto his horses gaue his guests for meat,
> Till he himselfe was made their greedie pray,
> And torne in peeces by *Alcides* great.
> So thought the Souldan in his follies threat,
> Either the Prince in peeces to haue torne
> With his sharpe wheeles, in his first rages heat,
> Or vnder his fierce horses feet haue borne
> And trampled downe in dust his thoughts disdained scorne. (5.8.31)

The Souldan, then, is the central figure in an allusive chain of overconfident tyrants captured in their common pride, immediately before their respective falls: Oenomaus on his chariot; Diomedes behind his horses; Philip surmounting the world in his *impresa* or conquering England with his ships. As the Souldan's fate is thrice sealed upon his entrance, the ensuing combat should present little or no difficulty for Spenser's reader.

Indeed, on a first reading, it hardly seems of consequence that the Souldan is not fed to his horses by Artegall/Hercules, as would best fit the Diomedes allusion, but that it is the British Arthur who defeats him. Somewhat more disconcerting, perhaps, is the manner of the tyrant's death at the end of the episode; dragged behind his broken chariot by his frantic horses and dismembered, the Souldan's ends up in the posture not of Diomedes, but of the far more sympathetic (if equally hapless) Hippolytus of classical tragedy. Still, we may explain away such glitches in an allusive sequence by asserting that individual allusions themselves are independent and transitory, and that Spenser need not feed the Souldan to his horses at the end of the sequence simply because he has compared him to Diomedes at the beginning.

Abandoned allusions, however, are strange fragments of authorship, and the questions they raise are not easily left behind: here, we wonder not only why the poet has abandoned his allusions, but why he has left them abortively in place. As the Herculean Artegall remains on the sidelines, disguised in a slain Saracen's armour, watching the combat between Arthur and the Souldan unfold, he testifies to the ease with which Spenser might have avoided any allusive conundrum by assigning each combatant his proper foe. Instead, the initial mismatch of the Souldan with Arthur sends the entire high-speed conflict off-track from the start, in constant danger of veering out of control. Complicating the critical identification of the fictional tyrant with Philip II and his Armada, for example, it seems unlikely that Spenser would have deemed relatively light English naval casualties enough to justify allegorically the wound suffered by Britain's prince (5.8.35.1–2). It was, moreover, the English ships that pursued the Armada, not the other way around, but it is Spenser's Souldan who chases Arthur, though the narration requires great readerly care if we are to follow the action and its implications for the historical allegory:

> Still when he [Arthur] sought t'approch vnto him [the Souldan] ny,
> His [the Souldan's] charret wheeles about him [Arthur] whirled round,
> And made him [Arthur] backe againe as fast to fly;
> And eke his [the Souldan's] steedes like to an hungry hound,
> That hunting after game hath carrion found,
> So cruelly did him [Arthur] pursew and chace,
> That his [Arthur's] good steed, all were he [Arthur's steed] much renound
> For noble courage, and for hardie race,
> Durst not endure their [the Souldan's steeds'] sight, but fled from place to
>   place. (36)

As so often in *The Faerie Queene*, the pronominal melee confuses the reader as to pursuer and pursued, but to one watching this fight, rather than reading it, there could be no confusion – quite simply, the charioteer chases the knight. Here we can perceive the narrator's obfuscation of the allegorical stakes of narrative, almost as if he were trying to wrench a story that should read nothing like propagandistic accounts of the Armada into their vein; the praise lavished on Arthur's "good steed," for instance, seeks – and fails – to cancel the narrative account of a present cowardice, which could even be the rider's own.[38] As Arthur merges with the Souldan, the continued faith of Spenser's Protestant readership in a decisive agency that will resolve and reward the justice of its imperial cause comes under increasing pressure.

That faith is nonetheless rewarded, of course, as soon as Arthur relies on his all-powerful, Ariostan shield, much as Lord Howard and his sailors had relied on a Protestant God, but even as the Souldan's horses are blinded, the poet's allusions unravel:

> Like lightening flash, that hath the gazer burned,
> So did the sight thereof their sense dismay,
> That backe againe vpon themselues they turned,
> And with their ryder ranne perforce away:
> Ne could the Souldan them from flying stay,
> With raynes, or wonted rule, as well he knew.
> Nought feared they, what he could do, or say,
> But th'onely feare, that was before their vew;
> From which like mazed deare, dismayfully they flew. (5.8.38)

The initial reference is to Phaethon; the Souldan's horses react to Arthur's incandescent shield as the horses of the sun react to Jove's lightning bolt in the second book of Ovid's *Metamorphoses*: *consternantur equi et saltu in contraria facto / colla iugo eripiunt abruptaque lora relinquunt* (*Met.* 2.314–15, "The maddened horses leap apart, wrench their necks from the yoke, and break away from the parted reins"). But Ovid's emphasis on the horses' immediate liberation from their reins and yoke does not quite match the way in which the Souldan's horses continue to pull his broken chariot and shattered body through five further stanzas. Indeed, in Ovid's account, Jove's lightning strikes Phaethon himself, killing him at once, while Arthur does not directly kill the Souldan (much as God and not Lord Howard had destroyed the Spanish Armada).[39] There is no clean break in the Souldan's case: the horses will not scatter, the chariot will not stop, the charioteer will not die.

As Spenser's narrative runs away with its own metaphors, swerving from reference to reference like the runaway vehicle each seeks to describe, the initial allusion to Phaethon, from the beginning of the *Metamorphoses*, is wrenched all the way over to Hippolytus, at the Latin epic's end. In the final book of Ovid's poem, Hippolytus himself narrates how he was dragged to death by his own steeds, terrified not by Jove's lightning, but by a bull sent by Neptune: *ego ducere vana / frena manu spumis albentibus oblita luctor / et retro lentas tendo resupinus habenas* (*Met.* 15.518–20, "I vainly strove to check them with the reins, flecked with white foam, and, leaning backward, strained at the tough thongs"). How strange, then, that after another stanza describing the horses dragging the Souldan over the rocks as he wrestles with the reins, Spenser suddenly refers explicitly, not to Hippolytus, but rather to the less appropriate Phaethon:

> As when the firie-mouthed steeds, which drew
> The Sunnes bright wayne to *Phaetons* decay,
> Soone as they did the monstrous Scorpion vew,
> With vgly craples crawling in their way,
> The dreadfull sight did them so sore affray,
> That their well knowen courses they forwent,
> And leading th'euer-burning lampe astray,
> This lower world nigh all to ashes brent,
> And left their scorched path yet in the firmament.
>
> Such was the furie of these head-strong steeds,
> Soone as the infants sunlike shield they saw … (5.8.40–41.2)

This overdetermined simile, bouncing between heaven and earth, ironically seeks to repair the broken metaphor of Phaethon, but even here there are significant glitches, for the longer the Souldan struggles like Hippolytus with his frantic horses, the more allusive distance he puts between himself and Ovid's Phaethon. It was the boy, not his horses, who was terrified into dropping the reins by the Scorpion (see *Met.* 2.195–200), and Spenser further emphasizes his belated allusion's sudden irrelevance by referring to Arthur's shield as "sunlike," since it was precisely *not* the sun that frightened Phaethon's solar horses. By clinging to Phaethon long after he is dead – by straining (and failing) to rein in these horses – Spenser's allusive method here bears an odd resemblance to the Souldan's inadequate horsemanship. But in keeping with Book 5's will to fragmentation, once Spenser's narrative slows down and we are presented with a final, static image, it is not of Phaethon's charred universe, but of Hippolytus's dismembered body:

> At last they haue all ouerthrowne to ground
> Quite topside turuey, and the pagan hound
> Amongst the yron hookes and graples keene,
> Torne all to rags, and rent with many a wound,
> That no whole peece of him was to be seene,
> But scattred all about, and strow'd vpon the greene. (5.8.42.4–9)

Or, as Ovid's Hippolytus himself narrates:

> excutior curru, lorisque tenentibus artus
> viscera viva trahi, nervos in stipe teneri,
> membra rapi partim partimque reprensa relinqui,
> ossa gravem dare fracta sonum fessamque videres
> exhalari animam nullasque in corpore partes,
> noscere quas posses: unumque erat omnia vulnus. (*Met.* 15.524–9)

> "I was thrown from my car, and while the reins held my legs fast, you might see my living flesh dragged along, my sinews held on the sharp stake, my limbs partly drawn on and in part caught fast and left behind, and my bones broken with a loud, snapping sound. My spent spirit was at last breathed out and there was no part of my body which you could recognize, but it all was one great wound."

Retold in the third person, this is exactly the Souldan's fate, and as if compelled by the violence of his own narrative, Spenser finally specifies the apt simile:

> Like as the cursed sonne of *Theseus*,
> That following his chace in dewy morne,
> To fly his stepdames loues outrageous,
> Of his owne steedes was all to peeces torne,
> And his faire limbs left in the woods forlorne;
> That for his sake *Diana* did lament,
> And all the wooddy Nymphes did wayle and mourne.
> So was this Souldan rapt and all to rent,
> That of his shape appear'd no litle moniment. (5.8.43)

In one sense, there is no problem here: the Souldan's demise, like the Armada's, is a fitting mess. As he has mutilated justice in his realm, so he is torn apart by violent allusions, and even the action itself – so confused and out of control, such tangled reins and so many broken bits of vehicle – surely justifies the breaking and intermingling of Ovidian references. The Souldan's death is somewhat like Phaethon's, somewhat like Hippolytus's, and ultimately like nothing at all because "no whole peece of him was to be seene." It is easy for the reader to reason away the allusive stakes; the villain was unjust, so why should we care if he evidently suffers like Hippolytus while the narrator insists he is punished like Phaethon? Should there not be a limit to intertextual reading? There may even be an element of stubborn presumption in wilful overreading; as Ovid's Hippolytus demands of his interlocutor, the self-pitying nymph Egeria, *num potes aut audes cladi conponere nostrae, / nympha, tuam*? (*Met.* 15.530–1, "Now can you, dare you, nymph, compare your loss with my disaster?").

**Mourning the Souldan: Allusive Counter-Narrative
and Excess Sympathy**

Hippolytus's rhetorical question does not satisfy Egeria, who weeps herself into a puddle, nor will Spenser permit us to ignore the signifying fissures opened up by his pointedly erratic allusivity. We remain aware that the allegorical representation of England's providential victory at sea simply has not required such acrobatic mythological references; a straightforward historical nod – say, to the battle of Salamis – would have sufficed. Even Golding's simplistic reading, that "In Phaetons fable unto syght the Poet dooth expresse / The natures of ambition blynd … / And how the weaknesse and the want of wit in magistrate / Confoundeth both his common weale and eeke his owne estate" (Golding, "Epistle," 71–2, 75–6), offers enough to undo Philip II's obvious *impresa*. Ultimately, Spenser's discordant comparisons of the Souldan to Hippolytus constitute an allusive counter-narrative to the sequence of Phaethon references his narrator seems more inclined to sanction. Despite the superficial similarity of their horse-drawn fates, the two mythological characters could not be less alike: the retrospective equanimity of Ovid's Hippolytus bears no resemblance whatsoever to Phaethon's unreflective hubris; the demigod's fabled chastity is offered as a distinctly Roman correction to the mortal boy's overweening recklessness.

Nor are their fates similar, for Phaethon receives an emphatically final epitaph, while Hippolytus is reassembled into immortal godhead as Virbius, a gentler, Italic Hercules.

Already in Ovid's poem – even without the Renaissance antipathy towards Phaethon – Hippolytus's virtue renders him automatically sympathetic.[40] It becomes especially difficult to declare that the Souldan deserves what he gets, when we reflect that, allusively as Hippolytus, the tyrant approaches benign immortality. When he reminds us that "for his sake *Diana* did lament, / And all the wooddy Nymphes did wayle and mourne," Spenser draws our attention to the problematic excess of sympathy triggered by his own reference.[41] A merciful Diana is indeed a rarity; by way of contrast, in the Faunus episode of the first canto of *Mutabilitie*, Spenser's portrayal of the goddess will refer us back to her vindictive punishments of Ovid's Callisto and Actaeon.[42] Here in Book 5, however, a surprisingly sympathetic Diana's homological relationship to Elizabeth/Cynthia renders this brief allusive contrast to the unapproachable Mercilla/Astraea almost nostalgic. Curious, too, is Spenser's depiction of Diana as unable to help Hippolytus, and there is a pointed contrast here to the first book of *The Faerie Queene*. According to Ovid's version of the myth, Diana calls upon Apollo's wisest son, Aesculapius (contrast Phaethon, Apollo's stupidest son), to revive her mutilated favourite, and for this crime against nature, Spenser's "sad *Aesculapius* far apart / Emprisond was in chaines remedilesse" in the hell of Book 1, where Duessa brings him the mortally wounded Sansjoy (1.5.36).[43] In this earlier episode, Spenser recounts the Hippolytus myth at length, including Theseus's remorse, Diana's salvific intervention, and Jove's excessive punishment of Aesculapius, who even voices his own complaint (37–42). In the unmetamorphic Legend of Justice, however, Diana simply mourns, and Aesculapius is nowhere to be found, not even in hell. The absence of the god of medicine, whom Ovid had incorporated into Rome as the final civilizing deity of the whole *Metamorphoses* (15.622–745), ensures that in Book 5 of *The Faerie Queene*, there are no physicians to reconstruct broken myths. There is marked contrast to the comic end of Book 4, where the sea-gods' physician Tryphon and Apollo himself were available to minister to the lovesick Marinell.

By likening the Souldan's "peeces" to the dismembered Hippolytus, then, Spenser shifts from Ovid's myth of resurrection to the darker accounts of tragedy and lyric. Hippolytus stays dead, of course, in the plays of Euripides and Seneca, but the most resonant precursor of Spenser's treatment is an image from one of Horace's most pensive odes. In this poem, Ovid's contemporary laments the definitive break between natural continuity and human mortality, contrasting the moon's self-renewal to the inevitability of our own deaths: *damna tamen celeres reparant caelestia lunae: / nos ubi decidimus / quo pater Aeneas ... / pulvis et umbra sumus* (*Odes* 4.7.13–16, "Yet the quickly changing moons recoup their losses in the sky; we, when we have gone down to the same place as Father Aeneas ... are dust and shadow"). Horace's Diana, though able as the moon to repair her own loss, as a personified goddess retains no power to resurrect Hippolytus: *infernis neque enim tenebris Diana pudicum / liberat Hippolytum* (25–6, "neither does Diana set Hippolytus free from the infernal darkness, for all his purity").[44] The Horatian helplessness of Spenser's Diana, in contrast to her divine agency in Ovid's version of the Hippolytus myth, thus contributes to an allusive recapitulation, at the heart of Book 5, of the dissonant sympathies of Duessa's petition to Aesculapius for Sansjoy's life in the opening book of *The Faerie Queene* – sympathies so disruptive to Redcrosse's allegorical quest that Spenser opted to leave the earlier episode unresolved. The Souldan's fate, on the other hand, is quite definite, yet it is described with a pathos that seems out of place in any straightforward allegorical reading of the Legend of Justice.

Although Spenser's disconsolate Diana derives from Horace's ode, "the wooddy Nymphs" who "wayle and mourn" return us once again to Ovid's myth of Phaethon, or more specifically to his weeping sisters, the Heliades, whose tears the poet calls *inania morti / munera* (*Met.* 2.340–1, "a useless tribute to the dead"). After all, if we search in Spenser's poem for the Souldan's body and fail to find it, we only follow Phaethon's mother and sisters in their own futile search: *Clymene ... totum percensuit orbem / exanimesque artus primo, mox ossa requirens / repperit ossa tamen peregrina condita ripa* (333, 335–7, "Clymene ... wandered over the whole earth, seeking first his lifeless limbs, then his bones; his bones at last she found, but buried on a river-bank in a foreign land"). Phaethon's body (left more or less in one piece, though Ovid playfully uses the plural *corpora*) has been buried by the local naiads, who have left a tombstone with his epitaph (325–8). Here the Heliades mourn for four months before metamorphosing into trees, while beside them Clymene laments helplessly (356–60). It is only a line, but given Spenser's prior emphasis on the Souldan's likeness to Phaethon, it would be difficult to maintain that there is no resonance between these "wooddy Nymphs" and Ovid's Heliades, suggesting furthermore an echo of Clymene in Diana's "lament."[45] While robbing Ovid's Diana of her agency by reducing her to Clymene's status, Spenser amplifies the goddess's sympathetic gesture by surrounding her with mourners.

The difficulty of reconciling these latent allusive, self-allusive, and generic sympathies to any propagandistic allegory on Spenser's part is only exacerbated by the cruel exemplum Arthur sets up in an effort to obscure them. Where Ovid's Aesculapius refashioned Hippolytus into a deity of the Roman springtime, Arthur erects the Souldan's battered shield and armour as an emblem of the Counter-Reformation's twilight:

> That mote remaine for an eternall token
> To all, mongst whom this storie should be spoken,
> How worthily, by heauens high decree,
> Iustice that day of wrong her selfe had wroken,
> That all men which that spectacle did see,
> By like ensample mote for euer warned bee. (5.8.44.4–9)

The unsignifying hollowness of Arthur's monument of divinely sanctioned victory reprises Spenser's original, inappropriate references to Phaethon, occluding once again the latent sympathy of the Hippolytus counter-allusion and the mourners around Phaethon's tomb.

The sympathies of Book 5, however, are recalcitrant, not easily erased by such a "moniment," which allusively is a weak parody of Phaethon's epitaph in the *Metamorphoses*, and which etymologically is also a "warning" to remember the Souldan's demise Mercilla's way. For all Arthur's efforts, Spenser here provides us with another example of the disturbing persistence of sympathetic qualities in Book 5's villains, reminding us in particular of the unfortunate Munera, butchered by Talus in the second canto. Jeff Dolven, troubled by the severed hands and feet that Artegall and Talus leave behind – "that all might them behold" – describes Munera's "sclender wast" (5.2.26.9, 27.1) as an "unallegorical middle, a surprising and touching detail," and concludes that "the allegory of justice struggles to contain this brief, humane rupture in its prosecutorial rigor."[46] The Souldan's demise rewrites Munera's sympathetic Petrarchan body as the allusive body of Hippolytus, and Spenser's emphasis is in both cases uncompromisingly corporeal. Even as we witness the just punishment of allegorical iniquity, we come uncomfortably close to pitying the victims – as fallen as we are – on whose flesh that punishment is enacted.[47]

Spenser's reader need not reenact all of these allusive acrobatics in order to feel this pity, as it is almost impossible not to register the contortions in the narrative wherever the poet compares his figures for injustice to Ovidian archetypes. The function of the allusions, however, remains obscure: are we to read them as Spenser's tactical containment of the threat that potential readerly sympathy poses to the proper workings of justice, or are they meant precisely to point the reader towards hidden intertextual pathways to that sympathy? The answer – what is at stake in this convoluted imitative process – has to do with the poet's shadowing forth of an all-important disconnect between the potential for readerly sympathy on the one hand, and the necessary failure of allegorical character agency on the other. These Ovidian allusions map Spenser's careful elision of undesirable agency from Book 5: Phaethon struck down by Jove; Hippolytus torn apart his own horses; Diana reduced to tears. Injustice is utterly powerless in each case, as the imitative poet crushes his own rebellious sources like Talus pulverising Artegall's physical foes. This would be a dull and programmatic intertextual violence if Spenser did not retain the swirling, compounding sympathies of the Ovidian account in each case, permitting us to look askance at Arthur's attempt to hide them behind a hollow decoy.

The problematic references circulating over the Souldan's (absent) remains are finally not about the poet so much as his reader, and it is worth asking who the ideal reader of the Souldan episode might be: is it the most careful and learned reader, who gets his or her copy of the *Metamorphoses* off the shelf in order to review the relative degrees of fitness of Spenser's warring allusions to Phaethon and Hippolytus? Or is Spenser's ideal reader here rather the casual reader who fails to notice the sympathies behind the similes, and can therefore simply root for the good guys? In other words, are we to chase these sympathetic ghosts or pass them by? Perhaps the conspicuous irrelevance of the entire car chase, with all of its backward glances at Ovid's *Metamorphoses*, is meant to push us towards elaborate intertextual readings like mine, only to trigger our awareness that we must finally reject them for our very identities (as English Protestants) to have meaning?[48] This last reader is not so far from the "gentleman" Stephen Greenblatt famously found Spenser fashioning, who "can secure … [the] self only through a restraint that involves the destruction of something intensely beautiful."[49] But if Spenser writes for this last, uncompromising reader – the one who, like the poet, insists upon the wrong allusion at the right time, in order to maintain control over the poem and the world behind it – why does he nevertheless permit this intolerable residue of sympathy to proliferate? Why does Spenser make it so difficult for his readers, and for himself, not to pity injustice? For though the Souldan is no Acrasia, and while no right-minded reader could be fooled, by a few bothersome allusions, into mourning the demise of a Catholic tyrant seeking the death of England's prince, Greenblatt's gentlemanly "restraint" becomes exponentially more difficult over time, as we turn our just wrath onto the Souldan's hysterical widow.

Adicia: Containing the Subversive Allusion

Perhaps fortunately, the unremitting action of this violent canto will not pause for such self-questioning, as Spenser carefully eliminates any intermission between episodes, reflecting the way in which the ubiquity of injustice limits our capacity even to gauge our responses to its countless iterations. Spenser's reference to Diana's lamentation for Hippolytus, as if bypassing the triumphant Arthur's intervening "moniment" of justice – so easily erected and so easily forgotten – signals the transference of the allusive counter-narrative from the vanished Souldan onto Adicia, who grieves for her husband as Clymene grieved for her missing child.[50] At the same time, the spectacle of the Souldan's empty armour may indeed draw our attention away from Spenser's sudden raising of the allegorical stakes, as it elides the important distinction between the Souldan, specifically figuring Philip II's aggression against England, and Adicia, generally embodying injustice itself, the principle behind that historical aggression.

Spenser's surprise decision to embody the antithesis to Book 5's central virtue in the immediately sympathetic body of the widow (long before we meet the promised arch-villain Grantorto, suitably hideous) brings the driving paradox of the Legend of Justice – the imposition of justice by fallen agents on a fallen and necessarily unjust world – to a moment of interpretive crisis. On the one hand, since nearly all the villains in Book 5 are torn to pieces, we can justly expect Injustice herself to meet the same fate as her husband. On the other hand, the hydra-like recurrence of injustice throughout Book 5 (and throughout the poem and the world beyond it) dictates that in order for the allegory to reflect reality, Adicia must survive it. Spenser's ostensible solution to this fundamental problem – Adicia's metamorphosis into a tiger, and her exile into the forest – is a brilliant and fully Ovidian compromise, but it may well leave the reader in the awkward position of pitying the tiger it would be much more natural to fear.

Of course, like the Souldan, Adicia fully deserves her punishment within the narrative, but even more than in the Souldan's case, her trip through Spenser's Ovidian slot machine scrambles any easy assessment of the range and nature of readerly responses to a hyperallusive text. Pursuing intertextual incoherence, Spenser adduces three prototypes for Adicia's grief, only to insist upon their equal insufficiency:

> Like raging *Ino*, when with knife in hand
> She threw her husbands murdred infant out,
> Or fell *Medea*, when on *Colchicke* strand
> Her brothers bones she scattered all about;
> Or as that madding mother, mongst the rout
> Of *Bacchus* Priests her owne dear flesh did teare.
> Yet neither *Ino*, nor *Medea* stout,
> Nor all the *Mænades* so furious were,
> As this bold woman, when she saw that Damzell [Samient] there. (5.8.47)

Within a couple stanzas, Spenser will identify Adicia unequivocally with Hecuba, transformed in Book 13 of the *Metamorphoses* into a rabid dog, following her revenge on the Thracian king Polymestor for murdering her last remaining child, Polydorus:

> As a mad bytch, when as the franticke fit
> Her burning tongue with rage inflamed hath,
> Doth runne at randon, and with furious bit
> Snatching at euery thing, doth wreake her wrath
> On man and beast, that commeth in her path. (5.8.49.1–5)

Before discussing the relative appropriateness of the chosen allusion, however, I want to linger for a moment on the discarded ones. What does Spenser gain by his inclusion of this extraneous stanza full of unapt allusions? What do we gain by remembering them, only to reject them? We can in any case assure ourselves that few *topoi* are as characteristically Ovidian as this explicit repudiation of insufficient mythology: this is, for example, the approach of Minyas's unnamed daughter, who at the beginning of the fourth book of the *Metamorphoses* considers three aetiological tales, only to reject them all in favour of the story of the origin of the mulberry's redness – the tale of Pyramus and Thisbe. This fictional weaver knows too many tales (*Met.* 4.43, *plurima norat*), but Ovid's reader may not remember each of them so well, such that the daughter of Minyas's decision to brush the abortive tales aside effectively banishes them from the mythological landscape and timeline (who remembers now the tale of Dercetis of Babylon?). A more mischievous poet in this regard than Virgil, Ovid is constantly describing what he has denied us through allusive *occupatio*, and in this odd stanza Spenser imitates the practice.

As he cycles through references to Ino, Medea, and Agave, we once again witness the poet's process of invention, his synoptic appraisal of the relative merits of various Ovidian myths as examples. At the same time, even as Spenser provides us with the sudden privilege of watching him at work, he annexes for himself a further layer of ambiguity, precisely because we must never stop judging in Book 5, and this includes judging the poet's choices. In the present instance, we know that this little catalogue must be something like Spenser's usual procedure for alluding to Ovid (perhaps after consulting the entries for *feminae furiosae* in his commonplace book), but it also reads as a parody of that procedure, if only because Spenser applies no principle of differentiation in the stanza, and shows no preference for any one simile over the others, rejecting them all equally. If we accept Spenser's apposition entirely on its own terms, we quickly find the obvious similarity: all of these women were murderers of children. The immediate resonance between Ino, Medea, and Agave, however, seems to end abruptly there, nor is it clear that any of these three anti-heroines prefigure very closely Adicia's present injustice, as she seeks vengeance on the messenger Samient.[51]

The more completely we read the individual allusions, the weaker Spenser's appositional triad becomes, for the sisters Ino and Agave are much more closely related to each other than they are to the fratricidal Medea, and Spenser widens the disparity by avoiding any reference to the dramatic versions of the Medea myth, in which she murders her own children by Jason. By their thematic and familial identity as the daughters of Cadmus and murderers of their children, Ino and Agave bracket "fell *Medea*" in the centre of the stanza, together pushing her forward into our cognizance and constituting a foil for her difference. The rage of Ovid's Ino, after all, was inspired by a Fury unleashed by Juno in revenge for her foster care of Jupiter's bastard son Hercules.[52] Similarly, Pentheus's dismemberment (in which Ino participates at *Met.* 3.719–22) was not his mother Agave's injustice, but Bacchus's vengeance through his "furious *Maenades*." The sisters are thus twice removed from the agency that motivates them, quite unlike Adicia, who, as Cora Fox has written, is effectively "the source of Mercilla's danger, the 'author' of Samient's wrong, and the epitome of the forces that resist justice and the just knights of book 5."[53] In contrast to Ovid's Ino or Agave – who never adjudicate anything, but are instead simultaneously condemned by others and robbed of their own judgment – Spenser's Adicia must be able to judge others in order to be unjust, her vindictive injustice thereafter to be judged by poet, knights, and reader.

With her consummate will to injustice, Medea indeed seems the most promising model for Adicia ("this proude Dame disdayning all accord," 5.8.22.3), given that Ovid's witch is the greatest agent and the fullest character among all the *Metamorphoses'* dubious heroines. A central figure, she combines both the Roman epic's universal impulse to metamorphosis and its destructive countermovement towards fragmentation and obliteration. Accordingly, Ovid sets Medea's rejuvenation of her aged stepfather Aeson (*Met.* 7.159–293) – presented explicitly as a metamorphosis – alongside her fraudulent persuasion of Pelias's daughters to mutilate their father in hope of reproducing the rejuvenating effect (297–349). Medea's singular agency, as the embodiment of the poem's twinned mythopoetic categories of form's renewal alongside form's annihilation, not only enables her to avoid both fates, but even earns her spells the same epithet – *coepta* (194, "undertakings") – which Ovid has already used to refer to his own poetry in the epic's invocation (1.2).[54] Of the three infanticides of the allusive stanza, then, the powerful Ovidian figure of Medea best approximates Adicia, the "mortall foe / To Iustice" and the real power behind the Souldan's throne (5.8.20.6–7).

Yet Medea's ambivalent presence at the centre of Ovid's poem renders Spenser's apparently uncomplicated allusion to her extremely problematic. In addition to sinning, Medea is famously sinned against, and the better side of the witch's nature could easily authorize an allusive counter-narrative, rife with ambiguous motivations and shared responsibility, opposing Book 5's increasingly shrill allegory of absolute justice. It is harder, after all, to forget Jason's extensive, culpable role in Medea's vengeful acts than to forget, say, the momentarily mad Athamas who chased Ino over the cliff.[55] At the same time, the Ovidian Medea's identity as an escape artist threatens to undo Book 5's cultivated sequence of references to myths of dismemberment and annihilation, confronting the allegory with a dangerous allusive model for Adicia, who as injustice herself must not exit the Legend of Justice unpunished. Although Spenser's brief reference to Medea initially seems much easier to contain than the Hippolytus intertext treated at such length in the preceding episode, the involved Ovidian negotiation over the Souldan's fate itself prepares us for an unusually close analysis of the stanza – bursting with italicized mythological examples – in which Medea appears at the centre. By his pointed retelling of Medea's unprovoked and unforgivable mutilation of her brother Absyrtus, Spenser would be seen to exclude all of these subversive aspects of the Medea story, but as an Ovidian campaigning on his imitative credentials, he must know that his ability to contain any allusion to such an extensive myth is quite limited.

Spenser knows, in other words, that while the characteristic Ovidian *topos* of explicitly discarding alternative mythological archetypes invites the reader to play the poet's allusive game, a decisive difference arises when the trope is applied by the Ovidian poet, rather than by Ovid himself, the original authority to whom Spenser's allusions refer. While the frame narrators of the *Metamorphoses* may pointedly exclude all but tiny summaries of undesirable myths (and even these myths are thereby set apart from those the poem does not treat at all), Spenser's narrator may not so simply mention Medea only to deny her any allusive significance. While he may ignore potential Ovidian points of reference, and no doubt does so on occasion, Spenser has no direct way of limiting readerly access to Ovidian models once he has made us aware, even momentarily, of their presence. Unlike the forgotten Dercetis, rejected in a moment by a frame narrator who prefers the tale of Pyramus and Thisbe, Medea alone has an enormous history, anchored in the *Metamorphoses* but stretching through the entire Ovidian corpus: her complaint in the *Heroides*; her cameos in the *Ars amatoria*; the all-but-lost tragedy of *Medea*. Like Hippolytus, she looks backward to classical Greece and forward to later Latin literature and beyond. Ovid's mastery of his mythographic material is absolute, but even he would have encountered difficulty in trying to exclude Medea from his epic as brusquely as Spenser does from Book 5, in that her mythological presence is so vast even within his own work that Ovid himself becomes an Ovidian – a poet imitating Ovid – when he writes of her.[56] Even so, Spenser is under no obligation to include her; he could simply choose Hecuba. Instead, he sandwiches Medea between safely irrelevant allusions to Ino and Agave.

Spenser renders his own allusion to Medea even more oblique by referring to her murder of the infant Absyrtus – "when on *Colchicke* strand / Her brothers bones she scattered all about" – in fact a story his reader will not find in the *Metamorphoses*, which pointedly skips the infamous fratricide, but only in other versions of the Medea myth, such as Ovid's gruesome description in the *Tristia*:

atque ita divellit divulsaque membra per agros
dissipat in multis invenienda locis.
neu pater ignoret, scopulo proponit in alto
pallentesque manus sanguineumque caput,
ut genitor luctuque novo tardetur et, artus
dum legit extinctos, triste moretur, iter.
inde Tomis dictus locus hic, quia fertur in illo
membra soror fratris consecuisse sui. (*Tr.* 3.9.27–34)

Then she tore [Absyrtus] limb from limb, scattering the fragments of his body throughout the fields so that they must be sought in many places. And to apprise her father she placed upon a lofty rock the pale hands and gory head. Thus was the sire delayed by his fresh grief, lingering, while he gathered those lifeless limbs, on a journey of sorrow. So was this place called Tomis because here, they say, the sister cut to pieces her brother's body.[57]

If we look for this kind of spectacular gore in Book 5 of *The Faerie Queene*, we find that it is not Medea and her kind who set up such "moniments," but the Faerie knights, who compel Sanglier to carry a severed head, mutilate Munera and nail her limbs to the lintel, behead Radigund, and display the Souldan's battered armour to his widow.

Spenser's surprising allusion to this part of the Medea story testifies to his deep reading of his Roman precursor, as it associates Faerieland with Ovid's obscure and grotesque aetiology for the wasteland of his final exile, where he found neither justice nor salvific metamorphosis, but only violence.[58] It is our loss if we rest satisfied with the Spenserian narrator's choice of Hecuba and forget about his rejected Medea, but if we follow the allusions, we may find that the landscape of Book 5 resembles Ovid's Tomis after all. But which landscape? Catholic Spain, the Low Countries, even England – all of these are present, for all suffer from or are threatened by injustice – but here the allusive register is especially Irish, or as McCabe describes the link between Spenser's Irish experience and his sense of himself as an Ovidian poet of exile:

The experience of writing from Ireland ... progressively displaced "Virgilian" with "Ovidian" perspectives as the would-be laureate became, or adopted the pose of, the critic in exile ... Spenser was quick to realize the literary benefits of writing from a "salvage soyl", of writing a sort of *Aeneid ex Ponto*, and Ovid's poetics of metamorphosis provided a perfect means of exploring the phenomenon of cultural "degeneration" that posed the single greatest threat to the Irish colonial enterprise.[59]

The Elizabethan poet, transplanted literally beyond the English Pale among the hostile Irish, increasingly resembles the Roman poet marooned in Pontus among the barbaric Getes.

I am not arguing here that Spenser demands we should follow his momentary allusion to Medea quite this far, or even that he himself has reconstructed Medea exactly as I have. I do, however, want to suggest that, by bringing Medea into his poem only to shove her out again, Spenser is not only foreshadowing what he will shortly do to his Adicia, but is in a larger sense appropriating an Ovidian poetics that anticipates and provides for the reader's open-ended interpretation of mythological reference. Whether or not we can remember each of Medea's many roles or identify her in all her significance as we read this episode, we do know that she signifies a great deal more than Spenser's recollection of her crime seems to want to admit.[60] At the same time, Spenser's italicized effort to contain Medea's subversive potential within a catalogue of discarded myths – his allusive damage control – testifies to the extent of that potential, to the damage Medea could so easily do to the allegory of justice.[61]

The Triumph of Justice

To be clear, Adicia's threat, coiled within her allusive identities, never translates to any immediate agency over the increasingly triumphal narrative of justice, as decreed by Mercilla and imposed by Arthur and Artegall. As she approaches "flaming with reuenge and furious despight" (5.8.46.9), Adicia attempts to murder the decoy Samient, compelling Artegall to disarm her – a sequence which shadows in narrative terms the allusive ferment underneath, as Spenser neutralizes the threat of Medea by substituting the metamorphosed Hecuba. Ovid's Hecuba, of course, is also a revenger, albeit a more vulnerable one: tearing out Polymestor's eyes for the murder of her son, she is pelted with stones by the king's subjects, until chasing them, she transforms into a dog, "howling in the feeldes of Thrace" (Golding, 13.685). The much-wronged Trojan queen, then, is no Medea, whose powers are akin to those of the poet, and who repeatedly escapes unpunished for her many crimes, nor is a dog pelted with stones as difficult to control as a witch in a flying car drawn by dragons.

Spenser purchases this diminution in allusive agency at the high cost of a corresponding amplification of readerly sympathy, or as Fox puts it, "This moment of Ovidian intertextuality and the specific comparison of Adicia's situation to Hecuba's destabilizes the allegorical meaning of the episode and to some degree the entire book by drawing sympathy to the conquered antiheroine."[62] One of the most frequent figures for misfortune and undeserved suffering in both classical and Renaissance literature, Hecuba generally evokes a sympathetic response of a unique and uncontainable magnitude.[63] Although Spenser alludes to the canine Hecuba – to the moment after her revenge, when she is once again impotent, no longer in possession of her vengeful agency – it is precisely at this moment that Ovid asserts, "Her fortune moved not / Her Trojans only, but the Greekes her foes to ruthe: her lot / Did move even all the Goddes to ruthe, and so effectually, / That Hecub to deserve such end even Juno did denye" (Golding, 13.685–8). Even the violent pagans and their unjust goddess can find pity for this woman; which of Spenser's readers will feel no pity at all for her, and is such a reader therefore just?

If so, it would be a stricter justice than the poet's, for although her lot is by no means to be envied, Spenser arguably treats his antiheroine with that rarest virtue of Book 5: clemency. Adicia, after all, is not beheaded, like Radigund before her or Duessa after her, but instead metamorphoses in a manner that is both quintessentially Ovidian and literally unprecedented; she does not become a dog, but a tiger:

> There they doe say, that she transformed was
> Into a Tygre, and that Tygres scath
> In crueltie and outrage she did pas,
> To proue her surname true, that she imposed has. (5.8.49.6–9)

This metamorphosis is Spenser's invention, unprecedented in the double sense that there are no specific classical myths of mortals becoming tigers, and that Adicia's transformation runs expressly counter to Book 5's proclivity for myths of annihilation. But while tigers do not run visibly or tangibly through Ovid's landscape like the canine Hecuba, they are nevertheless always on the minds of his characters as natural archetypes of injustice. Thus Byblis, seeking to persuade herself that her brother might still respond to her sexual advances, insists *neque enim est de tigride natus* (*Met.* 9.613, "For he is no tigress' son"); Scylla, resentful that Minos has abandoned her, claims his mother was an Armenian tigress (8.121); Medea herself, refusing to let her beloved Jason die in his quest for the Golden Fleece, cries *hoc ego si patiar, tum me de tigride natam … fatebor*! (7.32–3, "If I permit this, then shall I confess that

I am the child of a tigress ...”). In the most resonant of all such similes, Ovid compares Procne's murder of her own son to the killing of a
fawn by a tigress (6.636–7), thus associating the beast with infanticide.
Ovid's elegaic persona, on the other hand, condemns his own beloved
for performing an abortion on herself, comparing her to Philomela and
Medea, whose murders of their own offspring *not even* the Armenian
tigress would commit (*Am.* 2.14.29–36). In other words, even as Adicia's metamorphosis into a tiger likens her to the murderous mothers
of the earlier allusive stanza, it might also distinguish her, as a natural creature without reason, from their cruelty. Ovid authorizes either
interpretation.

As if in flight from such ambiguity, Spenser's narrator quickly distances himself from his own radical mythography, relying on a rhetoric
of indirect reportage – "There they do say" – which he occasionally
deploys as a hedge against accusations of poetic license.[64] This additional distance may save Adicia as much as the narrator, but in any case
it reflects poorly on Artegall, for only a vitiated justice fails to specify
the penalties it imposes on the condemned. Artegall, of course, would
seem to have no real control over where Adicia goes or what form she
takes (he has, after all, never witnessed a metamorphosis), but Spenser
does claim to control his allegory for injustice at the beginning of the
following canto:

> What Tygre, or what other saluage wight
> Is so exceeding furious and fell,
> As wrong, when it hath arm'd it selfe with might?
> Not fit mongst men, that doe with reason mell,
> But mongst wyld beasts and saluage woods to dwell;
> Where still the stronger doth the weake deuoure,
> And they that most in boldnesse doe excell,
> Are dreadded most, and feared for their powre:
> Fit for *Adicia*, there to build her wicked bowre.
>
> There let her wonne farre from resort of men,
> Where righteous *Artegall* her late exyled;
> There let her euer keepe her damned den,
> Where none may be with her lewd parts defyled,
> Nor none but beasts may be of her despoyled ... (5.9.1–2.5)

Quite aside from the Ovidian intertext of Hecuba's transformation and
the sympathy it evokes, or the troublesome transition from the simile

of Adicia "as a mad bytch" to her unprecedented metamorphosis into a tiger, Spenser's ostensible solution to the problem Adicia represents suffers from so many ironic malfunctions as to render allegorical the invincibility of her vice. Even as Artegall secures Adicia's absence from the court, he releases the tiger into the woods, where it is most at home and most powerful, reminding us of the Elizabethans' troubles in Ireland, where the cities and garrison towns were ordinarily defensible enough, while the countryside (where Spenser lived) was periodically overrun by Irish resistance fighters based in the woods and wilderness.[65] The narrator's insistence that we can safely "let her wonne farre from resort of men" is obviously self-belied by the fact that he has brought her back into the poem in order to tell us she is gone. And we might ask, into which of the poem's woods is Adicia driven: into the wandering wood of the very first canto? Into the great forest of the central books? Into the woods of the upcoming Legend of Courtesy – haunt of hired assassins, marauding bears, and cannibalistic tribes? Wherever she is left "to build her wicked bowre" (phrasing that can hardly reassure anyone who remembers Book 2's villainous Acrasia and her Bower of Bliss) – whether she invades her old court or lurks all around it – Adicia's metamorphosis grants her a functional immortality; like the Gealousie that was Malbecco, the rare aetiological resolution to narrative impasse comes at the cost of a permanent threat.[66]

The mere fact of metamorphosis within Book 5's fragmented landscape may finally be more significant than the specific form its subject takes: Spenser no sooner relates the rumor that Adicia has become a tiger than he reports her development into something even worse – "that Tygres scath / In crueltie and outrage she did pas" – demonstrating that injustice, left to itself, grows more dangerous with each passing line. The ambiguity of Adicia's ultimate status and shape implies the poet's continued incapacity to contain his own metaphors, insofar as Adicia's resemblance to the canine Hecuba of the *Metamorphoses* easily carries over to her resemblance to the regal Hecuba, whom Ovid compares to a "lioness" that "rages when her suckling cub has been stolen from her, and follows the tracks of her enemy, though she does not see him" (*Met.* 13.547–8, *utque furit catulo lactante orbata leaena / signaque nacta pedum sequitur, quem non videt, hostem*). Reverting from the dog to the lioness as we follow the source-text, we soon find the human queen again, or as Ovid writes of Hecuba upon her retrieval of Polydorus's corpse, *qua simul exarsit [ira], tamquam regina maneret, / ulcisci statuit poenaeque in imagine tota est ...* (545–6, "When now her rage blazed out, as if she still were queen, she fixed on vengeance and was wholly absorbed in the punishment her imagination pictured").[67] As a character, Adicia is at the mercy of Mercilla's narrative, but as an allusion she continues to haunt the empire that was once hers. The threat of her return, of course, is never realized in the poem as we have it, but her banishment is followed closely by the sudden reappearance of another villain, whom we have long since forgotten: Proteus.

Malengin: Proteus Minor

Like the Souldan and Adicia, Malengin (called "Guyle" in the headnote to 5.9) is a hyperallusive construct, but unlike his predecessors, he is primarily self-allusive in an intratextual sense – that is, he refers us most directly backward to the other villains of *The Faerie Queene*, not outward to competing figures from discrete texts.[68] This is not to say that he is not Ovidian; on the contrary, he not only epitomizes the *Metamorphoses* in his protean nature per se, but also in his metamorphic embodiment of the poet's commitment to self-revision. As a revised Proteus, Malengin is Spenser's variation on an Ovidian theme by Spenser, and in his flickering re-embodiments of injustice, his intricate thematic relations to the preceding episodes of the Souldan's demise and Adicia's exile are legion, such that he ultimately forms the third term in a permutating set of Ovidian myths of justice punishing injustice. Malengin is Talus's prey, now that Arthur has destroyed the Souldan and Artegall has driven Adicia from the poem, yet his fate is identical to the Souldan's: these villains, both pounded into indistinguishable fragments, bracket the singular metamorphosis of Adicia with Ovidian myths of annihilation. On the other hand, like Adicia, but unlike the Souldan, Malengin above all presents an allegorical principle (Spenser calls him "deceipt"), and he proves the 1596 poem's last protean, able to metamorphose endlessly and at will.[69] The pursuit of Malengin is, finally, a lengthy detour, not only from the respective quests of Arthur and Artegall, but likewise from the proper mission of Mercilla's herald Samient; although she alerts the knights to the "straunge aduenture, which not farre thence lay," she insists, "Were not ... that it should let your pace / Towards my Ladies presence by you ment, / I would you guyde directly to the place" (5.9.4.5, 7.5–7). When Arthur and Artegall with one voice insist on the adventure, they echo Redcrosse's will to errancy in Book 1, as Spenser couches the entire episode of Malengin's pursuit and demise as a digression from a digression, challenging the reader to find relevance in a narrative far off course. Ultimately, the greatest difficulty of reading the Guyle episode is locating it within the allegory of justice; why does Spenser include this narrative *fughetta*, chasing yet another iteration of protean injustice?

Malengin's accoutrements offer one clue, as his "many an yron hooke" and "great wyde net" link him to one of the most suspenseful episodes of the 1590 poem's Legend of Chastity, in which Florimell, fleeing the teeming threats to her chastity on land, takes refuge in the boat of a sleeping fisherman, only to undergo yet another attempted rape when the villain awakens. Although the serendipitous arrival of Proteus saves Florimell from her assailant, she finds herself besieged anew by the sea god himself, who in an unavailing effort to seduce her takes on the increasingly threatening forms of Faerie knight, king, giant, centaur, and storm, before imprisoning her in his undersea dungeon (3.8.20–43). The corresponding episode of Book 5, then, represents a variation on the earlier scene, as the knights offer the obliging Samient as "bait" for the fisherman Malengin. When they spring their trap, however, it is Malengin, not the knights, who reprises the role of Proteus, this time to escape punishment, whereas his predecessor sought to victimize Florimell through his power over metamorphosis.

By resisting Proteus, Florimell had testified to the superior power of her chastity, but the knights of the Legend of Justice do little to glorify Book 5's nominal virtue in their half-hearted re-enactment of the Proteus episode, for the Ovidian figure is now defined by his impotence. Indeed, Malengin is so overmatched by the agents of justice that the narrative turns farcical:

> There he [Talus] him [Malengin] courst a fresh, and soone did make
> To leaue his proper forme, and other shape to take.
>
> Into a Foxe himselfe he first did tourne;
> But he him hunted like a Foxe full fast:
> Then to a bush himselfe he did transforme,
> But he the bush did beat, till that at last
> Into a bird it chaung'd, and from him past,
> Flying from tree to tree, from wand to wand:
> But he then stones at it so long did cast,
> That like a stone it fell vpon the land,
> But he then tooke it vp, and held fast in his hand. (5.9.16.8–17)

This parody of Proteus flees or cowers alternately, and as Talus catches up to him, the tyrannical jailer becomes the apprehended fugitive. If the

Adicia episode obliged us to forget the antagonist's status as a widow –
as a wronged Medea – and to concentrate instead on her status as a
tiger, the Malengin episode requires us to pretend that a bush, a bird,
a stone, a hedgehog, are tantamount to the god of change in his most
terrifying aspects.[70]

If we feel as if the poet or his characters have learned something from
the Proteus of 1590, we might recall that although the ultimate origin
of any protean myth is Homer's *Odyssey*, the notion that Proteus himself teaches others how to arrest the protean is in fact Ovidian: in Book
11 of the *Metamorphoses*, Proteus reveals the secret to Pelias, frustrated
in his effort to rape the shapeshifting Thetis, advising, *"nec te decipiat
centum mentita figuras, / sed preme, quicquid erit, dum, quod fuit ante, re-
format"* (*Met.* 11.253–4, "And though she take a hundred lying forms, let
her not escape thee, but hold her close, whatever she may be, until she
take again the form she had at first"). In Ovid, the direct result of this
instruction is Pelias's rape of Thetis and the marriage of divinity and
mortality, resulting in Achilles's birth and in a sense providing a myth
of origin for epic itself. Spenser's Legend of Justice, however, seems
impossibly far from this epic fountainhead, and Artegall has effectively
unlearned the lesson long since imparted by Ovid's Proteus:

> So he [Talus] it [Malengin the stone] brought with him vnto the knights,
> And to his Lord Sir *Artegall* it lent,
> Warning him hold it fast, for feare of slights.
> Who whilest in hand it gryping hard he hent,
> Into a Hedgehogge all vnwares it went,
> And prickt him so, that he away it threw.
> Then gan it runne away incontinent,
> Being returned to his former hew:
> But *Talus* soone him ouertooke, and backward drew. (5.9.18)

However flat the knight's learning curve, his iron henchman has
adapted to all the shapes "Deceipt" himself can present. If we associate this absolute policing power over metamorphosis with the various
topical allegories critics have suggested for the Malengin episode – the
extermination of Irish bandits, for example, or the rooting out of Jesuit
agents – we are confronted by a wish fulfilment for the Elizabethan authorities, from London to beyond the Irish Pale. But the disproportion
between Artegall's ignorance of his prey's metamorphic capacity and
his enforcer's hyperawareness of it should trouble our confidence in
this blunt solution to the larger problem Malengin represents. After all,

it now requires four of Mercilla's agents to nullify one derivative protean, whereas Florimell alone could resist the infinite shapes of Proteus himself. At the same time, we might feel that Malengin's demise offers small consolation for the escape of Adicia – "Injustice" herself – into the wide woods of Faerieland.

After the bellowing torments of the Souldan and his wife's tragic pursuit of vengeance, such farcical touches as Malengin's last-ditch transformation into a hedgehog are disarmingly amusing. The villain's manifest harmlessness, however, cannot justify his exoneration; hence, Talus's rigour, as the projection of Artegall's uncompromising virtue, demands the suppression of sympathy, if not its annihilation, for fear of the villainous agency latent within it. There is a stubborn insistence here that injustice, having taken such unthreatening shapes – a hedgehog pricking Artegall's hand with its quills in an effort to flee – might at any time revert to the form of a tyrant, riding down his prey in a chariot with wheels of rotating blades, pulled by carnivorous steeds. Justice requires that all unsanctioned bodies must be pulverized into the same dust, and Malengin's near escape is too much for Talus, who makes everything sure:

> But when as he [Malengin] would to a snake againe
> Haue turn'd himselfe, he [Talus] with his yron flayle
> Gan driue at him, with so huge might and maine,
> That all his bones, as small as sandy grayle
> He broke, and did his bowels disentrayle;
> Crying in vaine for helpe, when helpe was past.
> So did deceipt the selfe deceiuer fayle,
> There they him left a carrion outcast;
> For beasts and foules to feede vpon for their repast. (5.9.19)

Only Talus's pre-emptive punishment reduces "Deceipt" himself to the "selfe deceiuer," to abnegation, to dust. The ambiguity remains, however, for we do not know in what form the villain meets his end; Spenser's hypothetical "would ... / Haue" allows us to envision either a further example of Book 5's iron-age policeman beating the suspect into "sandy grayle," or (alternatively) a Christlike threshing of the devil in his most outrageous form by the "instrument" of royal justice. Like so much else in Book 5, the resolution of the ambiguity is left to the reader, who is free to nod with grim approval at the allegory, laugh at the comedy, pity the colourful villain his grisly end, learn the lesson or resist it. But Spenser also tests our will to unmask and punish injustice:

When all the agency is ours, do we, like Talus, unfeelingly crush our foe when he is weak and pitiable, or do we, like Artegall, permit his escape and risk his recovery? Whatever we decide, Proteus's earlier departure is here reprised, but this time with emphatic finality. Upon Malengin's demise, Spenser abandons shapeshifting itself, which has so well served his poem's villains, from Archimago and Duessa to Proteus and Malengin. Even the Titaness Mutabilitie will not change form, only size, and in any case Malengin's outcast solitude – his pleas for mercy "when helpe was past" – testifies to the belatedness of his protean presence. He no longer belongs in Faerieland, and his pulverization comprises Spenser's decisive castigation of metamorphosis, a residue of paganism that might have led, ultimately, to the satanic serpent.

It is finally this continued access to diabolical agency that not only seals Malengin's fate, but explains his presence in the poem: this recapitulation of Proteus, however vitiated his threat, renders allegorical not injustice itself, but that vice's persistence, its recalcitrance, its adaptability to the efforts of justice as a virtue. The episode may be farcical for the ease of its resolution, but the terror of Malengin lies precisely in his throwaway, derivative status, his promise to return as something other than himself. Proteus's diminishment is counterbalanced by his immortality, rendering Talus's tactical victory pyrrhic – one head lopped off the hydra of injustice. We are shortly to witness the long-awaited execution of Duessa, the poem's most unreformed and ubiquitous villain, but what can Mercilla's capital judgment matter in this fallen world, where every sideways glance introduces a related, reminiscent villain to take the Queen of Scots' place? Book 5 assumes the world's infinite challenge to humanity's finite virtue of justice, presupposing the invincibility of sin in the face of human endeavour. Only divine intervention can save this Ovidian world, but Ovid's Astraea remains infinitely distant.

Murrogh O'Brien's Foster Mother

A little over halfway through his notorious prose dialogue, *A View of the Present State of Ireland*, for the benefit of his interlocutor – the model Englishman Eudoxus, eager to learn all he can about his queen's Irish dominions – Spenser's colonizing persona Irenaeus describes one Irishwoman's hysterical reaction to iron-age justice:

> At the execution of a notable traytor at Lymericke, called Murrogh
> O-Brien, I saw an old woman, which was his foster mother, take up his head,

whilst he was quartered, and sucked up all the blood that runne thereout, saying, that the earth was not worthy to drinke it, and therewith also steeped her face and breast, and tore her haire, crying out and shrieking most terribly.[71]

This distraught figure haunts Book 5 of *The Faerie Queene*, corresponding to Adicia as she seeks vengeance for her dismembered husband, "like an enraged cow ..., like raging *Ino* ..., as a mad bytch, when as the franticke fit / Her burning tongue with rage inflamed hath," like the unnamed Hecuba, like "fell Medea," and finally like nobody we know. Spenser's allegory of Justice requires that we approve such sights as Murrogh O'Brien's quartering, and accustom ourselves to such sounds as his foster mother's lamentations, in willing subjection to a comprehensive and unremitting ideology. Our readerly model, in effect, is Spenser's own Eudoxus in the *View*, whose response to Irenaeus's gruesome recollection is that of the armchair anthropologist:

> You have very well runne thorough such customes as the Irish have derived from the first old nations which inhabited the land ... It now remaineth that you take in hand the customes of the old English which are amongst the Irish ...[72]

As secretary to the brutal Lord Grey, whose administration of justice in Ireland he admired, Spenser must have seen many executions like that of Murrogh O'Brien, and probably witnessed the massacre of six hundred Spanish prisoners in one morning at Smerwick on 9 November 1580.[73] But does this participant in colonial justice, as a political author, expect his English reader, removed from such carnage and its motives, to respond like Eudoxus? Has he himself, even or especially with Irenaeus's eyewitness knowledge, learned to react with Eudoxus's exemplary dispassion, with understanding, with tacit approval, and without sympathy? And when Spenser refashions his own fallen world as poetry in Book 5 of *The Faerie Queene*, does he simply transmute Irenaeus's experience into allegory, and expect us still to approximate Eudoxus, or does the world look even darker when the poet portrays it?

I have argued here that, by altering his allusive process, Spenser makes room in his Legend of Justice for a sympathy all but missing from Irenaeus's anthropological anecdotalism or Eudoxus's civic curiosity. This sympathy is the volatile by-product of the forceful imposition of justice on the unjust; it is born with justice at the advent of injustice – at the Fall – and it is problematic because it is universal, applying not only to the victims of injustice, but to the deserving victims of justice. I do not wish to claim that in Book 5 the poet welcomes the sympathy he finds, or that he propagates and nourishes it, or resigns himself or his reader to feeling it; after all, he drives Adicia out of his poem. Spenser's insistent allusions to dismembered archetypes often seek thus to contain, disperse, or displace the sympathy they evoke. On the other hand, I am claiming that he knows such efforts are futile. For all his allegorical struggle to eliminate the residual sympathy accumulating with each permutation of injustice, Spenser never fails to register the inevitable recurrence of that sympathy, even if it always represents a threat to his allegory's impossibly distant, almost forgotten ideal. According to a single Ovidian dynamic, Spenser both erases the bodies of the unjust and records their names in *The Faerie Queene*; despite himself ("they say"), he lets Adicia live. Banishing the vengeful widow, refusing her allusive access to Medea's agency, relegating her to the past, transforming her into a beast – none of these measures can quite eliminate Adicia from Faerieland, through which she runs distracted like Hecuba. In *The Faerie Queene*, there is no ignoring Murrogh O'Brien's foster mother, however much Spenser tries to tell his story like Irenaeus, whether or not we try to read it like Eudoxus.

4 The Post-Metamorphic Landscape in Drayton's *Endimion and Phoebe* and *Englands Heroicall Epistles*

"*Rosamond* is so like Ovid that we catch ourselves trying to remember the Latin," wrote C.S. Lewis in 1954, reviewing Michael Drayton's 1597 collection, *Englands Heroicall Epistles*.[1] Like so many of his venerable declarations, the statement tells us more about Lewis himself than about the poet under discussion; the "we" is eminently royal, and the quiet joke – that Lewis can't be bothered to consult Ovid's original Latin – gives us a fair estimate of the amount of time we may devote to Drayton's bestseller: long enough to recognize the Elizabethan poet's successful imitation of his classical model, Ovid's *Heroides*, but not long enough to identify or interpret any specific allusions. From here, Lewis wanders into characteristic appraisals of the relative Drabness or Goldenness of Drayton's later poems, but had he paused over that first letter from Rosamond to Henry II (or, better yet, retrieved his Ovid from the shelf to compare the texts), he would have perceived that there isn't much Latin to remember after all; neither Rosamond's epistle nor Henry's response contain many passages directly indebted to the *Heroides*.[2]

Instead, Drayton sets this opening section of his volume – the first of twelve paired verse epistles fictionalizing the amours of the legendary couples of English history – in dialogue with another contemporary English poem: Samuel Daniel's *Complaint of Rosamond*, published in 1592. The case is similar with regard to the rest of Drayton's collection; Jane Shore's letter to Edward IV, for instance, only vaguely resembles any particular Ovidian source, but clearly responds to Thomas Churchyard's popular treatment of the scandalous affair in the 1587 *Mirror for Magistrates*. Subsequent letters, such as the exchange between Richard II and Isabel of Valois, likewise bear little evident relation to the *Heroides* – Ovid's epistolary interpolations into the mythological record from the perspectives of the wives and mistresses left behind by the patriarchal traditions of epic and tragedy.[3] Yet the central *Epistles* do present incisive psychological portraits of historical figures familiar to Elizabethans from recent dramatizations of the Wars of the Roses, including those of Shakespeare. A few of the *Epistles*, notably those of Matilda to King John and of Isabel de Ferrers to Roger Mortimer, resonate most insistently with other poems by Drayton himself (*Matilda the Faire* and *Mortimeriados*, published in 1594 and 1596, respectively).

Englands Heroicall Epistles, in other words, intervene not in the poetry of the past, but in that of the present. The Ovidian corpus (not limited to the *Heroides*) serves Drayton as a means rather than an end, as the periscope through which he observes the works of professional rivals, before torpedoing them if necessary with satire. This does not mean that Lewis is wrong to claim that Drayton is "like Ovid," nor am I suggesting that "the Latin" is generally expendable and can therefore be left on the shelf. On the contrary, Drayton himself acknowledges his debt to Ovid in the preface to the *Epistles*, referring explicitly to "OVID (whose Imitator I partly professe to be)," and his contemporaries readily identify him as the "English Ovid."[4] William Alexander's commendatory sonnet to the *Epistles*, which concludes "That OVIDS Soule revives in DRAYTON now," is characteristic of the volume's reception, and indeed follows the same conventional conceit of Pythagorean metempsychosis employed by Francis Meres in his praise of Shakespeare and by John Davies for his first prefatory sonnet to Chapman's *Banquet of Sense*.[5]

Such statements emphasize the synecdochal quality of early modern Ovidianism, as readers tended to identify those who adapt one element of the Roman poet's corpus with Ovid's wholesale "rebirth." Indeed, Meres, Alexander, and others, whose praise for their contemporaries automatically transmutes any imitation or translation into a full-scale instance of metempsychosis, ironically share the basic assumption of Ovid's detractors, whose animosity to erotic verse extends to a blanket condemnation of Ovid.[6] In stipulating that he only "partly professes to be" an Ovidian, Drayton seeks to forestall any such impulsive, uncompromising reception (for or against), and wishfully implies that the imitative poet fully controls the parameters of his engagement with a precursor. The *Epistles'* reader, it seems, is responsible for recognizing which aspects of Ovid's protean example Drayton endorses through imitation, and which he judiciously avoids. This task of differentiating Drayton's approved Ovidianism from undesirable alternatives, however, is not as difficult as it seems, for history as digested by the Tudor and Elizabethan chroniclers remains the reader's guide. If in his epistle the notorious King John invokes a rape-scene from the *Metamorphoses*, for instance, we suspect that Drayton does not approve that myth nor others like it; if Surrey's idealized beloved Geraldine echoes the prayers of Ovid's Penelope, on the other hand, we may safely assume a purer, more direct inspiration of the poet by his precursor. The *Epistles'* contemporary satirical aspect complements this retrospective assessment of historical figures as more or less trustworthy voices. We doubt the integrity of Ovidian voices corresponding to the personas of Drayton's Elizabethan rivals, while privileging his deviations from the norms those rivals have collectively established.

The following pages concern this strategically partial Ovidianism: Drayton's division of one synthetic "Ovid" into multiple, notionally discrete "Ovids" to be accepted or rejected by the reader on an individual basis. The latter category includes two familiar targets: first, Drayton clearly wishes to avoid the blatant, unprintable eroticism of Nashe's *Choice of Valentines* or Marlowe's *Elegies*, both condemned to the bonfire along with a host of satirical works in the Bishops' Ban of July 1599; second, Drayton seems equally determined to move beyond the Petrarchan tropes of conventional love poetry. To be sure, in *Ideas Mirrour* and other early efforts, Drayton too had embraced the rhetorical seductions of the sonnet sequences beloved by Elizabethan courtiers and those aspiring to their patronage. Often conflated with commonplace allusions to the *Metamorphoses* or its attendant early modern commentaries, such Petrarchan blandishments had long since migrated from courtly lyric to the epyllion, most influentially in Lodge's *Scillaes Metamorphosis* and Shakespeare's *Venus and Adonis*. By repudiating these most garish registers of amorous verse in the *Epistles*, Drayton hopes to demonstrate his professional maturity – in a sense, to prove himself Spenser's laureate rival, far above the likes of Lodge and Shakespeare.

At the same time, Drayton remains committed to popular poetry, forging a professional strategy that signals a clear shift away from manuscript and patronage culture, towards one of print and publication. While he prefaces each pair of *Epistles* with dedications to well-to-do patrons (again following Spenser's lead in the *Complaints* volume of 1591), increasingly Drayton proposes, as Andrew Hadfield remarks, "to cast his net wider in flattering a readerly public rather than a circle of powerful aristocrats, … connecting himself as poet to a readership and other poets, all through the interactive medium of print."[7] Accordingly, throughout the mature epistolary collection, Drayton reconstructs an

Ovid he may imitate in a positive manner, offering his readers a patriotic work well-attuned to contemporary fashion, neither prone to eroticism nor confused and adulterated with Petrarchan rhetoric. Drayton recognizes, however, that becoming England's "poet laureate in print" requires more than the rejection of hackneyed forms, the usual patriotism, and the gimmick of epistolarity. These aspects of the *Epistles* are mere adjuncts to the central "part" of Drayton's partial Ovidianism: the comprehensive depiction of a post-metamorphic landscape, everywhere haunted by Ovid's myths of bodily transformation, yet nowhere admitting the *nova corpora* of his poetry.

The post-metamorphic landscape of the *Epistles* might therefore appear altogether anti-Ovidian, but essentially Drayton expands upon the sense of cultural belatedness already apparent in Ovid's own work, enshrined in the humanist tradition since Petrarch, and evident in contemporary English epyllia and epics alike. Again and again, Drayton's epistolary wooers (usually male) show themselves fatally ignorant of the passing of the metamorphic world, while their wiser correspondents (usually female) lament its passage with unrestrained nostalgia. In the *Epistles*, the beloveds of English history already know what Shakespeare's Venus or the denizens of Spenser's Legend of Justice must learn so painfully – that the age of metamorphoses, like that of miracles, is finished. The ardent lovers, meanwhile, are made to learn this lesson through the inexorably unmetamorphic march of history. In itself, this effect is nothing new: Drayton's Eleanor Cobham, exiled for practicing witchcraft and conspiring against Henry VI, can no more sprout wings and fly to safety than Lavinia could regain her mutilated limbs in Shakespeare's theatre. By lending this trope an historical dimension, however, Drayton renders retroactive what is in fact an intertextual phenomenon. In other words, he projects onto English history the compounding inefficacy of this particular aspect of Ovidianism within the literature of his own culture; for Drayton, precisely because Lavinia could not metamorphose into a bird in 1592, Eleanor Cobham had all the less opportunity to do so in 1450.

Drayton, then, builds on the Ovidian techniques of his contemporaries, but at the same time he implies that they have not understood the implications of the end of metamorphosis for the practice of imitation. For Drayton, Ovidianism is more relevant than ever since the demise of metamorphosis, because once liberated from mythological narrative, the enterprising poet may lay claim to Ovidian authority by recalling other portions of the Ovidian corpus, especially the *Tristia* and *Epistulae ex Ponto*, which resonate even more strongly than the *Heroides* through the complaints of Drayton's tragic personas. At the same time, the ghosts of *Metamorphoses* continue to haunt the *Epistles*, offering history's castaways an alternative realm of what might have been, had mythology triumphed over history instead of fading into it. Such visions bring a strange combination of comfort and torment to Drayton's characters, until the collection becomes an echo chamber for the endless ambiguities of Ovid's poetry and the many imitations it fostered, themselves often highly ambivalent. Fittingly, then, Drayton's collection begins in an English labyrinth, superimposed over his rival Daniel's revision of the original labyrinth, built by Ovid's Daedalus at the lost centre of the *Metamorphoses*.

Rosamond's labyrinth, however, is only the gateway to the *Epistles* volume, which in its epic scope dwarfs not only Daniel's brief *Complaint*, but Shakespeare's renditions of episodes from the *Metamorphoses* and the *Fasti*, Chapman's *Banquet* (a "slight repast" rather than a feast in the Renaissance),[8] and the entire second wave of late Elizabethan epyllia, with their sense of Ovidian imitation as apprentice poetry. Even Spenser's *Faerie Queene*, in which so many allusions to the *Metamorphoses* are beaten down like Malengin or erased like Busirane's tapestries, can seem impoverished beside the multiple perspectives of the *Epistles'* narrators and their collective retrieval of Ovidian *copia*. In its most positive sense, then, the post-metamorphic landscape of the *Epistles* provides a backdrop for Drayton's laureate self-presentation, and this ambition likewise echoes Ovid, who after all had asserted his own cultural authority in the aftermath of mythology. By the end of the *Metamorphoses*, Augustus's presumptive stellification and godhead are all that remain of the *nova corpora* of the epic's opening lines, yet even in this defeat of mythology by history, Ovid finds a way to celebrate his poetic achievement. Declaring in the famous closing lines, "wherever Rome's power extends over the conquered world, I shall have mention on men's lips, and, if the prophecies of bards have any truth, through all the ages shall I live in fame" (15.877–9, *quaque patet domitis Romana potentia terris, / ore legar populi, perque omnia saecula fama, / siquid habent veri vatum praesagia, vivam*), the poet rockets from the identification of the empire itself with his epic to the confident prediction of his own immortality. For Drayton, this ambition constitutes the most desirable part of the "partial" profession of Ovidianism, as the basis of his own bid to "live in fame."

"Telling a story wholly of unkindness": *Endimion and Phoebe* as a Prelude to the *Epistles*

Drayton did not invent what I call the post-metamorphic landscape on his own or without practice. The landmark epyllia of the vogue's early years – Lodge's *Scillaes Metamorphosis*, Shakespeare's *Venus and Adonis*, and Marlowe's *Hero and Leander* – all capitalized on a growing sense of Ovidianism's ephemerality, and together heralded the collapse of metamorphosis as a narrative standard in the 1590s. As the second wave of epyllia followed, growing increasingly satirical by the end of the century, the common denominator remained an understood sense of literary apprenticeship, of Ovidian imitation in general and the epyllion in particular as the poetry of youthful ambition.[9] Most of these Ovidian debuts implied "graver labours" to come, following Shakespeare's lead by portraying the last metamorphosis or utmost aetiology. Often confined to the final few lines of a poem, presented as an afterthought or as a grudging concession to form, such outlandish metamorphic products as Cyril Tourneur's unicorn or John Weever's satyr had the ironic cumulative effect of perpetuating the trope.[10]

Drayton likewise published an epyllion, *Endimion and Phoebe*, in 1595, and it too is an apprentice work, but its debts are not to Shakespeare, and it prefigures the "graver labour" of *Englands Heroicall Epistles* by resituating Ovidian imitation squarely within a post-metamorphic landscape. As critics have shown, Drayton's version of the comic myth of the lunar goddess and her slumbering shepherd evinces a preference for Spenserian allegory over the usual erotic or satiric tendencies of the epyllion.[11] As the only Elizabethan epyllion in which the course of love indeed runs smooth, *Endimion* parodies the open-ended rhetorical displays and narratives of terminally frustrated desire so common to the genre. Whereas a mere strait of water had fatally separated Hero from Leander, even a synod of indignant Olympian gods cannot prevent Drayton's Phoebe from descending from her cosmic sphere in order to woo her mortal beloved. Again, while Shakespeare's Venus had memorialized the slain Adonis in a short-lived flower, Drayton's more fortunate goddess keeps Endymion "ever beautifull and yong" in sleep (*EP* 990).[12] Finally, in place of Scilla's monitory entombment at the climax of Lodge's poem, Drayton's idyll culminates in happy nuptials and a triumphal procession of the Graces and Muses. Having selected a nearly plotless myth, Drayton pads his poem with gorgeous pageantry, pastoral descriptions of the most unspoiled variety, and a Neoplatonic encomium on the mystical numbers three and nine.

In the midst of all this harmony, however, the Ovidian trope of metamorphosis sounds the only false note. Fittingly, it is Drayton's passionate shepherd, rather than his chaste goddess, who leads us down this dubious allusive path. Awakening to find his beloved by his side, but unaware of her divine identity, Endymion assumes the voice of "a man whom Love had learned [i.e., taught] Art," and speeds through the usual courtly blandishments, recounting his amorous "torments," affirming that the wind falls silent in deference to Phoebe's voice, and pleading for her "pity" (561–82). He next invents a cautionary tale:

> Behold (quoth he) this little flower belowe,
> Which heere within this Fountayne brim dooth grow;
> With that, a solemne tale begins to tell
> Of this fayre flower, and of this holy Well,
> A goodly legend, many Winters old,
> Learn'd by Sheepheards sitting by their folde,
> How once this Fountayne was a youthfull swaine ... (583–9)

Endymion narrates the anonymous swain's "unfortunate" love for "a fayre Nymph," his unavailing efforts to court her with the same strategies we have just seen Endymion himself employ, and his discovery that his professed sorrow, "Which might dissolve a rock of flinty harts," falls on ears "more deaf and hard then steele or stone" (591–6). These latter metaphors, of course, could easily derive from the Petrarchan tradition, but Endymion's increasingly metamorphic narrative renders them a pointed allusion to Lodge's petrified Scilla, "hard as flint."[13] Drayton's shepherd soon arrives at his tale's metamorphic climax: "The Gods at length uppon his sorrowes looke, / Transforming him into this pirrling Brooke, / Whose murmuring bubles softly as they creepe, / Falling in drops, the Channell seems to weepe" (599–602). It is exactly the wrong mythic model, as weeping oneself into a brook is generally the fate of Ovid's forlorn female characters, most prominently the incestuous Byblis (*Met.* 9.656).[14] But if Endymion's nameless swain suffers a fate as unprecedented as it is ludicrous, his hard-hearted nymph soon falls victim to an equally incongruous metamorphic punishment:

> And comming one day to the River side,
> Laughing for joy when she the same espyde,

> This wanton Nymph in that unhappy hower,
> Was heere transformd into this purple flower,
> Which towards the water turnes it selfe agayne,
> To pitty him by her unkindnes slayne. (605–10)

The aetiological flower, of course, has a pedigree reaching back to Ovid, but its purple colour identifies it most immediately with the ultimate metamorphosis of Shakespeare's Adonis, and Endymion's admonition to Phoebe is wholly inappropriate, insofar as it reminds the alert reader of the quintessentially unattainable male pursued by the least chaste of all goddesses.[15] Drayton's joke is less a retrospective critique of Ovid than a lateral parody of contemporary Ovidians, who would seduce their readers with inept or contrived allusions to metamorphosis.

Drayton's Phoebe listens eagerly to her shepherd's tale – "She … all this time attended, / Longing to heare" – but soon grows enraged upon detecting his artifice:

> Now like a jealous woman she repeats,
> Mens subtilties, and naturall deceyts;
> And by example strives to verifie,
> Their ficklenes and vaine inconstancie:
> Their hard obdurate harts, and wilfull blindnes,
> Telling a storie wholy of unkindnes. (611–18)

The joke appears to be as much on Phoebe and her jealousy as on Endymion and his falsity, but in any case the "Art" the shepherd employs identifies him with Ovid's *Ars amatoria* and with the unscrupulous, oversexed gods of the *Metamorphoses*, who often tell such admonitory tales to persuade reluctant nymphs to sleep with them.[16] Once implicated, Endymion's protest, that "all he spake was in good fayth and troth," inevitably seems suspect, as does his outlandishly chivalric vow of "secrecie, the crown of a true Lover" (624, 626). In the event, Endymion's sincerity hardly matters; Phoebe wants him, and ends all discussion by revealing her identity and transporting him first to heaven and finally to her bower on Mount Latmus. Her omnipotent intervention in her own amorous interest serves as one last parody of Shakespeare's Venus, who was left with nothing but a broken flower.

Despite the comic finale, Endymion's self-serving fiction of metamorphosis – anonymous, unverifiable, and lackluster in its delivery – amply illustrates Drayton's low opinion of the telltale Ovidian trope. The entire digression proves a parodic exercise in rhetorical vanity, utterly without consequence for what little plot the myth permits, and serving only to cast doubt on the antics of Petrarchan lovers and the "goodly legends" of shepherds. Insofar as these antics and legends correspond to the conventional genres of love poetry and pastoral, however, Drayton's satire proceeds beyond his rivals' work and towards self-satire, for his own publications prior to 1595 had consisted of eclogues and a sonnet sequence.[17] Associating Drayton's epyllion with his presumed relocation to London in 1595, Georgia Brown argues:

> *Endymion and Phoebe* enacts a rite of passage for Drayton, and through its composition he takes leave of his poetic youth, and particularly the pastoral and Petrarchan forms which are identified with his early career ... Urbanization requires new modes of identity and new forms of social and discursive authority for Drayton, and he uses the epyllion as a way of transforming pastoralism into the more appropriate forms of witty urbanity and sophistication."[18]

While conjectural, Brown's claim is compelling, given that the poem itself traces the shepherd's accession from a low pastoral landscape – "a Grove, / Which by the mount was shadowed from above" (*EP* 339–40) – to the lofty shrine of the goddess routinely identified with Queen Elizabeth. In this context, Endymion's misguided effort to seduce Phoebe, according to Ovidian "Art" and the aetiological ghosts of the pastoral tradition, appears especially retrograde. Drayton links the trope of metamorphosis to this implicit self-critique, and replaces the backward-looking, pagan myths of metamorphosis with the idealistic tropes of Neoplatonism: sublimation, apotheosis, rapprochement between human and divine.

Such priorities sound Spenserian, and critics have traditionally perceived Drayton as one of the first English poets to imitate Spenser in moving from pastoral to epic, progressing from the early *Shepheards Garland*, with its obvious debt to Spenser's youthful *Shepherdes Calender* and its hero Colin Clout, to the epic *Mortimeriados* three years later. By this account, *Endimion* looks away from rival epyllia, with their lubricous tales of passionate shepherds and randy goddesses, towards a still-distant Spenserian transcendence, which Drayton would only arguably achieve with the publication of the first part of his monumental *Poly-Olbion* in 1612.[19] The post-metamorphic landscape of *Endimion*, however, predates the cataclysmic Ovidianism of the 1596 *Faerie Queene*, and the most fruitful intertext for us to follow may not lead to Spenser, but (surprisingly) to Marlowe.

Hero and Leander, after all, is already set in a post-metamorphic landscape, for all its echoes of the *Metamorphoses*. While a blue and bumptious Neptune may still emerge from the poem's depths, Proteus – the avatar of metamorphosis itself – is merely "carvd" upon the wall of Venus's temple in Sestos. Whereas Homer's Proteus and Ovid's protean Thetis had exhausted their respective *nova corpora* in the unwanted embraces of mortals (*Od.* 4.434–61; *Met.* 11.221–65), Marlowe's frozen Proteus serves as an emblem of mutability arrested, pinned to the wall by art. The temple doubles eerily as the tomb of metamorphosis, for beneath the crystal "pavement" called "Venus's glass," the poet informs us, "There might you see the gods in sundrie shapes, / Committing headdie ryots, incest, rapes." Such quintessentially Ovidian metamorphoses as Jupiter transformed into a bull to entice and abduct Europa, or "Sylvanus weeping for the lovely boy / That now is turn'd into a Cypres tree," literally but inaccessibly underlie the poem.[20] Separated from Hero and Leander themselves, the supine metamorphic gods are relegated to the opposite side of the temple's ekphrastic floor. Elizabethan readers could find these figures elsewhere, of course, woven into the tapestries of Ovid's Arachne or Spenser's Busirane, but in *Hero and Leander* they are no longer supple intertexts, but congealed tableaux.

To be sure, Drayton's naive Endymion and coercive Phoebe appear paltry beside Marlowe's mythic lovers, but their antics may be of less moment to Drayton than his epyllion's reinstitution of Marlowe's post-metamorphic vision. In the *Heroicall Epistles*, Drayton stretches that vision across English history. Whether his narrators cling like Marlowe's Hero to bygone mythology, or like Leander stroll obliviously through the allusions all around them, they can never regain access to the other side of Venus's universal glass.

Rosamond Lost in the Allusive Labyrinth

The *Epistles* are experimental imitations, in that they introduce a wider public to a new Ovidianism. Drayton shares Spenser's sense of the utility of systematic allusion to the *Metamorphoses* as a means to self-revision and professional renewal, just as he shares Shakespeare's confidence in Ovid's durability under the public eye. But in the *Epistles* he also moves well beyond his own brief and frankly derivative *Endimion and Phoebe*, towards the open-ended format of the *Heroides* and the ambiguous frame-narration of the *Metamorphoses*. The Ovid Drayton finds through this exploration is the foster father of an epic unmooring, whose complex legacy disorients the *Epistles'* narrators even as they cite his myths. When Rosamond or Matilda or Jane Shore lose their bearings, it is Ovid's *Metamorphoses* in which they lose themselves, and due to the epistolary format, we register their insouciance in the first person.

To be sure, portions of the *Epistles* are familiar enough; at many points in the collection, as he divorces the "Heroicall" Ovid from more insidious precedents, Drayton amplifies his critique of the Petrarchan rhetoric that served Endymion so poorly in the 1595. Indeed, the ventriloquized wooing of Drayton's male correspondents derives less directly from Ovid's *Ars amatoria* than from the blazon and related Petrarchan tropes, rendered tiresomely familiar by centuries of courtly love and a decade of homegrown sonnet sequences.[21] In the most extreme parody of the collection, King John's bumbling efforts to seduce the chaste Matilda render comic the brutal tyrant Drayton had portrayed in his earlier, tragic treatment of the legend. John plunders the blazonic rainbow, declaring, "Now like I Browne (O lovely Browne thy Haire) / Onely in Brownnesse, Beautie dwelleth there. / Then love I Blacke, thine Eye-ball blacke as Jet, / Which in a Globe, pure Crystalline, is set," then on to white, and so forth (3.41–4). Soon enough, we sense that the unfortunate Matilda has retreated to a convent as much to avoid the king's rhetoric as to escape his lust; that she must nonetheless endure his letters (as surely as she will suffer death on his orders) effectively satirizes the cliché courtly language still employed in the mid-1590s by hack sonneteers like Bartholomew Griffin or the anonymous author of *Zepheria*.

In her angry reply to John's advances, however, Drayton's Matilda identifies such rhetoric not with the court or the sonnet, but with the nefarious influence of the *Metamorphoses* as a compendium of myths promoting sexual profligacy:

> Lascivious Poets, which abuse the Truth,
> Which oft teach Age to sinne, infecting Youth,
> For the unchaste, make Trees and Stones to mourne,
> Or as they please, to other shapes doe turne:
> Cinyra's Daughter, whose incestuous Mind,
> Made her wrong Nature, and dishonour Kind,
> Long since by them is turn'd into a Myrrhe,
> Whose dropping Liquor ever weepes for her;
> And in a Fountaine, Biblis doth deplore

> Her Fault so vile and monsterous before …
> She that with Phœbus did the foule Offence,
> Now metamorphos'd into Frankincense:
> Other, to Flowers, to Odors, and to Gumme;
> At least, Joves Leman is a Starre become:
> And more, they faine a thousand fond Excuses,
> To cloud their Scapes, and cover their Abuses;
> The Virgin onely they obscure and hide,
> Whilst the unchaste by them are deify'd … (4.135–44; 147–54)

Of course, this too is a "partial" reading of the *Metamorphoses*, which includes such exemplary virgins as Daphne and Diana, but the most striking aspect of this catalogue is its encyclopedic breadth.[22] It is as if Matilda, glancing ironically at Elizabethan allusive practice, has kept a commonplace book and perused it for Ovidian examples of lust, or has cherry-picked the most notorious trysts straight from Conti's *Mythologiae*. After all, only an attentive and determined reader of such texts could unearth Ovid's obscure aetiology for frankincense (originally the nymph Leucothoë, buried alive in a remote corner of the *Metamorphoses* for a dubious act of unchastity).

Matilda's very command of the lore she indicts, then, ironically affirms the universality of Ovid's influence; his myths have penetrated even the walls of her nunnery.[23] Yet as rhetorical means to persuasion, despite their cultural virulence, such Ovidian examples prove as ineffectual as the hackneyed Petrarchan tropes with which they are conflated, as if the blazon and its like were the historical consummation of the art Ovid pioneered.[24] Even Matilda's letter, which elsewhere achieves poetic flights the lowly John could never manage, becomes steadily less compelling as her Ovidian allusions pile up; citing those "Lascivious Poets," she is for once literally on the same page as her would-be seducer.

In their ostentatious efforts to avoid such irony, the female correspondents of the *Epistles* generally reject Petrarchan blandishments and Ovidian examples alike as rhetorical opportunism or downright fraud. Even the relatively unchaste Jane Shore condemns "*Romes* wanton Ovid," and urges the amorous Edward IV, who woos through such Petrarchan fashion accessories as ruby lips and teeth of pearl, to forget the "Rules" of Ovid's "Art," chiding him for "feigning" like a poet (18.103–6). In the *Epistles*, then, Drayton multiplies the artful but unsuccessful Endymion figure of his 1595 epyllion, while simultaneously ramifying the mythical chastity of Phoebe into the historically attested virtues of Matilda, Jane Grey, and their sister correspondents. The momentary petulance of the Arcadian shepherd here balloons into the tyranny of lustful princes, while the lunar goddess's nominal chastity, redistributed among historical subjects with every worldly reason to surrender their virginity, approaches correspondingly "Heroicall" proportions. Drayton's leap from mythographic aetiology to historical causality likewise amplifies the consequences of his characters' sophistical misuse of rhetoric and allusion; Endymion had invented his narcissistic admonition in the play-space of "Idea's Latmus" – and had literally failed to alter the course of the moon – but in the context of the chronicle, the errancy of princes leads inevitably to the civil strife and devastation Drayton treats in his *Legends* and epic verse. Where we once doubted Endymion's rhetorical evocation of a numinous mythological landscape, we now know to discount entirely the blandishments of historical figures whose vice or corruption threatened to ruin England.

Of course, neither Matilda nor Mistress Shore pen their own epistles; their explicit indictments of Ovid's more suspect precepts or racier myths are properly the poet's allusions.[25] As when Chapman explicitly invokes the myths of Diana's sexual proclivities in the *Shadow of Night*, even as he expels them from the allusive temple he erects to her chastity, Drayton's "partial" Ovidianism encompasses unexpected or flatly contradictory elements of the Ovidian corpus, such that the *Epistles* in general testify to a much broader intertextual engagement than the self-limited versions advocated by the collection's individual correspondents.[26] Unlike Chapman's *Shadow*, Shakespeare's *Venus and Adonis*, or his own *Endimion*, however, in the *Epistles* Drayton never settles on a central, representative myth, accorded a special currency or validity beyond the rest of the *Metamorphoses*. Instead, his more discerning correspondents insistently refuse any comfortable identification with particular Ovidian figures, and generally acknowledge the inefficacy of referential certitude. As Matilda rejects any Ovidian identity, so Shore refuses to listen to Edward's Ovidian "Art," and both resemble Phoebe as she reprimands Endymion for his self-serving tall tales of metamorphosis. With each new indictment of easy exemplarity, the unproblematic or admissible "parts" of Ovid's corpus grow fewer for Drayton. Ovidianism's utility accordingly appears to diminish as fast as the allusions proliferate, until even the correspondents' most direct invocations of the *Heroides*, such as Geraldine's appeal to the Surrey – "Then, as ULYSSES Wife, write I to thee, / Make no reply, but come thy selfe to mee" (22.181–2, adapting Penelope's admonition to her absent husband at *Her.* 1.1–2) – cease to be stable reference points by which to navigate historical contingency. The real Surrey, after all, was beheaded for treason, most unlike Ulysses, and Drayton amplifies the irony by placing his allusion to Ovid's comic opening epistle towards the tragic end of his own collection.

We need not wait for the end of *Englands Heroicall Epistles*, however, nor for Drayton's most obvious echoes of the *Heroides*, to engage questions of intertextual continuity or even integrity. Already in the opening exchange of the *Epistles*, between the fallen Rosamond and her royal paramour Henry II, Drayton frames a debate over the application of allusion: in what circumstances and to what extent may mythological paradigms, and Ovidian examples in particular, inform the perspective of the historical subject? Put another way, what exactly can the student of history learn from poetry? Despite the porous boundaries between Elizabethan conceptions of historical writing and poetry, the stakes of the problem are peculiarly high for Drayton, who by 1597 had already published three of his *Legends* and the first edition of his Lucanian national epic.[27] Once again, at issue is not Drayton's struggle with the ancients for authority, nor even his evaluation of the relative merits of various sources (as in Chapman's *Shadow*), so much as his promotion in the minds of readers and patrons of a taste for a distinctive Draytonian style, in preference to the familiar productions of rivals like Warner, Daniel, or that prolific author of sensational histories, Shakespeare.[28] Drayton advertises his own product, not as the most accountable or detailed historical writing – a niche increasingly occupied by the prose chronicles of Stow, Camden, and the like – but as the most responsible imitation of the most fashionable poetic model: Ovid.

Framing this debate over the relevance of Ovidian allusions to historical poetry, Rosamond emerges from the *Epistles'* opening exchange as an especially sensitive reader, while Henry proves self-willed and simplistic as he seeks to dispel her fear of his estranged wife, Eleanor of Aquitaine. Responding to his mistress's plaintive epistle from the labyrinth he has built for her confinement, the tyrant assigns each of his allusions a stable, uncompromising significance:

> Long since (thou know'st) my Care provided for
> To lodge thee safe from jealous Ellinor;
> The Labyrinths Conveyance guides thee so,
> (which onely Vaughan, thou, and I doe know)

> If she do guard thee with an hundred Eyes,
> I have an hundred subtill MERCURIES,
> To watch that ARGUS which my Love doth keepe,
> Untill Eye, after Eye, fall all to sleepe. (2.177–84)

As a miniature Mercury, the parenthetical Vaughan carries messages between the worldly king and the "Rose of the World," and in a broader sense, between the vanished labyrinths of myth and romance on the one hand, and those of English antiquity on the other. For the anonymous historian who provides learned commentary on the *Epistles*, Vaughan helps to anchor Drayton's poetry in the chronicles: "Vaughan *was a Knight, whom the King exceedingly loved, who kept the Palace at* Woodstock … *in whom he reposed such trust, that he durst commit his Love unto his Charge*" (180n).[29] With "a hundred subtill MERCURIES" like Vaughan at his disposal, Henry expresses confidence that all efforts by his jealous wife to keep Rosamond under surveillance will meet with the fate of Argus, the hundred-eyed watchman whom Juno commissions to guard Io – one of Jove's amorous conquests – in the *Metamorphoses*. The allusion, however, is inept (or is, at best, an example of royal dissemblance), for it is Henry who resembles Ovid's Juno, jealously confining Rosamond to the labyrinth and setting his spies to watch her, just as it is Eleanor, rather than Vaughan or any other agent of the king's, who will play Mercury by infiltrating the labyrinth and murdering, not the guard, but the prisoner herself. As the historical record corroborates this latter application of the Io myth, and fails to correspond to Henry's interpretation, the opening exchange of the *Epistles* seems once again to indict Ovidian allusion as empty rhetoric.

We must look to Drayton's Rosamond, then, rather than to Henry, for a demonstration of Ovid's contemporary relevance, as Rosamond is not primarily a creature of the chronicles, but a poetic construct of the 1590s. Drayton's principal source and target for the initial exchange of the *Epistles* is Daniel's *Complaint of Rosamond*, in which the heroine's ghost narrates her own tragedy, and Drayton's epistolary rendition of the legend, and the Ovidian motifs that drive it, are best deciphered in counterpoint to Daniel's treatment. In the earlier poem, by recounting her own fall, Rosamond's spirit, which lingers forgotten and marooned on the shores of Styx, hopes to win the favour of Daniel's beloved Delia, the addressee of the sonnet sequence preceding the *Complaint*. Only Delia's "indulgence" may prove sufficient to transport Rosamond's condemned soul to "sweet Elisian rest, / The ioyfull blisse for Ghosts repurified."[30] Thus dependent on Delia's favour, Daniel's Rosamond subordinates chronicle history to Petrarchan poetry, while Ovidian examples serve in a limited capacity as rhetorical devices for Henry and the envious crone he employs as his pander.

With a different set of generic priorities, Drayton finds more use for Ovid, though always with an eye on Daniel's poem. In both versions of the legend, the characters navigate the labyrinth by a "Clue" or "threed," but Drayton encourages the reader to follow that quaint thread further – that is, intertextually – through Daniel's *Complaint* to Daedalus's original labyrinth at the heart of the *Metamorphoses* (8.152–76). That Ovidian labyrinth, of course, once housed the all-devouring Minotaur, to whom Drayton's Rosamond compares herself, despite her outward beauty:

> Well knew'st thou what a Monster I would be,
> When thou didst build this Labyrinth for me,
> Whose strange *Meanders* turning ev'ry way,
> Be like the course wherein my Youth did stray;
> Onely a Clue doth guide me out and in,
> But yet still walke I circular in sinne. (1.87–92)

The *Epistles'* commentator provides further detail, as he seeks to demystify both Rosamond's labyrinth and its classical prototype:

> *The Labyrinth was framed by* Dedalus, *with so many intricate Wayes, that being entred, one could either hardly or never returne, being in manner of a Maze, save that it was larger ... out of the which,* Theseus, *by Ariadnes helpe, (lending him a Clue of Thred) escaped ...*
>
> Rosamonds *Labyrinth, whose Ruines, together with her Well, being paved with square Stone in the bottome, and also her Tower, from which the Labyrinth did runne (are yet remaining) ...* (87n).

As Vaughan may be found in the chronicles, so the foundations of Rosamond's labyrinth may be located on contemporary maps of England. For Drayton's commentator, the verifiable solidity of the *"square Stone in the bottome, and also her Tower"* supersedes the more nebulous testimonials of ancient mythology and allegory.[31]

These prosaic, antiquarian commentaries, however, remain in tension with the *Epistles'* poetic content, and it is not surprising that the commentator fails to follow Drayton's most important intertextual "Clue" – the proverbially circuitous Meander River, to which Rosamond compares her prison – to its Ovidian source:

> Non secus ac liquidus œrygiis Maeandros in arvis
> occurrensque sibi venturas aspicit undas
> et nunc ad fontes, nunc ad mare versus apertum
> incertas exercet aquas: ita Daedalus implet
> innumeras errore vias vixque ipse reverti
> ad limen potuit: tanta est fallacia tecti. (*Met*. 8.162–8)

> Just as the watery Maeander plays in the Phrygian fields, flows back and forth in doubtful course and, turning back upon itself, beholds its own waves coming on their way, and sends its uncertain waters now towards their source and now towards the open sea, so Daedalus made those innumerable winding passages, and was himself scarce able to find his way back to the place of entry, so deceptive was the enclosure he had built.[32]

Drayton has unravelled the "Clue" far enough that he may circumscribe Daniel's contemporary version of the labyrinth, rerouting us allusively back to its poetic origin in the *Metamorphoses*. At the same time, almost insensibly, Ovid's simile is transfigured as Rosamond's metaphor: even Daedalus's ancient labyrinth was only *like* the Meander that *is* Henry's Woodstock.

Rosamond's thread is no mere intertextual detail, however. For Daniel, the thread had functioned as an allusive umbilical cord; following the clue like Ovid's Theseus (or like Daniel's own Eleanor), the reader could navigate the twists and turns of literary influence, allowing access to the *Metamorphoses* as the scene's principal source, but also egress from that original Latin text back into the English complaint tradition. Presumably, Daniel had suppressed Ovid's associated metaphor of the Meander in order to prevent the river's metaphorical significance – its waters' disorienting habit of flowing "now towards their source and now towards the open sea" – from overwhelming the thread's primary significance as a navigational aid between texts and genres. By restoring the Meander to the intertextual labyrinth (even pluralizing Ovid's singular *liquidus Meandros* as "strange *Meanders*"), Drayton plays Daedalus to Daniel's Theseus, winding the passages back up into unnavigable circularity. Like Rosamond, we may follow the "Clue" back to the *Metamorphoses*, but by doing so we only imprison ourselves anew in that labyrinthine text, wandering among its countless reiterated myths. Her convoluted poetic syntax, arriving at the *hyperbaton*, "But yet still walke I circular in sinne," confirms her disorientation despite the thread.[33] Where Daniel has demonstrated anew the penetrability of the labyrinth, Drayton renews its mystery.

The determinacy of Daniel's labyrinth corresponds to his deployment of classical allusions throughout the *Complaint*, so as to anchor Rosamond to mythological archetypes: in particular, she associates herself with Amymone and Io, victims of divine rape depicted on the "Casket richly wrought" sent to her by Henry on "the day before the night of my defeature" (*Comp.* 379–80). A perverse variation on the traditional *cassone* – the richly decorated "hope chest" presented to a bride by her husband in fifteenth-century Italy – Henry's casket admonishes Rosamond to abandon her resistance to his advances, and fore-ordains her submission.[34] Of the figures depicted, Amymone, raped by Neptune, is far the more obscure, as she is unattested by Ovid and by most mythographers.[35] Daniel's ghostly Rosamond, however, dwells upon her example, appealing to the sympathies of the narrator-persona and the *Complaint*'s larger audience:

> *Neptune* came and caught her:
> From whom she striu'd and struggled to be gone,
> Beating the aire with cries and piteous mone;
> But all in vaine, with him she's forc'd to go;
> Tis shame that men should vse poore maidens so.
>
> There might I see described how she lay …
> Her teares vpon her cheekes (poore carefull Gerle,)
> Did seeme against the Sunne Christall and Pearle. (*Comp.* 388–93, 398–9)

After a further stanza of Petrarchan adornment, Daniel's prone Amymone gives way in Rosamond's ekphrastic recollection to Ovid's familiar myth of Io, "Turn'd to a Heiffer, kept with iealous eyes" (412).

In one sense, Daniel's depiction of the Io myth comes closer than Amymone to the traditional content of Renaissance *cassoni*, which, as Leonard Barkan observes, commonly featured dubiously domesticable myths like the rapes of Proserpina or Europa, as part of a "recuperated paganism," which "speaks to all those powerful natural drives that operate so triumphantly in the Ovidian world."[36] Even this recognizable Io, however, falls short of the conventional imagery of the *cassone*, the shape of which "required multiple figures with a narrative to connect them," as Malcolm Bull attests.[37] Ovid's elaborate myth of Io easily accommodates the kind of storyboarding Bull describes, yet in

Daniel's poem the "other squares" of Henry's casket, far from depicting an unfolding narrative, portray a static emblem of "Transformed *Io*," confined to her bestial shape, under the hundred "iealous eyes" of Argus, the watchman appointed by the furious Juno. Daniel's tyrannical Henry, in other words, short-circuits Ovid's well-known account of Io's liberation, according to which Mercury assassinates Argus on Jupiter's order, and though Juno for a time continues to torment her mortal rival, Io is ultimately rehabilitated, returned to human shape, and worshipped as a goddess.[38] As if ignorant or forgetful of this comic denouement to Ovid's Io story, Daniel's Rosamond interprets Henry's *cassone* as a mirror of her own tragedy:

> These presidents presented to my view,
> Wherein the presage of my fall was showne,
> Might haue fore-warn'd me well what would ensue,
> And others harmes haue made me shun mine owne.
> But Fate is not preuented, though foreknowne.
> For that must hap, decreed by heauenly powers,
> Who worke our fall, yet make the fault still ours. (*Comp.* 414–20)

Rosamond's conclusion subtly decontextualizes her *Complaint*, for in the *Metamorphoses* Io's innocence is never questioned except by Juno, and even she relents at Jupiter's entreaty. By incorporating Io's reverse metamorphosis, Ovid signals his poetic prerogative to vary his treatment of mythological archetypes, allowing them to meander on occasion from human to bestial form and back. In Daniel's *Complaint*, by contrast, any invocation of the gods and their amours leads directly and irrevocably towards bestiality, towards Rosamond's "defeature." If Ovid's tale of Io's rehabilitation retains any resonance for Daniel's heroine, it lies beyond the poem itself, in her expressed hope that the *Complaint* may find a sympathetic audience to restore her reputation. Pending that transformative reception, Io and Amymone alike present Daniel's Rosamond only with dire portents, without room for the ambiguity Drayton cultivates in his epistolary revision.

Towards the end of her letter to Henry, Drayton's Rosamond refers back to the admonitory *cassone* she received in Daniel's *Complaint*, in what at first appears an unsubtle and opportunistic bit of borrowing:

> In that faire Casket, of such wond'rous Cost,
> Thou sent'st the Night before mine Honour lost,
> Amimone was wrought, a harmelesse Maid,

> By Neptune, that adult'rous God, betray'd;
> She prostrate at his Feet, begging with Prayers,
> Wringing her Hands, her Eyes swolne up with Teares … (1.153–8)

While Drayton imports most of these details directly from Daniel's *ekphrasis*, he replaces Amymone's artificial tears of "Christall and Perle" with the more realistic variety, in keeping with the *Epistles'* animus against Petrarchan embellishment. Drayton's Rosamond moreover introduces this more human, less beautified Amymone in order to spin the casket's original rhetorical function – its declaration of absolute sexual power over its recipient – improbably towards an exoneration of the king: "This was not an intrapping Bait from thee, / But by thy Vertue gently warning mee, / And to declare for what intent it came, / Lest I therein should ever keepe my shame" (159–62). According to this revision of the *cassone*, a beneficent Henry (the antithesis of Daniel's brutal Neptune) has sought to preserve his beloved from Amymone's fate. As she turns her attention next to the panel depicting the metamorphosed, closely guarded Io, Rosamond prophetically equates Ovid's Juno (not pictured) with the murderous Eleanor:

> And in this Casket (ill *I* see it now)
> Was *Ioues*-loue *I-o* turnd into a Cowe.
> Yet was she kept with *Argus* hundred eyes,
> So wakeful stil be *Iunos* iealousies;
> By this I wel might haue fore-warned beene,
> T'haue cleerd my selfe to thy suspecting Queene,
> Who with more hundred Eyes attendeth mee
> Then had poore *Argus* single eyes to see.
> In this thou rightlie imitatest *Ioue*,
> Into a beast thou hast transformd thy loue.
> Nay worser farre; (degenerate from kind)
> A monster, both in body and in mind. (163–74)

Drayton presses even orthography into his labyrinthine revision of Daniel's *cassone*, as the rhyme-words "*Ioue*" and "loue" mirror one another, though the italic slant sends a significant ripple through the reflection.[39] The second "loue," however, is already a pun so strong as to reflexively metamorphose Henry himself "into a beast," for readers (ostensibly including Henry) may opt to misread the line, "Into a beast thou hast transformd thy *Jove*" – that is, Rosamond suggests that by loving her so ardently, Henry has fallen from his own divinity into bestiality. Is the lowercase "loue," then, Rosamond herself or Henry's desire for Rosamond? Is the "monster" the Minotaur haunting the Dedalian Labyrinth, or Henry "degenerating" from a divine Jove to a base lover? Scanning backward and forward from that "monstrous" rhyme, Drayton's reader is confronted by multiplying ambiguities, by literal metamorphoses inhabiting the text itself: the serpentine *s* intervening in "*Ioues*-loue"; a faintly audible pun on the "lowing" of cattle; even the "turning" of that absolute *I* of "*I-o*" into the horned *C* of "Cowe." Like the passageways of a Labyrinth, Rosamond's seemingly straightforward allusions to Ovid and Daniel – indeed, the very letters constituting her epistle – lead us from a finite linearity to an endless circularity.

The chronicler John Stow had likened the labyrinth of Woodstock "unto a knotte in a garden," and the local or momentary suggestions of metamorphosis throughout Drayton's *Epistles*, even on the elemental level of orthography, indeed resemble the topiary "knots" of Tudor horticulture. In Rosamond's epistle in particular, Drayton transforms the subterranean labyrinth into a poetic garden with an Ovidian centre:

> Here, in the Garden, wrought by curious hands,
> Naked DIANA in the Fountaine stands,
> With all her Nymphes got round about to hide her,
> As when ACTEON had by chance espy'd her:
> This sacred Image I no sooner view'd,
> But as that metamorphos'd Man, pursu'd
> By his owne Hounds; so, by my Thoughts am I,
> Which chase me still, which way soe'r I flye. (1.139–46)

Such a fountain actually existed in England, though Drayton would have heard about it only by report, as it was located in the Privy Garden of the royal palace at Nonsuch, designed under Henry VIII and redecorated in the 1580s. The fountain imitated continental models, depicting the chaste Diana at her bath, observed by the lascivious Actaeon in the midst of his transformation into a stag, prior to his dismemberment by his own hounds (*Met.* 3.138–252).[40] Whether or not we associate Drayton's fountain directly with the monument at Nonsuch, we perceive first of all that this central Ovidian feature is Drayton's addition to the labyrinth of Daniel's *Complaint*, hence an intertextual departure from the conventions of prose chronicle and mythographic poetry alike.

Even as he pushes the semi-historical Rosamond deeper into the myth-scape of the *Metamorphoses*, however, Drayton resists the easy moralizations of the Actaeon story commemorated in allegorical tableaux like that at Nonsuch, where a signpost admonished visitors to avoid the voyeuristic hunter's fate by refusing to indulge "the temptation to baseness" and "the serpent's view." Instead of describing a monitory statue of Actaeon undergoing metamorphosis for his transgression, Drayton's Rosamond takes Actaeon's crime and punishment upon herself; in a sense, she reproduces Ovid's myth in the absence of metamorphic evidence, for all her suffering is self-imposed by way of simile: "as that metamorphos'd Man, pursu'd / By his owne Hounds; so, by my Thoughts am I, / Which chase me still … " Visitors to Nonsuch, like readers of the *Metamorphoses*, were warned against transgression by the image of Actaeon, manifestly doomed by his sprouting horns, but Drayton's frantic Rosamond invents her Ovidian identity without the corroboration of metamorphosis. No literal hounds, but only her own "Thoughts" – that is, only her memories of Ovid's myth – chase her from the garden and pursue her through the labyrinth. Her hysteria notwithstanding, Drayton's addition of the fountain of Diana pushes his heroine beyond the precedents of Amymone and Io, established by Daniel in the *Complaint*, and renews her access to the wider *Metamorphoses*, to mythology as a whole. In intertextual terms, Drayton's allusion to Actaeon is a thread that disappears into the Ovidian tapestry, implying the applicability of any number of myths to the historical Rosamond's seduction, captivity, and murder.

Yet even as Drayton recommits himself, his heroine, and his readers to the *Metamorphoses*, distinguishing his own work from that of Daniel, he seals off an even more important escape route from Ovidian indeterminacy, in pointed contrast to Shakespeare. By progressing from *Venus and Adonis* to *The Rape of Lucrece*, Shakespeare had advertised his graduation from the cartoonish myths of the *Metamorphoses* to the legends of the *Fasti*, ostensibly more sober and less fanciful. At the crucial moment in Rosamond's letter, however, Drayton introduces a new character in the person of a maid, who inquires as to the significance of a mural depicting Lucretia's suicide. Rosamond begins to explain, "Why girle (quoth I) this is that Roman Dame …" (99), only to cut her explanation short upon recognizing the irony of her own insuperable difference from that Shakespearean paragon: "With that I sent the prattling Wench away, / Lest when my lisping guiltie Tongue should hault, / My Lookes might prove the Index to my Fault" (102–4). To the Elizabethan reader, Rosamond's prophylactic dismissal of Lucretia – lest that "prattling Wench" (or any other audience) register her manifest incongruity with the proverbially chaste figure depicted ekphrastically behind her – has less to do with ancient history than with contemporary poetry. Unlike Shakespeare, Drayton will not flee from the irresolution of myth to the resolution of history, but will instead leave open the gate into Ovid's labyrinth.

The opening exchange of *Englands Heroicall Epistles* thus yields a new and surprising answer to our original inquiry as to which "parts" of the Ovidian corpus Drayton "professes" to imitate: primarily those passages in the *Metamorphoses* that tend towards indeterminacy or outright misdirection; those myths provoking a global crisis of identity among the poem's wandering characters, while compounding the disorientation of its readers. In other words, Drayton does not troll the classical tradition for stable archetypes, so as to assign his historical subjects their corresponding locations along the linear narrative of chronicle. On the contrary, he seeks an Ovidian authority to meander between the labyrinths of literary imitation on the one hand, and the chronicle tradition on the other, in the process corroborating the personal sense of vertigo described by his bewildered historical subjects.

Drayton's Rosamond, then, promises a richer Ovidianism than that abused by Henry II in both the *Complaint* and the *Epistles*, yet there remains a disturbing self-destructive quality to her allusive approach, which never avails her any escape from her fate. This sense of epistolary impotence, moreover, is itself Ovidian, for as Alessandro Barchiesi writes of the *Heroides*:

> The reader must make … incisions into a given framework that cannot be modified, such that the existence of the epistle will not have any effect upon it. Indeed this narrative context is decided elsewhere, in those literary texts … upon which Ovid has chosen to operate. In other words, the narrative autonomy of the letter is curiously interwoven with its pragmatic impotence, and the impotence implied by the context moves every letter into the realm of illusion.[41]

Rosamond's tendency to range ever further through the labyrinth of mythology, only to multiply dead ends, would seem to corroborate Barchiesi's stark assessment; her epistle suffers as much as any of the *Heroides* from "pragmatic impotence," which tends to overwhelm her "narrative autonomy." But as Laurel Fulkerson and others have argued, several of the epistolary "authors" in the *Heroides* work to reverse this effect, seizing a degree of autonomy despite the apparent hopelessness of their situation within a prescripted mythology, endeavouring to "create from scratch a tradition of women's writing (in direct competition with men's writing)."[42] This strategy, too, finds its corollary in *Englands Heroicall Epistles*: Rosamond may languish in despair, but another of Drayton's "authors," the disgraced Eleanor Cobham, though little more than an afterthought in the chronicle tradition, attempts a veritable coup through her allusions to the *Metamorphoses* and the *Tristia*.

Eleanor Cobham Dreams of Metamorphosis

Exploiting the immediate success of his *Heroicall Epistles*, for subsequent editions Drayton added three further pairs of epistles to the original nine, rounding up to the traditional epic numbers of twelve (pairs) and twenty-four (total epistles). These additions compound the ambiguities Rosamond sets in motion in the collection's opening exchange, and move even further from what we might call historicity towards a passionate Ovidian errancy, as each character's allusions to mythological archetypes in general, and to the hapless lovers of the *Metamorphoses* in particular, reflect a personal loss of historical perspective – in this context, a loss of selfhood. "I am not I," declares the exiled Eleanor Cobham in the most striking of the new letters, addressing her husband, Humphrey of Gloucester, likening her physical deterioration to metamorphosis:

> Saw'st thou those Eyes, in whose sweet cheerefull Looke
> Duke HUMPHREY once such joy and pleasure tooke,
> Sorrow hath so despoyl'd them of all grace,
> Thou couldst not say, this was my EL'NORS face:
> Like a foule *Gorgon*, whose dishevel'd Hayre
> With every blast flyes glaring in the Ayre ...
> My lanke Brests hang like Bladders left unblowne,
> My Skin with lothsome Jaundize over-growne;
> So pin'd away, that if thou long'st to see
> Ruines true Picture, onely looke on mee. (13.6, 163–8, 171–4)

Accused of witchcraft as part of a conspiracy to assassinate Henry VI and place Gloucester on the throne, Cobham died in exile, and though Drayton might easily have portrayed her in the midst of her transgression, self-betrayed by a plainly culpable letter and sentenced to public shaming on her way out of London (so Shakespeare had staged Cobham's penance in *The First Part of the Contention*), he depicts her instead languishing on the empire's outer margin. Forgoing drama and dynamism in favour of history's fatal aspect and plaintive resonance, Drayton renders Cobham the antitype to his Rosamond, signalling her difference through her allusive relation to an alternative set of Ovidian sources. While a few of the *Heroides* – for example, Briseis's unavailing appeal to Achilles to take her back – postdate the personal tragedies of their putative "authors," most are interpolated into the classical tradition so as to portend catastrophe (or, more rarely, reconciliation). The *Epistles'* opening exchange is characteristic, as we all but hear the vengeful Eleanor of Aquitaine approaching while Rosamond reads Henry's false assurance of security. By contrast, Cobham's complaint from disaster's aftermath most immediately recalls the *Tristia* and *Epistulae ex Ponto*, Ovid's final elegies from exile. Here, more than anywhere else in Drayton's collection, the Roman poet's unanswered pleas for a reprieve provide the model for epistolary futility.

The *Tristia* and *Ex Ponto*, however, also provide Drayton's Cobham with a strange new access to myths of metamorphic power and momentous self-assertion, through allusions to the great sorceresses of the classical tradition. Having pretended to witchcraft prior to her banishment, Cobham now dreams of the unlimited potency implied by her own lost fictions, echoing Ovid's exilic persona and his envy for Medea's ability to fly from disasters of her own making (*Tr.* 3.8.3–4). Despite possessing no more historical agency than Rosamond, Cobham presents herself allusively as the countertype to her predecessor, who had embraced her victimization by identifying with Amymone, Io, and Actaeon. For Drayton, in other words, witches like Circe or Medea serve not merely as archetypes for metamorphic power, but as the allusive repositories of ambiguity: ambiguous motives, gender roles, and degrees of agency. Renouncing her magic only at sword point, Homer's Circe promptly falls in love with Odysseus and redirects him towards Penelope and home, but by an alternative reading she sends him and his sailors straight to Hades. A descendent of Homer's unruly original, Ovid's Medea is yet more troublesome (as we have seen in the case of Spenser's allusively inscrutable Adicia); primarily a tragic figure, she invites both sympathetic and antipathetic readings, and enjoys a godlike agency in her power over mortality and metamorphosis alike.[43]

By pursuing such ambiguous precedents, Drayton's readers soon re-enter the intertextual labyrinth familiar from the collection's opening epistles, with roundabouts and dead ends located not only in the classical tradition, but in the most current Renaissance poems. Even Cobham's scrofula is allusive; contracted from a long literary tradition – the punitive leprosy suffered by Robert Henryson's Cressida, for instance – it most immediately recalls the shamed Duessa of Spenser's *Faerie Queene*:

> Her crafty head was altogether bald,
> And as in hate of honorable eld,
> Was ouergrowne with scurfe and filthy scald ...
> Her dried dugs, lyke bladders lacking wind,
> Hong downe, and filthy matter from them weld;
> Her wrizled skin as rough, as maple rind,
> So scabby was, that would haue loathd all womankind. (*FQ* 1.8.47.1–3, 6–9)

Herself derived from the witches of the epic tradition, Spenser's enchantress, at first glance, appears a more obvious villain than the lovesick Circe or jilted Medea. Like her immediate prototypes, Ariosto's Alcina and Tasso's Armida, Duessa serves a romantic function as an impediment to the hero's progress, a spur to his errancy. As an allegory for the tempting hypocrisies of Catholicism, moreover, she has no right to the sympathy of Spenser's Protestant readers, who should instead applaud her exemplary doom, meted out by Una, the embodiment of Reformed truth. Blasting his repentant Cobham with the same "lothsome" skin and deflated breasts as Spenser's witch, Drayton links his epistle to this emblematic juncture in *The Faerie Queene*, where Duessa is not so much a character within a dynamic narrative as the admonitory "face of falshood" (49.4), held aloft by Truth for England's edification.

From one perspective, then, the confessional epistolary voice of Drayton's Cobham echoes Una's definitive judgment against Duessa in *The Faerie Queene*. Depending on the degree of credence Drayton's reader lends to centuries-old, politically motivated charges of witchcraft, Cobham may further be held responsible for Henry VI's fatally weak disposition, but in any case, historically her actions precipitated her own downfall as well as that of her husband Gloucester, England's Lord Protector. She bears considerable responsibility, in other words, for the Wars of the Roses, which resonated so strongly with the Elizabethans – including Drayton, who portrayed the conflict in his *Mortimeriados* –

as they faced the prospect of their monarch's death without an heir. As Danielle Clarke observes, "the epistles clearly gesture towards Elizabeth as the apotheosis of the historical trajectory that they traverse, whilst providing a timely reminder of the importance of dynastic security."[44] To the extent that Cobham and her fellow correspondents serve this "clear," exemplary function, however, the Elizabethan reader's capacity to resolve their allusive identities grows more urgent, and Drayton rarely makes such judgments easy. As Clarke notes elsewhere, "Although the form and structure of the epistles is orderly and controlled, the lines of descent are not, as Drayton splices together sources, themselves often uncertain, and incorporates self-conscious allusions to other poets."[45] Can we untangle these "lines of descent" into a coherent account of Drayton's historical revision and allegorical critique of his own culture? Is Cobham, for instance, included in the "trajectory" of the *Epistles'* evolving narrative of Elizabeth's "apotheosis," as an agent who unwittingly catalyses the imperial triumph of the Tudors? Or is she rather outside that trajectory, exhibited like Spenser's Duessa as a timeless, admonitory counter-example, personifying an errant path the nation must not follow?[46]

Even if such a pointed opposition projects too stark an ambivalence onto a work tending elsewhere towards propaganda, there can be little question that Drayton courted seditious interpretations of his poem by depicting so clearly English history's most notorious witch. After all, by 1598, enemies of the regime had begun to revive early anti-Tudor propaganda slandering Elizabeth's mother, Anne Boleyn, as a witch, and despite the continued efforts of court poets to depict the queen as Diana, she grew increasingly easy to associate with the hags and crones of literature. As the French ambassador André Hurault, Sieur de Maisse, reported candidly in 1597, "Her bosom is somewhat wrinkled ... As for her face, it is and appears to be very aged. It is long and thin, and her teeth are very yellow and unequal compared with what they were formerly."[47] Ultimately, Drayton's portrait of Cobham suggests rather than insists upon its own interpretation as a slanderous topical allegory for Elizabeth; contemporary readers might just as easily associate Drayton's hag with the long-dead Mary Stuart or, most straightforwardly, read Cobham as her historical self. But much as Spenser's lukewarm praise of Elizabeth through the allegory of the 1596 *Faerie Queene* allows for seditious reading, so Drayton cultivates the ambiguities of Cobham's self-portrait, and his troublesome allusions to the anti-heroines of classical epic amplify the effect.

Drayton's Cobham, in other words, operates on at least three allusive levels. Most directly, as a figure from the chronicles, she is rooted in English history, like the stony ruins of the commentator's castle of Woodstock, and her epistolary voice remains an impotent complaint from exile. For early modern readers, however, accustomed to interpreting poets' ambiguous renderings of historical figures allegorically as comments on their contemporaries, Drayton's Cobham might not have lingered isolated and inert in the fifteenth century, but might instead have evoked more troubling associations with the present, as Elizabeth herself had interpreted Shakespeare's *Richard II*.[48] Finally, in the less plaintive, more vindictive portions of her epistle, Cobham achieves an allusive resonance with the radically freethinking witches of classical mythology – with Homer's Circe and Ovid's Medea, both survivors irrepressibly central to the epic tradition. Just as Spenser's Ovidian allusions threaten to subvert the triumphal allegory of his own Legend of Justice, so the periodic recourse of Drayton's ventriloquized authors, not only to myths of metamorphosis but also to myths of witches capable of metamorphosing the epic poems around them, awakens dormant readerly sympathies, and hints at character agencies seemingly remote from English history's unmetamorphic record, including magic, revenge, escape, and immortality.

In one sense, of course, the powerlessness of Drayton's Cobham – her unbridgeable distance from the metamorphic witchcraft she would practice – renders any topical interpretation moot, history having passed beyond her malevolence:

> O, that I were a Witch but for her [i.e., Queen Margaret's] sake!
> Yfaith her Queeneship little Rest should take;
> I would scratch that Face, that may not feele the Ayre,
> And knit whole Ropes of Witch-knots in her Hayre …
> Or take me some such knowne familiar shape,
> As she my Vengeance never should escape.
> Were I a Garment, none should need the more
> To sprinkle me with Nessus poys'ned Gore;
> It were ynough, if she once put me on,
> To teare both Flesh and Sinewes from the Bone:
> Were I a Flower, that might her Smell delight,
> Though I were not the poys'ning *Aconite*,
> I would send such a Fume unto her Brow,
> Should make her mad, as mad as I am now. (13.107–10, 115–24)

Ranging furiously through the *Metamorphoses* in pursuit of an apt model for her vengeful fantasy, Cobham begins by imagining herself a witch and immediately displays sufficient cunning and cruelty for her chosen role. A strange pathos overtakes her lurid reverie, however, as she registers her incapacity to effect any of the metamorphoses required for the execution of her plots against Queen Margaret's beauty, status, and life. Cobham, in other words, may not be a witch at all, but a mere hag; though she resembles Circe in her will to debase her foes, and Medea in her proclivity for violence, she remains impossibly distant from either archetype, lacking their power over the natural world. Hence the awkward conditional clauses hobbling her efforts to express her rage ("O, that I were a Witch … ," "Were I a Garment… ," "Were I a Flower … "), which culminate in the concession, "Though I were not the poys'ning *Aconite*," referring to the noxious *Aconitum* concocted by Ovid's Medea for her attempt on the life of Theseus (*Met.* 7.404–24).[49] Wishing in vain for a fraction of Medea's witchcraft (if not her poisons, at least a psychotic to drive Queen Margaret mad), Drayton's Cobham registers her absolute removal from Ovidian models. In view of these intertextual contrasts, the reader is tempted to view Cobham as an epistolary afterthought, her innocuous hysteria recalling the helpless invective of the fashionable complaint genre.

In her name as in her rhetoric, however, Drayton's Eleanor recalls the original Eleanor of English history: Eleanor of Aquitaine, the estranged wife of Henry II, avenging herself on none other than the fair Rosamond, whose plaintive epistle opens Drayton's collection. As an addition to the 1598 edition of the *Epistles*, after the volume's initial success, Cobham is a belated figure in every sense, reprising not only the furious Eleanor of the first edition, but that villain's original in Daniel's *Complaint of Rosamond*:

> Enrag'd with madnesse, scarce she [i.e., Eleanor] speakes a word,
> But flies with eager furie to my face,
> Offring me most vnwomanly disgrace.

> Looke how a Tygresse that hath lost her Whelpe,
> Runnes fiercely ranging through the Woods astray:
> And seeing her selfe depriu'd of hope or helpe,
> Furiously assaults what's in her way,
> To satisfie her wrath, (not for a pray)
> So fell she on me in outragious wise,

> As could Disdaine and Iealousie deuise.
> And after all her vile reproches vsde,
> She forc'd me take the Poyson she had brought ... (*Comp.* 586–97)

As Cobham fantasizes, "I would scratch that Face, that may not feele the Ayre, / And knit whole Ropes of Witch-knots in her Hayre," she replaces both Rosamonds – Daniel's and Drayton's own – with her present nemesis, Margaret of Anjou. Although the latter only shields her face from the elements as required by convention, Cobham's allusive alchemy equates her with Rosamond hidden in the labyrinth, a motif reflected in the threatened "Witch-knots." Enlarged from exile in her furious dream, Cobham's "vile reproches" are heard at last and her poisons "forc'd" down her victim's throat.

In this attenuated intertextual sense, Cobham's allusive fantasy even promises her accession to the royal status she has always desired. After all, her namesake, Daniel's Eleanor, is herself clearly modelled on Ovid's Hecuba, as she avenges herself on her son's murderer, the tyrant Polymestor. In Golding's translation:

> ... tamquam regina maneret,
> ulcisci statuit poenaeque in imagine tota est,
> utque furit catulo lactente orbata leaena
> signaque nacta pedum sequitur, quem non videt, hostem,
> sic Hecube, postquam cum luctu miscuit iram,
> non oblita animorum, annorum oblita suorum ... (*Met.* 13.545–50)

> As though shee still had beene a Queene, to vengeance shee her bent
> Enforcing all her witts to fynd some kynd of ponnishment.
> And as a Lyon robbed of her whelpes becommeth wood,
> And taking on the footing of her enmye where hee stood,
> Purseweth him though out of syght: even so Queene Hecubee
> (Now having meynt her teares with wrath) forgetting quyght that shee
> Was old, but not her princely hart, to Polemnestor went,
> The cursed murtherer ... (Golding, 13.654–61)

Ovid's Hecuba proceeds to scratch out Polymestor's eyes, and in her feverish imagination, Drayton's Cobham participates in this primal vengeance, so consummate as to elevate her "as though shee still had beene a Queene." Nor does she identify with Hecuba via some remote path through the Ovidian labyrinth; on the contrary, as Lynn Enterline reminds us, the passage ranked among the most commonly assigned to Elizabethan schoolboys by humanist pedagogues: a "'mirror' or 'example' for pupils to imitate – a lesson for young men learning to develop their own style."[50] Cobham's fantasy is thus a variation on one of the central Ovidian tropes of the 1590s, recalling Spenser's description of the "mad bytch" Adicia metamorphosing into a "Tygre" (*FQ* 5.8.49.6–7), and resembling Hamlet's urgent desire that the players should "come to Hecuba." As Shakespeare's Gertrude describes the "bodiless creation" of her son's "ecstasy" (*Hamlet*, 2.2.481, 3.4.128), implying that he "stands outside himself," so Drayton's Cobham describes her madness as "a sudden Extasie" – a transportation to the other Eleanor's time, place, and identity. In a sense, then, Cobham dreams of more than mere metamorphosis; she dreams of an Ovidian triumph over English history itself.

Of course, it is only a dream, for every reader knows Eleanor Cobham's historical fate, and Drayton's commentator is standing by to remind those who might forget. As an Ovidian figure, Cobham advances well beyond Rosamond and her serial self-victimization as Io, Actaeon, the Minotaur, and so forth. She achieves a new allusive register among self-empowered figures, who would fly, seize the throne, and take revenge, but that is as far as Drayton will allow metamorphosis to impinge upon the historical record. For an exultant few lines, Ovid's myths allow Cobham to imagine an alternative history, but she has already lived and died in this one.

"But thou scornst to stay under one title"

Three decades after the *Epistles'* first publication, in an elaborate dedication to a miscellaneous anthology of Drayton's late verse, Ben Jonson recalled the earlier volume as an Ovidian tour de force:

> But then, thy'epistolar *Heroick* Songs,
> Their loues, their quarrels, iealousies, and wrongs,
> Did all so strike me, as I cry'd, who can
> With vs be call'd, the *Naso* [i.e., Ovid], but this man?[51]

The lines echo the more immediate testimony of William Alexander's prefatory sonnet to the 1600 edition of the *Epistles*, "That Ovids Soule revives in Drayton now," and they amount to effusive praise from Jonson, who elsewhere advised aspiring poets to "make choise of one excellent man above the rest, and so to follow him, till he grow very *Hee*: or, so like him, as the Copie may be mistaken for the Principall" (*Timber*, 2469–71). C.S. Lewis's judgment, that "Rosamond is so like Ovid that we catch ourselves trying to remember the Latin," corroborates across the centuries these contemporary testimonies to Drayton's lasting success as Ovid's imitator.

Jonson's formula for poetic glory, however, requires the all-important precondition that the imitator must first "make choise of one excellent man above the rest," and if Drayton seems distant and amorphous to us now, perhaps it is because he never committed to Ovid as his "choise," but remained as indecisive as his own epistolary heroines. Jonson's commendatory verse, after all, sets Drayton's Ovidianism in the context of a long, protean career of serial imitation, as each successive element of the 1627 anthology recalls to Jonson's mind a different classical persona – Drayton-as-Ovid appears alongside Drayton-as-Theocritus, as "Rurall *Virgil*," Orpheus, Lucan, and Homer – until Jonson surrenders, "But thou scornst to stay / Vnder one title" (28, 47–8). Stretching nearly to a hundred lines, Jonson's poem ultimately betrays his consternation, as if the very thought of prefacing such a miscellaneous volume seems foreign to a poet who had translated Horace's *Ars poetica*, affected Horatian rusticity in his odes, and even staged himself as Horace. Far easier for a poet like Jonson to praise Chapman for progressing naturally from translating Homer to translating Homer's contemporary, Hesiod, or to applaud Shakespeare for his singular excellence beyond all precedent.[52]

By contrast, Jonson's Drayton shows himself too protean to bear any particular, lasting excellence, an ironic consequence of his "partial" Ovidianism; his care in avoiding his contemporaries' easy, synecdochal reception of any imitation of the Ovidian corpus as the singular reincarnation of Ovid's soul. Recapitulating the paradoxical voices of the *Heroides* and the more wayward myths of the *Metamorphoses*, Drayton may well have distinguished himself from his peers – that is, from the readiness of Marlowe, Shakespeare, or Chapman to declare themselves participants in or fugitives from the Ovidian vogue of the 1590s – but the eclectic ventriloquism of the epistolary mode may also have impeded Drayton from establishing any more positive poetic identity. Again, in critical retrospect, Drayton's publications suggest a career developing in the growing shadow of Spenser's achievement: the younger poet departs from the pastoral of the *Shepheards Garland*, progresses up Diana's Neoplatonic mountain in *Endimion and Phoebe*, claims laureate status with the publication of *Poly-Olbion*, and returns to Faerieland in several of the more celebrated poems in the late miscellany prefaced by Jonson. A professional poet's committed identity as a Spenserian, however, may not have been readily apparent to most Elizabethan and Jacobean readers. The patterns of humanist pedagogy, supplemented by the examples of classicizing figures like Jonson, encouraged the literate to associate modern poets all but exclusively with ancient models, making it difficult for readers to recognize or substantiate any new poet's claim to contemporary laurels.

Like his own Eleanor Cobham, then, Drayton proves an adept juggler of the *Metamorphoses*, but does not thereby approach any central authority, whether classical or modern. He dreams of a transitory Ovidianism of professional convenience – a partial imitation leaving room for other and better imitative choices as he and his audience evolve – but the *Epistles* proved, if possible, too successful, for Ovid and Drayton-as-Ovid alike remained popular. In edition after edition, as Drayton added to the original volume's contents and readdressed it to new patrons, he reinforced his Ovidian identity, even as he sought new ones. As a result, we remember him as an Ovidian, or as a nobody. It would take a very different kind of poet – one who meant to replace Ovid rather than imitate him, even "partially" – to win the recognition of his peers and the judgment of posterity as someone new. That poet was John Donne.

5 The Brief Ovidian Career of John Donne

At least under certain historical conditions, such as those underwriting the Ovidian vogue of the English 1590s, it makes little sense to refer to the straightforward rise and fall of a particular literary influence. Indeed, a host of outlying examples disrupts this convenient parabolic model, in some cases even inverting it; we might, for example, set Shakespeare's 1593 rendering of the Adonis-flower as a terminal aetiology – a stillborn metamorphosis forecasting the end of the vogue, even in its youth – against Drayton's bestselling transcription of Ovidian epistolarity at the turn of the seventeenth century. Hence, in the preceding chapters, I have sought to redefine Ovidianism as a centre of cultural gravity, nebulous enough to allow a poet like Spenser to choose new "Ovids" to suit new poetic occasions, yet compelling enough to draw even a reluctant imitator like Chapman into Ovid's orbit.

A cursory glance at John Donne's poetic evolution from Elizabethan elegist to Jacobean divine, however, seems to contradict this claim, and to reaffirm a more straightforward sense of Ovidianism's rise and fall. Coming of age at the height of the Ovidian vogue in the mid-1590s, Donne had actively cultivated the contrarian, libertine persona popular in his aristocratic milieu at the Inns of Court, and had circulated his urbane, sexually knowing elegies among a like-minded coterie. In the broadest sense, then, critics like Alan Armstrong are correct to claim that "to Donne ... the brilliant, irreverent wit and light-hearted cynicism of Ovid proved congenial."[1] Scrutinizing Donne's poetic activity during his years at Lincoln's Inn, however, Arthur Marotti discerns an early, strategic departure from traditional models:

In his elegies, Donne displays a youthful iconoclasm, sometimes a cynicism, as he adjusted his pieces to the interests and attitudes of his peers, replacing Ovid's Rome with Elizabethan London and the mythological metaphors of Roman elegies with multiple allusions to contemporary social, economic and political realities ... Certainly in turning to this poetic form, Donne was competitively engaged in the practice of producing modern versions of classical genres, a sport in which other Inns authors indulged. But it is misleading to view Donne, as Roma Gill does, as basically "a scholar engaged in the respectable academic pursuit of imitating Ovid."[2]

Following a close reading of Donne's "To his Mistress Going to Bed" as the counterpoint to its Ovidian model, *Amores* 1.4, Marotti concludes, "While Ovid's elegy is an imaginatively excited (if brief) poem about satisfying sexual experience, Donne's is a curiously antierotic treatment of a sexual encounter."[3] Extrapolating this reading across Donne's early poetic output – that is, preceding his 1601 elopement with the socially superior Anne More and his consequent disgrace – Marotti helps us to account for Donne as an intermittent anti-Ovidian, accomplishing with vastly more sprezzatura than Chapman the repudiation of the mythographic style and vitiated eroticism then in fashion. That such a "contrarian" attitude appealed to the self-flattering avant-gardism of Donne's coterie partly explains the ease with which he assumed this anti-Ovidian posture. Unlike Chapman or Drayton, Donne was not obliged to feed the popular appetite for mythology at all, nor flatter particular patrons' Ovidian foibles as directly as, say, Shakespeare addressing *Venus and Adonis* to the Earl of Southampton.

But Donne is not merely a more capable Chapman writing for a more encouraging audience, nor does the term "anti-Ovidianism" sufficiently define his response to the vogue for Ovidian imitations. He is instead the period's premier *post*-Ovidian, who continues to capitalize on his readers' sense of the vogue's ephemerality. Recasting that ephemerality as obsolescence, Donne indicts Ovidianism implicitly as no longer relevant to the erotics or poetics of his cultural moment; he begins, in other words, where Shakespeare concluded *Venus and Adonis* – by acknowledging the sterility of traditional imitative models. The distinction of this post-Ovidian posture from the anti-Ovidianism of contemporaries like Chapman or the young Ben Jonson is subtle, but it is no less a posture: Donne would be perceived as no longer in need of Ovidian influence, as existing in advance of literary fashion itself.

In practice, however, this post-Ovidian posture required and prioritized a critical (albeit strictly limited) mass of Ovidian allusion – an immediately recognizable foregrounding of the models Donne would be seen to have surpassed already. In this regard, the young Donne differed fundamentally from the poet to whom he is most often compared, George Herbert, who indeed had little use for Ovid beyond such dismissive statements as, "I envie no mans nightingale or spring; / Nor let them punish me with losse of ryme, / Who plainly say, *My God, My King*."[4] While Herbert reached (at least ostensibly) for an axiomatic "plainness" infinitely above style itself – a vertical, asymptotic goal – Donne portrayed himself as having arrived already at a more perfect expression of his society's present condition, envying his contemporaries' Ovidian nightingales and Petrarchan springs just enough to improve upon them. If Donne evolved into a poet like Herbert – over time, between reigns, or along the trajectory of a professional career that would lift him to his own pulpit – his youthful self-fashioning against the backdrop of the previous century's Ovidian vogue remained fundamental to his own narrative of metamorphic reformation. As the Dean of St. Paul's and author of the *Holy Sonnets* and *Devotions upon Emergent Occasions*, Doctor Donne reoriented his contemporaries' sense of his excellence, ascending infinitely above Ovid where once he had merely left Ovid behind. By the end of that process, however, Jack Donne of Lincoln's Inn, far from vanishing, had become for Doctor Donne and his eulogists what Ovid had been for the poets of the 1590s – that is, the bygone centre of literary fashion, against whom a present fashionability could be constructed.

Disowning Ovid in the Epigrams and Elegies

In 1633, at the end of the posthumous first edition of Donne's poems, Thomas Carew could eulogize his late friend as England's premier anti-Ovidian:

> But thou art gone, and thy strict lawes will be
> Too hard for Libertines in Poetrie.
> They will repeale the goodly exil'd traine
> Of gods and goddesses, which in thy just raigne
> Were banish'd nobler Poems, now, with these
> The silenc'd tales o'th'Metamorphoses
> Shall stuffe their lines, and swell the windy Page,
> Till Verse refin'd by thee, in this last Age,
> Turne ballad rime, Or those old Idolls bee

Ador'd againe, with new apostasie ...[5]

Carew's perfect verbs – the Olympian pantheon "exil'd" and "banish'd,"
the *Metamorphoses* "silenc'd," and English verse "refin'd" – register
Donne's ultimate success at distinguishing his own poetry from the
Ovidianism of "this last Age." Already in his elegy, Carew reverts ironically to the poetic "Libertinism" antedating Donne's "just raigne," permitting "th'Metamorphoses" to "stuffe" his own lines. Less apparent
than the present strength of Donne's disavowal of Ovidianism, however, is the process by which the reformed poet came to triumph over
those "old Idolls" in the first place – the "strictness" and "hardness" of
the "lawes" he imposed upon himself in order to resist any impulse to
backslide.

Donne himself gives us a curious account of this process in a 1608
verse epistle to his friend Edward Herbert, George's brother. In a pe-
destrian satire, "The State progress of Ill," the elder Herbert had likened
the world to a perverse "Ark of *Noah*," in which dwell "few Men, and
many Beasts," to which Donne replies:

Man is a lumpe, where all beasts kneaded bee,
Wisdome makes him an Arke where all agree ...
How happy'is hee, which hath due place assign'd
To'his beasts, and disaforested his minde!
Empail'd himselfe to keepe them out, not in;
Can sow, and dares trust corne, where they have bin ...[6]

Reorienting Herbert's satirical image, Donne affirms the human capacity to become "an Arke where all [beasts] agree," but emphasizes too
the mental discipline required to achieve that "happy" state, that "disaforested ... minde." As man herds his constituent beasts into their "due
place," he recolonizes portions of his mind for his own cultivation. The
beasts of youth are here depicted as threatening the harvest, rather than
assisting it, and man "Can sow, and dares trust corne" only "where
they have bin" but no longer are. The initial herding of the beasts into
the ark is now revealed to have been the prelude to their total exclusion
from civilized society, not so much domestication as an uncompromising effort to "keepe them out, not in."

Without unduly equating the shape of Donne's literary development
to this single poem's hindsighted advice to a fellow poet, we may perceive in Donne's early work patterns suggestive of such a long-term

project of self-cultivation, with Ovidian imitation among the "beasts" evacuated from the intellectual forest. Specifically, Donne's youthful elegies undermine and ultimately usurp Ovid's pre-eminent status as an erotic didact – the *praeceptor amoris* of the *Ars amatoria* and *Amores*[7] – while his experimental epic, the *Metempsychosis: or the Progress of the Soul*, despite its fragmentary form, systematically marginalizes Ovid's *Metamorphoses* as an intertext, irreverently proclaiming Donne's own epic authority instead. In both cases, the Elizabethan poet colonizes territory previously occupied in the cultural imagination by Ovid and his early modern imitators; "empail[ing] himselfe" in order to "sow" his own "corne" unmolested.

Three of Donne's epigrams capture this process of intellectual enclosure at an early stage, in which the mythographic Ovid is still visible, if only barely. As vestiges of the Ovidian vogue, they neatly illustrate the imitative poet's sense of his own evolution:

Hero and Leander:

Both rob'd of aire, we both lye in one ground,
Both whom one fire had burnt, one water drownd.

Pyramus and Thisbe:

Two, by themselves, each other, love and feare
Slaine, cruell friends, by parting have joyn'd here.

Niobe:

By childrens births, and death, I am become
So dry, that I am now mine owne sad tombe.[8]

Without their titles, these compressed, paradoxical couplets – pure conceits – could fit neatly into any number of Donne's more characteristic lyrics, but in their nominal subjects (as in their strict form) the mythographic epigrams seem garishly out of place in the midst of Donne's larger poetic corpus.[9] Although they can be read as experimental verse or as a young poet's trying-on of Ovidianism, the assurance of the couplets' epigrammatic structure instead suggests that they are residual from the process of purging Ovid while "disaforesting" the mind. All three poems are also, after all, epitaphs – the poet's ventriloquization of dead voices, by definition the last words on their subjects. Alternatively, we may read the mythographic epigrams as radically reduced versions of the *Heroides*, Donne's virtuosic compression of the self-elegizing lamentations of Ovid's heroines.[10] Several of Ovid's epistles, notably those of Phyllis and Dido, suggest this very rhetoric of compression, the closure of complaint with a self-ascribed epitaph; others, like the twinned epistles of Hero and Leander, are exercises in narrative dilation, cues for the Elizabethan authors of epyllia.[11]

For the young contrarian Donne, however, such myths instead challenge the poet to maintain strict rhetorical economy, stripping away centuries of digressive retelling and allegorical accretion to extract each myth's kernel of paradox. M. Thomas Hester notes, for example, "the Empedoclean circularity of [Hero and Leander's] immersion in the four elements" in the epigram's mere two lines – the universe bottled in a rhymed couplet.[12] In the case of Pyramus and Thisbe, it takes Ovid's frame-narrator over a hundred hexameter lines to tell her intentionally long-winded myth (*Met.* 4.37–166), whereas Donne again packs his double epitaph into two pentameter lines.[13] The epigrammatic version of "Niobe" likewise reduces Ovid's long account in the *Metamorphoses* to the space of an emblem without an image.[14] In the single phrase, "By chilldrens birth, and death," Donne records both the grounds for Niobe's notorious pride and its punishment, while the second and final line undoes the permanence of Ovid's weeping rock, declaring Niobe dry, as if Donne had both outlasted Ovid's vision and disabused us of his myth.

While Donne's epigrams may thus be read as a parody of Ovid's prolix style, his choice of three myths treated at such length by other Elizabethan poets – Marlowe in *Hero and Leander*, Shakespeare in *Romeo and Juliet* and again in *Midsummer Night's Dream*, and Chapman in *Ovid's Banquet of Sense* – gestures suggestively at contemporary literary culture. Yet even as he exposes the mythographic and rhetorical logorrhoea of professional Ovidians, Donne asserts his pre-eminence over rival epigrammatists. Ovid, after all, wrote in many genres, but never in epigrams (so far as we know), and when Jonson, John Davies, and others adapted the form, they naturally looked elsewhere, mainly to Martial, for their Latin models. Donne, by contrast, adapts the most digressive classical poet to the least expansive poetic form, as his three couplets respond simultaneously to the contemporaneous vogues for Ovidianism and for the epigram.

The explicitly Ovidian personae of the mythographic couplets, however, remain uncharacteristic of Donne, for whom the classical world seems smaller, more sparsely populated, and less frequently visited than it does for almost any other Elizabethan secular poet.[15] On the rare occasions when Donne does invoke a pagan name or two, he often alludes around Ovid to more obscure mythographers, or even to the denigrators or debunkers of mythology. In the valedictory elegy "On his Mistress," Donne writes:

> Thy (else Almighty) beautie cannot move
> Rage from the Seas, nor thy love teach them love,
> Nor tame wilde Boreas harshnesse; Thou hast reade
> How roughly hee in peeces shivered
> Faire Orithea, whom he swore he lov'd ... (19–23)

About to sail from England, the persona admonishes his beloved not to expect her "(else Almighty) beautie" to calm the seas for his safe passage, and recounts the story of how the North Wind, Boreas, accidentally killed his own beloved, Orithea, while attempting to ravish her. The names are most familiar from the sixth book of the *Metamorphoses*, but in that version of the myth, Boreas does not kill Orithea, but rather succeeds in kidnapping her and making her his bride. Donne's allusion is not to this best-known, Ovidian version of the myth, but rather to a passage in Plato, that foe of licentious poets.[16] In the dialogue *Phaedrus*, when the impressionable Phaedrus asks Socrates whether he believes the tale of Boreas and Orithea, Socrates replies that "If I disbelieved, as the wise men do, I should not be extraordinary." Rationalizing the myth, he provides the ultimate source for Donne's allusion by suggesting that Orithea was blown over a cliff by a gust of wind. Socrates then rejects this version as well, with characteristic sarcasm:

> I, Phaedrus, think such explanations are very pretty in general, but are the inventions of a very clever and laborious and not altogether enviable man, for no other reason than because after this he must explain the forms of the Centaurs, and then that of the Chimaera, and there presses in upon him a whole crowd of such creatures, Gorgons and Pegas, and multitudes of strange, portentous natures. If anyone disbelieves in these, and with a rustic sort of wisdom, undertakes to explain each in accordance with probability, he will need a great deal of leisure. But I have no leisure for them at all ... (*Phaedrus* 229 C–D)

For Donne, there is enough raw material in the real world for the poet's purposes; to invent new forms, or to rehabilitate old ones, is to unleash superfluous beasts into the mind's forest; "Man ... a lumpe where all beasts kneaded bee" becomes lumpier with each additional centaur. By accessing Plato's irreverent passage through the Boreas allusion, Donne, like Socrates, effectively dismisses euhemerism – allegoresis taken to its rationalizing extreme – in addition to mythology. His satirical gaze thus comes to include those latter-day Ovidians who would force a discredited account of a vanished cosmos onto physical and metaphysical realities.

Donne has, in other words, little direct use for metamorphosis as metaphor. Indeed, his metaphysical similes tend to bypass or deflect metamorphosis as a trope; put another way, we might say that nymphs transform into rivers in Ovidian poetry, whereas in Donne's early poems the inconstancy of the mistress may be compared to a river's flow, as in the elegy "Oh, let mee not serve so" (ll. 21–34). The natural world and our human sense of it come to replace the mythological middlemen of the pagan universe, for who needs the lunar goddess Diana when we have the "trepidation of the spheares" ("A Valediction: forbidding mourning," l. 11)? Why lament Pyramus and Thisbe, who can only come together in death, when the motion of a mathematician's compasses can figure the living reunion of parted lovers? Unimpressed and unimpeded by metamorphosis, Donne is able to focus his attention instead on the erotic elegy – that is, on that aspect of the Ovidian vogue most germane (and most threatening) to his ambitions as an Inns-of-Court poet. This does not mean merely that Donne considers himself a better *praeceptor amoris* than Ovid, but moreover that he sees in this particular Ovidian mode an opportunity to distinguish himself from rival poets writing less innovative erotic verse for the same audiences and patrons. If he disregards the *Metamorphoses* as demotic, or dismisses the *Amores* as outmoded, it is less to ignite his own poetic lights in the study, than to distinguish his elegies and their select audience from the vulgar Ovidianism of the marketplace – in other words, to elevate his own work above Marlowe's translations, Shakespeare's imitations, Chapman's obsessive citations, and so on. No less than for his peers, for Donne Ovidianism remains emphatically a present-tense phenomenon, as the common vertex in relation to which all secular poets of the 1590s identify themselves. To appear to ignore Ovid's influence is not therefore to disengage fully from the Ovidian vogue, but rather to show oneself in a new relation to the culture organized around it.

"Practice *my* Art": Special Ed for Modern Lovers

For Donne, in his self-appointed capacity as the new *praeceptor amoris*, Ovidian prolixity was not merely a stylistic fault, but reflected a systemic cultural failure. In the ribald elegy "Love's Progress," Donne addresses Ovid's didactic model most forcefully, strictly opposing his persona's erotic precepts to those of the original *praeceptor amoris*, neither improving nor expanding upon the teachings of the *Ars amatoria* and the *Amores*, but instead repudiating them and replacing them.[17] When Donne claims at the outset of his elegy, "Who ever loves, if he do not propose / The right true end of love, he's one that goes / To sea for nothing but to make him sick" (1–3), he glances with an allusive disdain at his predecessor's lack of self-control, or as Ovid confesses in the *Amores, Nam desunt vires ad me mihi iusque regendum; / auferor ut rapida concita puppis aqua* (*Am.* 2.4.7–8, "I lack the strength and will to rule myself; I am swept along like a ship tossed on the rushing flood").[18] Donne proceeds to apply the image of the bear-whelp – the early modern period's ubiquitous natural sign for shapelessness – in order to question the decorum of the Ovidian erotic mode and to demonstrate the inadequacy of metamorphic figurations of erotic love: "Love is a bear-whelp born, if we o're lick / Our love, and force it new strange shapes to take, / We erre, and of a lump a monster make" (4–6). And while Donne's dictum, to "preferr / One woman first, and then one thing in her" (9–10), echoes Ovid's advice in the *Ars amatoria – Elige cui dicas 'tu mihi sola places'* (*Ars am.* 1.42, "choose to whom you will say, 'You alone please me'") – it simultaneously lampoons the hypocrisy of the otherwise promiscuous Ovidian posture, ridiculing the persona of the *Amores*, endlessly in love with all women for each quality.[19]

As "Love's Progress" continues, Donne replaces Ovid's protracted foreplay with an uncompromisingly direct approach to the object of his passion:

> ... But if we
> Make love to woman; virtue is not she:
> As beauty'is not nor wealth: He that strayes thus
> From her to hers, is more adulterous,
> Then if he took her maid ... (23–7)

Here, as in many of his other secular poems, Donne abruptly dismisses feminine beauty, virtue, and wealth as the commonly sanctioned proxies for the actual, purely sexual worth of the opposite gender. Ridiculing all men who would prove vulnerable to such extra-corporeal distractions, this is only the first of several moments in the poem in which Ovidians and Petrarchans are satirized simultaneously.[20] Donne's satire extends all the way back to the ancient *praeceptor* and his original affair with his beloved's maid. In the *Amores*, Ovid's philandering persona first defends himself to Corynna's face from the accusation that he has slept with her slave, yet in the following poem attempts to blackmail the maid into providing him with further sexual favours (*Am.* 2.7, 8).[21]

Throughout the first half of "Love's Progress," then, Donne portrays Ovid allusively as the least of all lovers. He is the adulterous weakling to whose lowly status the true male lover will be reduced, should he waste his time on his mistress's more exalted (yet more superficial) qualities, rather than focusing – as is proper for the seducer – on what Donne here scurrilously calls her "centric part." Inverting the usual rhetoric of celestial beauty, Donne writes:

> ... Search every spheare
> And firmament, our *Cupid* is not there:
> He's an infernal god and under ground,
> With *Pluto* dwells, where gold and fire abound:
> Men to such Gods, their sacrificing Coles
> Did not in Altars lay, but pits and holes.
> Although we see Celestial bodies move
> Above the earth, the earth we Till and love:
> So we her ayres contemplate, words and heart,
> And virtues; but we love the Centrique part. (27–36)

In every way unlike the winged, all-powerful deity who oversees Ovid's poetic efforts (*Am.* 1.1.1–5) and who rides in triumph through the Ovidian corpus, Donne's Cupid – "our *Cupid*" – exists only in a feminine "hell," in the "pits and holes" where men must "lay" their "sacrificing Coles." The various endearing traits of Ovid's endless loves in the *Amores*, the amorous poet's flickering visions of the female form – whether modest, bold, austere, learned, simple, urbane, rustic, tall, short, nude, well-dressed, blonde, brunette, Corynna, Corynna's "dusky" (*fusca*) maid – are reduced in Donne's elegy to a female body so empty, negative, and unresponsive that the "progress" of the male persona's love becomes tantamount to necrophilia. The beloved's supine posture lends itself to Donne's favourite corporeal metaphor of the map, yet he refuses to pause (or to let his reader pause) at "the streight *Hellespont* betweene / The *Sestos* and *Abydos* of her breasts" (60–1), thereby abruptly dismissing the Ovidian and Marlovian myth of Hero and Leander. "Progress" in "Love's Progress," entails a relentless sailing forward, through the Hellespont; to swerve to either shore – towards Hero's Sestos or Leander's Abydos – is to risk drowning prior to consummation.

As the persona's apprentice lover approaches the object of his erotic voyage, he is further warned against dwelling on the geography of the female body, lest the voyage and poem end prematurely. Donne writes:

> Yet ere thou be where thou wouldst be embay'd,
> Thou shalt upon another Forest set,
> Where many Shipwrack, and no further get.
> When thou art there, consider what this chace
> Mispent by thy beginning at the face. (68–72)

Ovid had insisted in his *Ars amatoria*, *Crede mihi, non est veneris properanda voluptas, / Sed sensim tarda prolicienda mora* (2.717–18, "Believe me, love's bliss must not be hastened, but gradually lured on by slow delay"). For Donne, writing to his own amorous novices in the 1590s, that time-honoured, patient approach to eros defeats itself, takes too long, leads nowhere. He fills the vacuum with his own unlovably efficient *ars amatoria*:

> Rather set out below; practice my Art,
> Some Symetry the foot hath with that part
> Which thou dost seek, and is thy Map for that
> Lovely enough to stop, but not stay at;
> Least subject to disguise and change it is ... (73–7)

Having rejected the Petrarchan lover's conventional approach to his beloved's hair, face, lips, neck, breasts, belly, and waist, thus eliminating the sonneteers' paralytic corporeal obsessions, Donne's *praeceptor* does not opt instead for the urbanity of the equally discredited precepts of Ovid. Rather, he insists, "practice *my* Art," which begins at the opposite end of the woman's body: at the foot, which for Donne is "Least subject to disguise and change" – that is, least metamorphic. The "Map" of the woman's unspectacular lower torso does not confront Donne's erotic voyager with the synaesthetic obstacles that so bedeviled the former journey's progress through her upper hemisphere: her lips' "Syrens," her breasts, or her "fair Atlantick Navell" (55, 61, 66). Here is only an "empty and Ætherial way" (89), permitting the lover direct access to the lower, more desirable of the "Two purses" that "Rich Nature hath in women wisely made" (91–2).

Of course, according to early modern erotic norms, every heterosexual male lover's goal is ostensibly the same, whether he looks to Ovid, Petrarch, or Donne for poetic advice on how to penetrate. But where Petrarchans fall woefully short of that goal, Ovidians prove fast learners; at the climax of the *Ars amatoria*, the original *praeceptor* congratulates himself on his own success at playing the pander:

> Conscius, ecce, duos accepit lectus amantes:
> Ad thalami clausas, Musa, resiste fores.
> Sponte sua sine te celeberrima verba loquentur,
> Nec manus in lecto laeva iacebit iners.
> Invenient digiti, quod agant in partibus illis,
> In quibus occulte spicula tingit Amor.

> Lo! the conscious couch has received two lovers: tarry, O Muse, at the closed door of their chamber. Of their own accord, without your aid, they will utter eloquent speech, nor will the left hand lie idle on the bed. Their fingers will find what to do in those parts wherein Love secretly dips his darts. (*Ars am.* 2.703–8)

Ovid's muse leaves her poet's youthful lovers to their own mutual desires in a private bedroom. As she waits patiently outside the door, she might be eavesdropping, but in any case she is delighted at her own *praeceptor*'s pedagogical accomplishment – at the apprentice lovers' consummation of their loves. Ovid's male protégé, naturally and inevitably, will find his goal, so the poet counsels confidence: *Cum loca reppereris, quae tangi femina gaudet, / Non obstet, tangas quo minus illa, pudor. / Aspicies oculos tremulo fulgore micantes, / Ut sol a liquida saepe refulget aqua* (719–22, "When you have found the place where a woman loves to be touched, let not shame prevent you from touching it ... You will see her eyes shooting tremulous gleams, as the sun often glitters in clear water"). These lovers look into each others' eyes in their ecstasy, and afterwards, the voyeuristic *praeceptor* approves of their performance: *tum plena voluptas, / Cum pariter victi femina virque iacent* (727–8, "then is pleasure full, when man and woman lie vanquished both together").

But no eyes meet in the silent bedroom of Donne's imitation; the poem is addressed only to the male lover, whose attention is to remain fixated on the "Centrique part" alone. The cynicism of this revised art of love offers no such parity as that which blesses Ovid's couple; here is no pleasure for the woman at all, no post-coital reverie for the couple, nothing but the man's conquest of the map beneath him.

The unapologetic misogyny of "Love's Progress," however, should not be allowed to obscure the more intelligent implications of Donne's parody of erotic poetry in general and Ovidianism in particular. The poem does not merely offer precepts as a practical guide to the male reader's sexual pleasure, but satirizes both Petrarchan hypocrisy and the obsolescence of the *Ars amatoria*'s idealism. The original *praeceptor amoris* is to be repudiated, not because his precepts were foolish or unworkable, but instead because early modern London is not imperial Rome, and *amor* has changed very much for the worse over the centuries. Ovid's beloved Corynna, for all her fickle nature, has become an ideal (she had a name, at least), and bears as little resemblance to the objectified women of Donne's elegies as she will to the unreachable beloveds of the *Songs and Sonnets* in later years. Donne's male readers, meanwhile, are themselves among his satirical targets, as they are the unseaworthy voyagers of "Love's Progress," prone to shipwreck before reaching their forgotten goal. Alongside its cynicism, Donne's elegy offers a depressing realism: how unlikely, indeed, the vision of one of Donne's readers – a young spark of the Inns – rhapsodizing his true love's virtues or achieving mutual ecstasy after a protracted courtship; how much simpler to advise a concupiscent male reader to pursue instead only one moment and locus of sexual contact, reducing all of his desires to one desire; and how shameful and fallen the society where this is the norm, where the muse can no longer listen at the bedroom door. The failing schoolboys of the 1590s require instruction even in bed, and must be goaded to their unromantic goal by a stern schoolmaster.

Even as he satirizes Ovidian and Petrarchan personae, however, Donne leaves open the possibility of self-parody, implying that Elizabethan society is so drastically impotent that even its *praeceptor amoris* cannot follow his own advice. In "Love's Progress," as the *praeceptor* prohibits the ordinary lover's odyssey through "the streight *Hellespont* betweene / The *Sestos* and *Abydos* of her breasts, / (Not of two Lovers, but two Loves the neasts)" (60–2), the additional half-line actually renders this incidental treatment of the Hero and Leander myth longer than Donne's more comprehensive epigram of the same period. The parenthetical line moreover pauses, however briefly, to compliment the beloved's breasts in hyperbolic, Petrarchan fashion. Such frequent digressions conspire to make the poem's "upper torso" – from the "Forest" of the beloved's coiffure to the second "Forest" of her pubic hair, where "many Shipwrack" – considerably longer than the "lower torso" of the final section, on which the reader is nonetheless encouraged to focus more attention. While rapid progress through "this empty and Æthereal way" is much of the *praeceptor's* point, the majority of his own time is spent lingering on the beloved's foot, and though he cautions against lingering over the foot too long, he himself devotes eight more lines to its sex appeal (73–86). The poem, then, can be read as an indictment of the very notion of a *praeceptor amoris*, or even of a male poet capable of navigating the female form without foundering. As an *ars amatoria*, "Love's Progress" seems as apt to produce podiphiles as womanizers.[22]

Satire, of course, inheres in the subgenre of the *ars*, but in his other elegies, as in "Love's Progress," Donne eagerly demonstrates his precursor's obsolescence and irrelevance. "Love's War," for instance, may recall Ovid's *Amores* 1.9, *Militat omnis amans* ("Every lover is a soldier"), but Donne's poem in fact comprehensively subverts the rhetoric of the Latin original, opposing Ovid's equation of lover and soldier with a barrage of contrasts between luxury and combat: "Other men war that they their rest may gayne; / But wee will rest that wee may fight agayne. / Those warrs the ignorant, these th'experience'd love, / There wee are always under, here above" (33–6). Admittedly, after the quick and joyless sex of "Love's Progress," with its exclusive focus on the lower torso, we might find some encouragement in Donne's thus turning love rightside-up again. As in the *Amores*, some of Donne's elegies read as satires on sexual impotence, while others celebrate bedtime romps with the preferred mistress of the moment. Even in "Love's War," however, the Ovidian intertext at best remains implicit, and in any case, the association of *amor* with *arma* is so commonplace that its provenance may safely be ignored. By the end of "Love's War," as in "Love's Progress," we may feel that Ovid never existed, that only John Donne ever taught the art of love, or as he insists at the beginning of yet another elegy, "*I taught thee to love*." There can be only one *praeceptor amoris*.

Metempsychosis: **Ovid and the Poet's Progress**

Neither Ovid nor Donne limited themselves to love poetry, however, nor did Donne simply abandon his youthful elegies for the mature introspection of Christian asceticism without a second glance at the Roman poet's principal work, the *Metamorphoses*. Donne too attempted an epic of sorts – the *Metempsychosis, or the Progress of the Soul* – though he abandoned it in 1601, having completed only one canto. Eighteen years later, Ben Jonson reminisced about the project to William Drummond:

> The Conceit of Dones transformation or μετεμψυχοσις was that he sought the soule of that Aple which Eva pulled, and therafter made it the soule of a Bitch, then of a sheewolf & so of a woman. his generall purpose was to have brought in all the bodies of the Hereticks from the soule of Cain & at last left it in the body of Calvin. of this he never wrotte but one sheet, & now since he was made Doctor [i.e., of theology] repenteth highlie & seeketh to destroy all his poems.[23]

Perhaps because he was drunk (alcohol being "one of the Elements in which he liveth," as Drummond reports), Jonson's recollection proves inaccurate in almost every detail, from the number of pages Donne completed to the projected identity of the transmigrating soul's ultimate heretical host.[24] Easily lost among the errata is Jonson's misremembering of the poem's subtitle: "The Progress of the Soul," according to the posthumous 1633 edition of Donne's poems (which begins with the *Metempsychosis*) – but Jonson recalls it as "Dones transformation." The error is small, but significant, in that the word "transformation" was synonymous in the period with "metamorphosis,"[25] and thus could easily be associated with Ovid's endlessly influential epic. But Donne, when he began his own epic in 1601, apparently wished to mute, if not avoid this association – more precisely, he wished his coterie readers to perceive him as having already progressed beyond Ovid's influence. Consequently, the fragment he produced constitutes the first major post-Ovidian text of the seventeenth century, and arguably marks the pivotal moment in what Carew later celebrated as Donne's "just raigne," in which "the goodly exil'd traine / Of gods and goddesses ... / Were banish'd nobler Poems."

Yet Donne's decision to design a post-Ovidian epic around the concept of metempsychosis – that is, the Pythagorean doctrine of the immortal soul's transmigration through an endless series of bodily hosts – remains counter-intuitive, for even in the absence of metamorphosis (or "transformation") as a discursive stepping stone, it is only natural for the Elizabethan reader to associate metempsychosis directly with Ovid's *Metamorphoses*, which after fourteen books arrives at a climactic celebration of the soul's immortality via metempsychosis, delivered by the character of Pythagoras himself. Ovid's portrait of the venerable Greek philosopher is ambivalent; Pythagoras's dissertation begins with a shrill and rather ludicrous defence of vegetarianism – for by eating meat, one might consume the soul of an ancestor – but approaches sublimity as he proclaims, "a god inspires my lips" (*Met.* 15.143, *deus ora movet*), prompting him to affirm that "our souls are deathless" (158, *morte carent animae*).[26] Hence, while the doctrine of metempsychosis received its share of attention from ancient philosophers, and became (importantly for Donne) a target of early Christian apologists like Irenaeus and Tertullian,[27] Ovid's version retained its preeminence as the consummate poetic formulation of metempsychosis. To refer in verse to the transmigration of the soul was necessarily to allude to the *Metamorphoses*.

Donne's determination to supersede Ovid's epic pre-eminence is evident from the prefatory epistle he appends to the *Metempsychosis*, which militates against this obvious association of Pythagorean doctrine with the *Metamorphoses*, and subtly but irreparably undermines the traditional authority of Ovid's account. Specifying that "the Pithagorian doctrine doth not onely carry one soule from man to man, nor man to beast, but indifferently to plants also," Donne's learned preface has prompted scholars like Janel Mueller to seek out sources far more obscure than the *Metamorphoses*, reconstructing an elaborate intertextual framework of early Christian polemicists and subsequent commentators.[28] Significantly, however, as Mueller observes, "in all of the tradition about Pythagoras, ... Ovid's portrayal comes closest to being a source for the *Metempsychosis*, [though] even here the parallels are more those of tone and perspective ... than of philosophical substance."[29] Yet even if the "philosophical substance" of Donne's poem lies an erudite league beyond the *Metamorphoses* – in remote allusions to Tertullian's diatribe against the Pythagorean heretic Carpocrates, for example – source-hunting scholars have overlooked the most immediate irony of Donne's emphasis on the psycho-habitability of plants: namely, that the vegetarianism advocated so anxiously by Ovid's Pythagoras is rendered moot by the addition of vegetables to the metempsychotic smorgasbord. By obviating the occasion of his speech, Donne's epistle retroactively bars Ovid's Pythagoras his entrance into the epic tradition.

Thus circumventing Ovid's Pythagoras, Donne colonizes long-occupied generic space, in which to develop his own cynical brand of epic authority. After all, as the last and longest-winded frame-narrator of the *Metamorphoses*, Pythagoras assumes the role of the poem's ultimate champion, at once translating the serial metamorphoses of mythological history – the epic's first fourteen books – into the perennial mutability of our own experience. Ovid's Pythagoras moreover promises his disciples the renewal of the bloodless golden age, to be ruled (paradoxically) by a Roman civilization triumphant over time and change: *urbem et iam cerno ..., / quanta nec est nec erit nec visa prioribus annis* (*Met.* 15.444–5, "I see even now a city ... than which none greater is or shall be, or has been in past ages"). Cartoonish from one angle, Pythagoras represents, in another sense, the pinnacle of Ovid's poetic career; as the legendary philosopher boasts, *iuvat ire per alta / astra* (147–8, "it is a delight to take one's way along the starry firmament") – a triumphal sentiment which easily upstages the anticlimactic, *de rigeur* quality of the *Metamorphoses'* closing praise for the presumptively deified emperor Augustus.[30]

The *Metempsychosis'* first stanza alone, however, short-circuits each aspect of the prophetic optimism of Ovid's Pythagoras. Donne's poem begins:

> I Sing the progresse of a deathlesse soule,
> Whom Fate, which God made, but doth not controule,
> Plac'd in most shapes; all times before the law
> Yoak'd us, and when, and since, in this I sing.
> And the great world to his aged evening;
> From infant morne, through manly noone I draw.
> What the gold Chaldee, or silver Persian saw,
> Greek brasse, or Roman iron, is in this one;
> A worke t'outweare *Seths* pillars, bricke and stone,
> And (holy writt excepted) made to yeeld to none. (1–10)

The epic parameters are all-inclusive, as Donne invokes both the "Fate" of classical tradition and the "God" of the Judeo-Christian tradition, while encompassing "all times" and superimposing the westward trajectory of empire over the conventional degeneration of the four metallic ages of human history. We may further measure the poet's ambition by his stylistic innovation, for the ten-line iambic stanza, culminating in a triple rhyme and an alexandrine, overtakes and outdoes both the Italianate epic's *ottava rima* and the metrical intricacy of Spenser's celebrated stanza.[31] Yet even as they demonstrate poetic virtuosity, these opening lines reveal what Donne is prepared to exclude from the

Metempsychosis; specifically, he sets "holy writt" safely beyond his unorthodox narrative, while leaving pagan mythology behind by skimming over the ancient civilizations, here reduced to fleeting adjectives for bygone ages. Ovid's *Metamorphoses* nevertheless figures crucially in this stanza as the *ne plus ultra* of epic achievement, the allusions confirming Donne's transcendence beyond poetic convention.

Indeed, Donne's allusive engagement with Ovid in this stanza alone is fivefold: first, the opening line's "deathlesse soule" evokes Pythagoras in the final book of Ovid's poem; second, the projected scope of the *Metempsychosis* matches the ambitious epic parameters of the *Metamorphoses'* invocation; third, Donne's emphasis on "most shapes" recalls Ovid's commitment "to tell of bodies changed into new forms" (*Met.* 1.1–2, *In nova … mutatas dicere formas / corpora*); fourth, Donne's recitation of the four metallic ages corresponds to the well-known story of the world's devolution in the *Metamorphoses'* opening book; fifth, Donne's confidence in his epic's immortality approximates Ovid's ultimate boast at the end of the *Metamorphoses*, that "wherever Rome's power extends over the conquered world, I shall have mention on men's lips, and, if the prophecies of bards have any truth, through all the ages shall I live in fame" (15.877–9, *quaque patet domitis Romana potentia terris, / ore legar populi, perque omnia saecula fama, / siquid habent veri vatum praesagia, vivam*). The individual tropes, of course, are commonplace, but as in his earlier elegies, Donne's Ovidian allusions here are mutually implicated and ultimately systematic; to paraphrase Shakespeare's Hippolyta: transfigured so together, they grow to something of great constancy.[32]

Donne's method is thus not to isolate specific intertextual passages for piecemeal revision, but rather to gesture broadly at comfortable cultural attitudes – generally acknowledged, but rarely challenged or questioned by poets or their readers – which he may then undermine and explode, clearing space for his own fresher, wittier constructions. Unlike, say, Jonson importing a line from Horace, or Ovid himself rendering bathetic some exemplary scene from the *Aeneid*, Donne often prefers that his reader's recollection of a particular source passage remain foggy, as his allusions are cast nets for cultural norms, rather than spearguns aimed at precursors or rivals. Before we come to Donne's poetry, we know well enough that the mistresses of the Petrarchan tradition are overdone and Ovid's cartoonish divinities outmoded, but for this very reason, Donne does not want us to narrow our sense of his satirical targets to Stella herself or Jupiter alone.

Hence, perhaps, the opening stanza's allusive feint away from Ovid and towards Josephus, who records that the descendants of Adam's son Seth "made two pillars; the one of bricke, and the other of stone; and ingraved in each of them such things as they had invented, to the end if that of bricke should bee abolished by the ouerflowes and rage of waters, that other of stone should remaine."[33] This apocryphal embellishment on what Donne parenthetically terms "holy writt," however, is tantamount to the standards of poetic immortality Ovid sets for himself at the end of the *Metamorphoses*: *Iamque opus exegi, quod nec Iovis ira nec ignis / nec poterit ferrum nec edax abolere vetustas* (*Met.* 15.871–2, "And now my work is done, which neither the wrath of Jove, nor fire, nor sword, nor the gnawing tooth of time shall ever be able to undo"). Where Ovid unwittingly limited his poem's influence to the spatial and temporal boundaries of empire, however, the Josephan "pillars" of the *Metempsychosis* are not subject to earthly vicissitude. According to this formulation, Donne's epic authority exponentially exceeds that of Ovid, even as it falls short of "holy writt," and Ovid's consequent erasure is enacted by Donne's refusal to allude directly, again depriving the reader of easy access to the *Metamorphoses*.[34]

Against this nebulous Ovidian backdrop for the *Metempsychosis'* opening stanza, we find that Donne reduces the infinite forms of the *Metamorphoses* to "most forms," while relegating the "great world" of Pythagoras's vision to a fleeting temporality – an epic teleology already arrived at "aged evening," precisely where the reader would expect the poet to begin conventionally *in medias res*. Donne thus condemns his "deathlesse soule" – a relatively direct echo of Ovid's *morte carent animae* (*Met.* 15.158, "souls free from death") – to a fate worse than death: to the perpetual freefall of the postlapsarian condition, beyond redemption so long as "holy writt" is "excepted." Such a counsel of despair is far from the paradisiacal vision of Ovid's Pythagoras, whose pagan promise of redemption-through-vegetarianism had in any case depended upon the Roman empire's everlasting hegemony – a fallacious prophecy which Donne exploits sardonically by identifying Rome not with the golden age, but with the iron.

While the allusive network of the *Metempsychosis*'s opening stanza thus denigrates Ovid's self-proclaimed legacy, much as Donne's prefatory epistle had undercut the authority of Ovid's Pythagoras, the poem's ensuing narrative quickly develops into a parody of the metamorphic machinery of the Roman epic. Properly speaking, the first pivotal passage in Donne's narrative – as the transmigrating soul, having "fled" from its original home in the Edenic apple at the instant of the Fall, is rehabilitated in the mandrake root (121–30) – qualifies as parthenogenesis, rather than metamorphosis, yet the passage reads curiously like a lazy pastiche of countless scenes of transformation in the poetry of Ovid and his early modern imitators:

> His right arme he [i.e., the incipient mandrake] thrust out towards the East,
> West-ward his left; th'ends did themselves digest
> Into ten lesser strings, these fingers were:
> And as a slumberer stretching on his bed,
> This way he this, and that way scattered
> His other legge, which feet with toes upbeare ... (141–6)

While this description of the mandrake's growth recalls such classic Ovidian episodes as Lycaon's gradual degeneration into a wolf, or Myrrha's limb-by-limb arborification, Donne's myth of the mandrake subtly inverts the Ovidian paradigm, for here the aetiological result is the botanical simulacrum of a man. At the same time, the satirical element of Donne's aetiology corresponds neatly to the essentializing quality of Ovidian metamorphosis; for Donne, as for Ovid, the transforming subject's final shape makes manifest his or her predominant character trait or flaw.[35] Specifically, Donne's man-drake presents a travesty of human nature, created in God's image, but fallen into a subterranean form, not only commensurate with our lowest (i.e., vegetable) soul, but naturally given to ill; "His apples kindle, his leaves, force of conception kill," Donne writes, reminding us of the early modern association of the mandrake with lust, madness, and the lapsarian apple (150).[36] Hence, Donne's parody of Ovidian metamorphosis merges seamlessly with his satirical allegory:

> A mouth, but dumbe, he hath; blinde eyes, deafe eares,
> And to his shoulders dangle subtile haires;
> A young *Colossus* there hee stands upright,
> And as that ground by him were conquered
> A leafie garland weares he on his head
> Enchas'd with little fruits, so red and bright
> That for them you would call your Loves lips white;
> So, of a lone unhaunted place possest,
> Did this soules second Inne, built by the guest,
> This living buried man, this quiet mandrake, rest. (151–60)

From one angle a tumorous incarnation of biblical commonplaces indicting heretics and hypocrites (e.g., Ps. 115:4–8, Ps. 135:15–18, Jer. 5:21), Donne's insensible mandrake further satirizes the pretensions and conventions of fashionable contemporary poetry: from the garland for which every poet strives, through the hackneyed metaphors of Petrarchan sonneteers – "your Loves lips" leeched of their colour by the mandrake's vampiric berries – arriving finally at the neat paradox of the "living buried man." Skillfully weaving the mandrake episode into the epic framework of the *Metempsychosis*, Donne recounts how Eve uproots and "kills" the mandrake in order to soothe her ailing child (unnamed, but readily identifiable as Cain), thus in a wider paradoxical sense feeding the first murder victim to the first murderer.

Donne's satire, then, pursues a host of targets, among which Ovidianism is only one, yet the *Metamorphoses* in particular proves convenient for Donne as the protean universal source, suited to diverse satiric occasions. Indeed, what Mueller terms the "philosophical insubstantiality" of Ovid's Pythagoras may well have rendered the *Metamorphoses* all the more attractive to Donne as a straw source text. Having largely ignored Ovid's epic elsewhere in his early work, Donne would here be seen to vault over its pervasive cultural influence. Hence he reinscribes vegetarianism – Pythagoras's unlikely ticket back to the golden age – as the foredoomed prelapsarian state of Eden:

> … man did not know
> Of gummie blood [i.e., sap], which doth in holly grow,
> How to make bird-lime, nor how to deceive
> With faind calls, hid nets, or enwrapping snare,
> The free inhabitants of the Plyant aire. (211–15)

The passage provides at least a faint echo of Ovid's Pythagoras, who taught that in the golden age (in Golding's 1567 rendering), "Then birds might safe and sound / Fly where they listed in the ayre" (Golding, 15.106–7, *Tunc et aves tutae movere per aera pennas*). The Edenic context of the *Metempsychosis*, however, precludes any sense of homecoming, as Donne replaces the productive nostalgia of Ovid's prophet with his own persona's cynicism and regret. Indeed, despite Donne's emphasis in the prefatory epistle on the suitability of plants for the soul's transmigration, the *Metempsychosis* quickly devolves into a mythological record of carnivorousness, not as natural selection, but as a moral allegory for the degeneration of the fallen soul over time. Hence, Donne describes a series of increasingly voracious fish, culminating in the all-consuming leviathan as a metaphor for the corrupt courtier:

> He hunts not fish, but as an officer,
> Stayes in his court, at his owne net, and there
> All suitors of all sorts themselves enthrall;
> So on his backe lyes this whale wantoning,
> And in his gulfe-like throat, sucks every thing
> That passeth neare. Fish chaseth fish, and all,
> Flyer and follower, in this whirlepoole fall … (321–7)

While the whale has been read as a figure for the self-aggrandizing Earl of Essex or as Elizabeth's rapacious councillor Robert Cecil, Donne subordinates any topical significance to his broader satiric allegory, accounting such gluttony merely one among the vices for which the poem's degenerate animals kill and are killed.[37]

Significantly, however, Donne laces his moralistic beast fables with allusions to Ovid; his portrayal of the proverbially lustful sparrow, for instance, as the first carnivore of the *Metempsychosis*, resembles in miniature the original arch-villain of Pythagoras's vegetarian diatribe:

> A mouth he [i.e., Donne's newborn sparrow] opes, which would as much
>   containe
> As his late house, and the first houre speaks plaine,
> And chirps alowd for meat. Meat fit for men
> His father steales for him, and so feeds then
> One, that within a moneth, will beate him from his hen. (186–90)

To which we might compare:

> heu quantum scelus est in viscera viscera condi
> ingestoque avidum pinguescere corpore corpus
> alteriusque animans animantis vivere leto! (*Met.* 15.88–90)

> Oh, how criminal it is for flesh to be stored away in flesh, for one greedy body to grow fat by eating the body of another, for one live creature to go on living through the destruction of another living thing!

While Donne's reflexive " … meat. Meat …" reproduces the cannibalistic effect of Pythagoras's overwrought rhetoric – technically a triple

polyptoton (*viscera viscera* … / … *corpore corpus* / … *animans animantis*) –
his sparrow proceeds quickly from gluttony to lust, in a passage echoing Myrrha's sophistical defence of incest in the *Metamorphoses*:

> Already this hot cocke [i.e., the sparrow], in bush and tree,
> In field and tent, oreflutters his next hen;
> He asks her not, who did so [l]ast, nor when,
> Nor if his sister, or his neece shee be;
> Nor doth she pule for his inconstancie
> If in her sight he change, nor doth refuse
> The next that calls; both liberty doe use;
> Where store is of both kindes, both kindes may freely chuse. (193–200)

This incestuous sparrow hatches, in a sense, from the brain of Ovid's
anti-heroine:

> … coeunt animalia nullo
> cetera dilectu, nec habetur turpe iuvencae
> ferre patrem tergo, fit equo sua filia coniunx,
> quasque creavit init pecudes caper, ipsaque, cuius
> semine concepta est, ex illo concipit ales. (*Met.* 10.324–8)

> Other animals mate as they will, nor is it thought base for a heifer to en-
> dure her sire, nor for his own offspring to be a horse's mate; the goat goes
> in among the flocks which he has fathered, and the very birds conceive
> from those from whom they were conceived.

While the other Ovidian allusions in the *Metempsychosis* resonate exclusively with the beginning or end of the Roman epic, the sparrow's
resemblance to Myrrha derives uniquely from the main body of Ovid's
text – that is, from a myth culminating in metamorphosis, rather than
metempsychosis. While we may dismiss this simply as an exception
(the passage does not, after all, recount Myrrha's ultimate transformation into a tree), it is suggestive that Donne has ventriloquized Myrrha's
argument before, in the elegy entitled "Change," where his scurrilous
persona demands rhetorically, "Foxes and goats; all beasts change when
they please, / Shall women, more hot, wily, wild then these, / Be bound
to one man … ?" (11–13). Donne's return to this Ovidian commonplace
in the *Metempsychosis* – his cannibalization of his own prior imitation of
an illegitimate progenitor – not only helps us to relate his abortive epic
to his elegies, but further suggests that by the turn of the seventeenth

century Ovidianism itself could be figured as a freakish combination of voracity and incestuousness.[38]

Fittingly, then, Donne's increasingly violent narrative leaves off at the intersection of bestiality, incest, and morbid fecundity, with the rape and insemination of Cain's sister Siphatecia ("willing halfe and more," we learn at line 485) by an ape possessed by the poem's vicious soul. Donne writes:

> And whether by this change she [i.e., the deathless soul] lose or win,
> She comes out next, where the Ape would have gone in [i.e., Siphatecia's
>   vagina] …
> Keeping some quality
> Of every past shape, she knew treachery,
> Rapine, deceit, and lust, and ills enow
> To be a woman. *Themech* she is now,
> Sister and wife to *Caine, Caine* that first did plow. (491–2, 506–10)[39]

Although Donne has by now abandoned the parodic language of metamorphosis, in favour of a genealogical account of the sinful soul's propagation, this penultimate stanza of the *Metempsychosis* continues to evoke the opening lines of the *Metamorphoses* – specifically, Ovid's intention "to tell of bodies changed into new forms" (*Met.* 1.1–2, in nova… *mutatas dicere formas / corpora*). The word "change," simultaneously recalling Donne's original adaptation of Ovid's Myrrha in the context of elegy and the sparrow passage earlier in the *Metempsychosis*, is recapitulated here at the termination of the epic fragment. Donne associates this last soul's ultimate inconstancy with "every past shape," such that a fully protean history is channelled, through metempsychosis, into the vicious constitution of the feminine. The poisonous mandrake, the lustful sparrow, the gluttonous leviathan, the rapacious ape, and all the other "past shapes" of Donne's poem – their vices metempsychotically interbred – provide "ills enow / To be a woman." As the physical "changes" of metamorphosis and metempsychosis are subsumed into the "changing" character of the Donnean mistress, we find we may look forward as well, from this final passage of the *Metempsychosis*, towards the *Songs and Sonnets* of Donne's poetic maturity, or at least towards certain less-than-gracious lyrics in that collection, such as "Woman's Constancy":

> Now thou hast lov'd me one whole day,
> To morrow when thou leav'st, what wilt thou say?

> Wilt thou then Antedate some new made vow?
> Or say that now
> We are not just those persons, which we were?
> … Or, your owne end to Justifie,
> For having purpos'd change, and falsehood; you
> Can have no way but falsehood to be true?
> Vaine lunatique, against these scapes I could
> Dispute, and conquer, if I would,
> Which I abstaine to doe,
> For by to morrow, I may thinke so too. (1–5, 11–17)

Finally without form, now an abstract vice, feminine "change" is associated appositionally with "falsehood," but as Donne's persona confesses his own fickle nature at the end of the poem, we find the predisposition to change has grown universal. All men, like all women, have eaten of the metempsychotic apple.[40]

The Metamorphosis of Elegy: Ovid as "Fall Guy"

The *Metempsychosis* is best read not as the repudiation of the *Metamorphoses*, but as the epic counterpart to Donne's own erotic elegies – indeed, as their completion or perfection, however incomplete the epic itself. By proceeding from elegy to metempsychosis, while all but eschewing metamorphosis, Donne effectively teleports from Ovid's apprenticeship to the pinnacle of his poetic achievement – to the vision of Pythagoras – which he then debases with satirical brutality. Having inverted Ovid's epic peak into his own satirist's trough, we might well have expected Donne to continue to mark his poetic evolution in allusive counterpoint to Ovid's career, as his decade of poverty and disgrace in the early seventeenth century corresponds strikingly to the Roman libertine's interminable exile at the beginning of the common era. Yet the exilic Ovid, who haunts Spenser through the 1590s, and who lingers in Chapman's *Banquet of Sense*, vanishes entirely from Donne's corpus. On the contrary, while occasional echoes of the elegiac *praeceptor amoris* infiltrate the *Songs and Sonnets* (in "The Indifferent," for instance, which recalls *Amores* 2.4), the Jacobean Donne turns increasingly away from Ovid – as indeed he turns away from all his pagan precursors – so as to be perceived by his readers (or, by then, the audiences of his sermons) not as gazing backward at the poetry of the past, nor even scanning the horizon of contemporary secular literature, but staring steadfastly upward towards heaven.[41] Or, as he proclaims to God himself in the *Devotions upon Emergent Occasions*:

> Thou art a *figurative*, a *metaphoricall God* too: a *God* in whose words there is such a height of *figures*, such *voyages*, such *peregrinations* to fetch remote and precious *metaphors*, such *extensions*, such *spreadings*, such *Curtaines* of *Allegories*, such *third Heavens* of *Hyperboles* … as all *prophane Authors*, seeme of the seed of the *Serpent*, that *creepes*; thou art the *dove*, that flies.[42]

Graced with such heavenly copia, what need has the elected Dr. Donne for Ovid's profane myths or serpentine rhetoric?

For the general reader of the *Devotions*, which unlike the elegies or *Metempsychosis* were published during Donne's lifetime, this *ars poetica* ironically appears artless; we overhear nothing but the Dean of St. Paul's expostulating with God. In his public sermons, as in the *Devotions*, Donne likewise propagates a mythic image of himself as the beneficiary of divine rhetoric, with the Bible as his single, sufficient source; as he declares in a 1623 sermon on the Psalms, "Nothing is more demonstrable, then that if we would take all those Figures, and Tropes, which are collected out of secular Poets, and Orators, we may give higher, and livelier examples, of every one of those Figures, out of the Scriptures, then out of all the Greek and Latine Poets, and Orators."[43] Even the trope of metamorphosis itself undergoes an absolute, Pauline "change" by 1626, when Donne preaches before King Charles:

> That God should seale to me that Patent, *Ite prædicate omni Creaturæ, Goe and preach the Gospell to every Creature* … That if I finde a licentious Goat, a supplanting Fox, an usurious Wolfe, an ambitious Lion, yet to that creature, to every creature I should preach the Gospel of peace and consolation, and offer these creatures a Metamorphosis, a transformation, a new Creation in Christ Jesus … This is that which ministerially and instrumentally he hath committed to me, to shed his consolation upon you, upon you all …[44]

It is a totalizing myth of anthropomorphosis; as priest, Dr. Donne mediates between Charles and Christ, or by extension between England and Heaven, all the more perfectly because he has performed his own transformation from beast to man to divine – from Jack Donne to Dr. Donne – before this very court. To be sure, for some among Donne's audience (perhaps even for Charles, who after all simply inherited this libertine-cum-theologian from his father), such a sermon would sound impersonal – not a poet's evolution so much as every Christian soul's epiphany: the "consolation" is the same as that offered by any priest to his congregation. To the better informed, however – to Jack Donne's aging coterie, for instance, or to younger admirers of Dr. Donne like Thomas Carew or Izaak Walton – the trope of metamorphosis remains fraught in the context of a sermon preached by the author of the *Metempsychosis*.

Whether or not he means to slander his friend and rival, Jonson's remark to Drummond that "since he was made Doctor, [Donne] repenteth highlie & seeketh to destroy all his poems" portrays Donne much as he represents himself late in his career – as hyperaware of the irony of having aspired to his "God of metaphors" on the backs of the classical poets in general, and of the Ovidian corpus in particular. For Jonson, such a compromised position translates directly into anxiety, but Donne may well have recognized an opportunity in the long memories of his audiences and patrons.[45] When in 1619 Donne honoured Sir Robert Ker's request for copies of his poems, he enclosed the 1608 manuscript of his defence of suicide, the *Biathanatos*, and included instructions for the preservation of this curious, unsolicited gift:

> It was written by me many years since; and because it is upon a misinterpretable subject, I have always gone so near suppressing it, as that it is onely not burnt: no hand hath passed upon it to copy it, nor many eyes to read it… Keep it, I pray, with the same jealousie; let any that your discretion admits to the sight of it, know the date of it; and that it is a Book written by *Jack Donne*, and not by *D*[r.] *Donne*: Reserve it for me, if I live, and if I die, I only forbid it the Presse, and the Fire: publish it not, but yet burn it not; and between those, do what you will with it.[46]

While the *Biathanatos* is prose rather than poetry, Donne's letter belies Jonson's conclusion to Drummond (also in 1619) that Donne "seeketh to destroy all his poems," and helps us measure how far Dr. Donne indeed "repente[d]" his youthful persona. The image of the mature Donne holding his learned defence of Christianity's least forgivable sin over the fire, only to pull it back repeatedly, is evocative, but delivering it to one of King James's favourites with instructions to preserve it is hardly a retraction. Reading it instead as an advertisement (albeit targeting a patron, rather than the reading public), we might recollect a similar moment in Ovid's *Tristia*, in which the poet recalls burning his own *Metamorphoses* when exiled from Rome:

> haec [opus] ego discedens, sicut bene multa meorum,
> ipse mea posui maestus in igne manu ...
> quae quoniam non sunt penitus sublata, sed extant –
> pluribus exemplis scripta fuisse reor –
> nunc precor ut vivant et non ignava legentum
> otia delectent admoneantque mei. (*Tr.* 1.7.15–16, 23–6)

> These verses upon my departure, like so much that was mine, in sorrow I placed with my own hand in the fire ... These verses were not utterly destroyed; they still exist – several copies were made, I think – and now I pray that they may live, and that they may delight the industrious leisure of readers and remind them of me.

The final subjunctive, *admoneant*, warns even as it advertises – let the *Metamorphoses* "admonish through me" – and whatever the irrecoverable truth of Ovid's account of his epic's destruction, its survival and continued success prove the "sorrowful" poet's greatest consolation, such that he permits himself a reverie of re-inscription:

> orba parente suo quicumque volumina tangis,
> his saltem vestra detur in urbe locus.
> quoque magis faveas, haec non sunt edita ab ipso,
> sed quasi de domini funere rapta sui. (35–8)

> All you who touch these rolls bereft of their father, to them at least let a place be granted in your city! And your indulgence will be all the greater because these were not published by their master, but were rescued from what might be called his funeral.

Donne did not go so far as to burn the *Biathanatos*, nor any of his poems, so far as we know, but then again, he had no need to commit them to the fire, as his professional recovery allowed him to recalibrate the narrative of his own soul's progress, from the erotic elegies and satirical epic of his Elizabethan youth to the *Holy Sonnets* and sermons of his Jacobean redemption.

At the same time, Donne's coterie remained available to him throughout the period of his disgrace, and upon his death his admirers were prepared to promote his narrative, neatly summarized in the epitaph at the end of Carew's elegy:

> *Here lies a King, that rul'd as hee thought fit*
> *The universall Monarchy of wit;*
> *Here lie two Flamens, and both those, the best,*
> *Apollo's first, at last, the true Gods Priest.*[47]

Like his fellow elegists, Carew testifies to Donne's conversion from pagan "Flamen" to Christian "Priest," but he also undermines that easy coming of age, as his epitaph leaves us contemplating a textual grave in which two Donnes are interred: the learned divine buried alongside (or atop) the Ovidian laureate.[48] Not only does the pagan corpus occupy the same grave as the churchman's fleshly remains, but according to Donne's favourite Pauline doctrine of the body's reconstitution and reunification with the soul on Judgment Day, Jack Donne will always be with us, and will rise with the saintly doctor after all.[49] The Ovidian "Flamen" (an emphatically pagan term) is resurrected and his self-corrupted corpus exposed in the *Poems of J.D.* Hence, perhaps, the lingering ambiguities of Carew's double epitaph: the celebration of a worldly man as "King," the uncorrected subjection of "the universall Monarchy" to human wit, the syntactically retroactive implication that "the true Gods Priest" remains one of "two Flamens," and the tendency of the appositional phrase "at last" to unite the disparate gods of poetry and Christianity. Hence too the irony of Carew's earlier warning, that "Libertines in Poetrie ... will repeale the goodly exil'd traine / Of gods and goddesses, which in thy just raigne / Were banish'd nobler Poems," for by the end of his elegy Carew has himself reintroduced Apollo, embodied in the sacerdotal person of John Donne.

Conclusion: "It sticks strangely, whatever it is"

Simultaneously the most decadent cliché of the late Renaissance and the period's most fruitful poetic ground, Ovidianism was no longer a retrospective mode by the middle of the English 1590s, but was rather the premier means of locating oneself among peers and rivals, themselves visibly invested in striking imitative postures relative to the established fact of Ovid's celebrity. In this sense, the self-divided attitude towards Ovidianism already on display in Shakespeare's *Titus Andronicus* typifies a larger truth about the rapidly evolving literary culture of the late Elizabethan period: at this transitional moment – as private patronage was giving way to market-driven professionalism, as new audiences developed and old ones splintered – a nimble, readily adjustable allusive posture proved indispensable to ambitious young poets like Shakespeare, Marlowe, or Drayton. Ovid's centrality, as the common site of so many competing acts of poetic self-fashioning and self-revision, results most immediately from the straightforward fact of his popularity within the cultural moment. Quite simply, Ovidian poetry sold.

In a deeper sense, however, Ovid's popularity as a model for imitative poets originates in the protean capacity of his corpus; in his manifold identities as erotic elegist, epic celebrant of a pagan cosmos, urbane representative of the aristocratic lifestyle, plaintive and hopeless exile. At the same time, the Ovid of the Renaissance was not merely (nor even primarily) a figure of his own construction; he was also the beneficiary – at times, the victim – of the medieval and early modern impulse to inscribe multiple new identities on the legendary figures of the classical world. Hence, he became the serial moralizer of the didactic tradition, the arch-villain of anti-poetic diatribes, the master and slave of courtly love, the admonitory embodiment of wasted genius. With so many recognizable faces, Ovid became the allusive reference point *par excellence*; the Elizabethan poet first chose his Ovid, then defined himself in relation or in contradistinction to that figure, yet remained free to self-revise allusively, in accordance with a developing career and in response to an evolving readership. Hence, while certain Ovidian postures would continue to signal a poet's immaturity or prodigality, others could reflect professional growth, mastery, or a return to personal or cultural origins.

The first years of the seventeenth century, however, saw a trend in certain literary circles towards the repudiation of Ovidianism, in the wake of the Bishops' Ban on satires in 1599 and in the midst of official reaction to the Essex rebellion. Ovid fared especially badly on the stage, during the famous "War of the Theaters," as playwrights like Thomas Dekker, John Marston, and Ben Jonson indicted one another for an intellectually impoverished reliance on the poetry of the past. In his 1601 comedy *Poetaster*, Jonson even dramatized the historical exile of Ovid himself as part of a broader attack on his rivals' tastes and abilities. In the same year, a pair of poems by Jonson appeared in Robert Chester's miscellany, *Love's Martyr*, testifying most emphatically to the end of Ovid's cultural authority.

In the first poem of the pair, entitled *"Prœludium,"* we find Jonson at his most bilious, violently rejecting the Ovidian pantheon; indeed, vomiting up a bolus of gods:

> *We must sing too? what* Subiect *shal we chuse?*
> *Or whose great* Name *in* Poets Heauen *use,*
> *For the more* Countenance *to our Actiue* Muse?

> Hercules? *alasse his bones are yet sore,*
> *With his old earthly* Labors; *t'exact more*
> *Of his dull* Godhead, *were Sinne: Lets implore*

> Phœbus? *No: Tend thy* Cart *still. Enuious Day*
> *Shall not giue out, that we haue made thee stay,*
> *And foundred thy hote* Teame, *to tune our Lay*

> *Nor will we beg of thee,* Lord of the Vine,
> *To raise our spirites with thy coniuring Wine,*
> *In the greene circle of thy Iuy twine.*

> Pallas, *nor thee we call on,* Mankind Maide,

That (at thy birth) mad'st the poore Smith *afraide,*
Who with his Axe *thy* Fathers *Mid-wife plaide.*

The emetic litany soon proceeds beyond decorum, in the manner of the
"biting satire" of the late 1590s:

Go, crampe dull Mars, *light* Venus, *when he snorts,*
Or with thy Tribade *Trine, inuent new sports,*
Thou, nor their loosenesse, with our Making *sorts.*

Let the old Boy *your sonne ply his old Taske,*
Turne the stale Prologue *to some painted Maske,*
His Absence *in our* Verse *is all we aske.*

Hermes *the cheater, cannot mixe with vs,*
Though he would steale his sisters Pegasus,
And rifle him; or pawne his Petasus.

Nor all the Ladies *of the* Thespian Lake,
(Though they were crusht into one forme) could make
A Beauty *of that* Merit, *that should take*

Our Muse *vp by* Commission: *No, we bring*
Our owne true Fire; Now our Thought takes wing,
And now an Epode *to deepe eares we sing.*[1]

The poem's hysteria gives way in the final tercet, with its promise of
a more digestible satire in the calmer Horatian mode, which duly follows. As Jonson's "Thought takes wing," he strikes the familiar attitude
of the Ovidian debutant, like Shakespeare promising "graver labour" to
come, though to a general reader rather than to any particular patron.[2]
In one sense, then, the "*Prœludium*" can hardly be said to constitute
an Ovidian poem at all, as Jonson here, in unmistakable fashion, purges
his verse of the false gods of the *Metamorphoses*.[3] A less categorical view,
however, responds to the poem's overwhelming ironies, beginning with
the strangely epic quality of the purge; it is a catalogue akin to the scandalous tapestries of Arachne and Busirane in the most irreverent passages of Ovid and Spenser. Indeed, the dissonance of the "*Prœludium*"
can hardly be corrected by the programmatic imitation of Horace which
follows, as the corrupt pantheon has already spilled onto the page. Hercules is presented as a syphilitic with aching bones; Apollo as drawing

a "Cart" instead of the chariot of the sun; Hermes as a cheater, thief, and spendthrift; Bacchus (elsewhere glowingly invoked by the tippling Jonson) as a conjurer; Mars simply as "dull." The goddesses are presumed guilty of sexual perversion – Minerva of cross-dressing and Venus of "inventing new sports" with the three Graces, her "Tribade trine." Jupiter and Diana, both identifiable with Queen Elizabeth, conspicuously escape censure, though given the efficiency with which Jonson vomits up each god, tercet by tercet, we get the impression that he could easily have included either of them. For all its vitriol, then, the *"Prœludium"* is fundamentally an inclusive poem, with space for any classical deity, even the nine Muses "crusht into one forme."

However much damage the "Epode" can repair, in the *"Prœludium"* Jonson corresponds to the "Libertine in Poetrie" lambasted by Carew in his elegy on Donne. Jonson "will repeale [i.e., recall] the goodly exil'd traine / Of gods and goddesses" – ironically in the act of exiling them – and he permits the "silenc'd tales o'th'Metamorphoses / ... [to] stuffe [his] lines, and swell the windy Page."[4] The colic aspects of Carew's latter metaphors point to Jonson's notorious scatological tendencies, but properly speaking, Jonson's Ovidian posture is emetic.[5] The *"Prœludium"* does not recall Donne and his deft usurpations of Ovid's cultural roles, so much as Nashe's apologetic sonnet to Lord Strange – his "longing to unlade so bad a fraught" as *The Choice of Valentines*. By rejecting with such violence the divine syphilitics and tribades of "Ouids wanton Muse," Jonson empties himself, like Nashe's troublesome dildo, in preparation for a more sublime performance.[6] The latent sexuality of the final lines of the *"Prœludium"* hint at the modern significance of the poem's title: "foreplay."[7]

Unlike Nashe, however, who abandons the imitation of Ovid after a single exercise in impotence, Jonson all but admits his addiction to Ovid; the violent emetic posture of *"Prœludium"* is that of an addict prescribing himself an unhealthy and unworkable cure. Of course, Jonson is better known for having administered such medicine not to himself, but to Marston, his rival in the "War of the Theaters," in the final scene of the *Poetaster*. Marston, lampooned onstage as the poetaster Crispinus, is made to vomit his store of affected terms and phrases in the presence of Augustus himself, who approves the medical intervention by Horace/Jonson, and of the laureate Virgil, who recommends the procedure. Notably, Crispinus does not vomit gods and goddesses, but his plight nonetheless stages the uncontrolled emetic posture of Jonson's own *"Prœludium."* Ovid himself, after all, has already been purged from the stage of *Poetaster* for the crime of impersonating the gods, in a scene reminiscent of Chapman's *Banquet of Sense*. Jonson's satirical targets, then, are many and varied: the character Ovid contains aspects of Marlowe, Shakespeare's Romeo, and other violators of poetic decorum, all of whom are disgorged from the stage upon the banishment of their representative, nor have critics yet established the degree to which we are meant to sympathize with Ovid's fall from Caesar's grace.[8] Throughout the confusion, however, what remains clear is the simultaneous necessity and futility, for Jonson, of portraying the end of Ovid's influence over him, again and again, *ad nauseam*. As Virgil observes of an uncooperative verbal affectation during poor Crispinus's most protracted heave, "It stickes strangely, what euer it is" (*Poetaster*, 5.3.517–18); the same might be said of Jonson's Ovidianism.

That Ovidianism "stickes strangely" for Jonson is not, however, a purely psychological phenomenon, though there is clearly an element of obsession in his approach to his sources. As a series of imitative postures, Jonson's Ovidianism approximates not Nashe's single premature ejaculation, but Shakespeare's continuous rediscovery of the lingering utility of Ovidian postures in all their variety. Like his friend and rival, Jonson employs the trope of the Ovidian poet's (false) retraction and dubious commitment to more wholesome material. Both poets likewise play with the apocalyptic implications, in *Venus and Adonis* and "*Prœludium*," of the end of metamorphosis and the departure of the gods. As we have seen, however, these too are imitative postures, because both Shakespeare and Jonson remain prepared to redeploy Ovidian allusions or tropes whenever required. Such postures seem at times compulsory, as in the sad cases of Lavinia or Crispinus; at times irresistably desirable, as when Aaron delights in his role of Ovidian "tutor" (*Titus*, 5.1.98), or when Jonson's own Ovid begins *Poetaster* with an anachronistic tribute to the late Marlowe (as the translator of *All Ovids Elegies*); at times opportunistic, as when Jonson and Marston alike preface their satires with tales from the *Metamorphoses*, only to repudiate them in the sequel.

Despite such satirical formulations, by the beginning of the seventeenth century Ovidian imitation clearly meant more than any one of these motivations or the consequent striking of any single posture could express. More organically, practicing Ovidian imitation meant possessing the protean quality of striking that series of postures best calculated to create and recreate relationships – associations and distinctions – between one's own poetry and the poetry of rival proteans. Jonson's Ovidianism, after all, incorporates further postures in addition to the emetic hysteria of "*Prœludium*" and *Poetaster*. Jonson turns to Ovid as occasion dictates, for example, in the opening lines of the "Execration upon Vulcan," as he laments the fiery destruction of his personal library. He likewise turns to Ovid as his monarch dictates, as he reveals in the argument to his latest masque, *Chloridia* (1630), drawn from the *Fasti*, "the king and queen's majesty having given their command for the invention."[9] Even when freed entirely from occasion or compulsion, Jonson proves a subtle weaver of Ovidian intertexts, as when he declares the poet's divinity in his commonplace book, *Timber, or Discoveries*, by combining sentiments from the *Ars amatoria* and *Fasti*,[10] or again in his astonishing allusion to the plight of Ovid's Marsyas at the climax of his lyric, "To Heaven," the Christian prayer which closes his most powerful collection of verse, *The Forest*.[11]

Such local touches and interwoven strands are far, perhaps, from the metempsychotic claims of commendatory sonneteers like Davies and enthusiasts like Meres, who find in Chapman, Drayton, or Shakespeare the re-embodiment of Ovid himself. Jonson's friend and critic Edmund Waller, however, did recognize him as England's latest Proteus, despite the loud insistence with which Jonson himself rejected such an association in "*Præludium*," *Poetaster*, and many other works. Following Jonson's death in 1637, Waller meditated on his legacy:

> The sundry postures of thy copious Muse
> Who would express, a thousand tongues must use;
> Whose fate's no less peculiar than thy art;
> For as thou couldst all characters impart,
> So none could render thine, which still escapes,
> Like Proteus, in variety of shapes;
> Who was nor this, nor that, but all we find,
> And all we can imagine, in mankind.[12]

Waller's sentiment is compliment enough to a playwright and actor, of course, though it is also the opposite of the "centred self" that several critics, following Thomas Greene, have identified as the Jonsonian ideal.[13] Assessing Jonson's achievement, Waller proves deaf to the "*Epode to deepe eares*," listening instead for the zany pantheon of the "*Præludium*"; he applauds the Ovid of the *Poetaster*, while ignoring the play's Horace. He affirms, finally, that Ovidianism requires a "copious Muse," prepared to strike "sundry postures," and his tribute, though unlikely to win Jonson's own approval, provides us with one of the most perceptive and revealing contemporary reflections on the Ovidian vogue.

Notes

Introduction: "Note how she quotes the leaves"

1 The princes' fictional education mirrors or at least parodies Shakespeare's own; see the classic account in T.W. Baldwin, *William Shakspere's Small Latine & Lesse Greeke*, esp. 2.417–55.

2 Shakespeare, *Titus Andronicus*, ed. Waith, 3.2.80–4. References to *Titus* are to this edition, and are provided parenthetically. Editors continue to debate the date of the play's composition, the likelihood of authorial collaboration, and the integrity of the various texts; indeed, this scene, included in the 1623 Folio but absent from earlier quartos, is especially suspect (the clumsy repetition of the verb "to go" in these lines hints at the difficulties involved). On the textual issues, see not only Waith's introduction, esp. 39–43, but also Jonathan Bate's introduction to the Arden edition of the play, esp. 95–103. For extensive arguments that George Peele, rather than Shakespeare, wrote the first act of *Titus*, see Brian Vickers, *Shakespeare, Co-Author*, 148–243. I find sufficient continuity between the confused text of the first act and the remainder of the play to support critical claims regarding the evolution of characters and their allusive tendencies, but I recognize that this does not necessitate Shakespeare's sole authorship; for a judicious account, see Patrick Cheney, *Shakespeare's Literary Authorship*, 70 and 70n13.

3 James, *Shakespeare's Troy*, 51. James discusses the "deformation" of the *Aeneid* as the textual foundation for the "late Roman society" of the play, analyzing the refiguring of the family tomb of the opening scene into the bloody pit of the central acts. The latter she identifies with Ovidian "narrative and critical practice, … which substitutes, inverts, confuses, appropriates, swallows up, and engenders meanings" (64).

4 The only exception to this self-imposed rule is my discussion of Nashe's *Choice of Valentines* in the first chapter, because Nashe's effective withdrawal from participation in the vogue provides a useful contrast to Shakespeare's serial responses to Ovid's celebrity.

5 At the beginning of his *Ars amatoria*, Ovid declares *ego sum praeceptor Amoris* (1.17, "I am Love's teacher"), referring to the anthropomorphic Cupid (*puer*), though elsewhere he freely substitutes *magister* for *praeceptor* and the abstract *amor* for the god *Amor*. Hereafter I will refer to the "*praeceptor amoris*," following the general sense employed by most Elizabethan authors.

6 On the vogue and its origins, including an analysis of the use of Ovid's poems in Elizabethan schools, see Bate's *Shakespeare and Ovid*, esp. 21–5. Colin Burrow writes, "School-children in England and Europe were encouraged to learn Latin verse composition by translating verses of Ovid into the vernacular, and then translating them back into Latin prose. They would then be required to structure their prose translation into a metrical and rhetorically shaped approximation of their original, so that (ideally) they might 'have made the very same' poem as Ovid originally wrote" ("Re-embodying Ovid: Renaissance Afterlives," in *Cambridge Companion to Ovid*, ed. Hardie, 304). Jeff Dolven, however, identifies instances of the suppression of Ovid's texts in Elizabethan schools and in humanist educational treatises from the continent (*Scenes of Instruction in Renaissance Romance*, 60–1, 116–17).

7 On Golding's translation, see Raphael Lyne, *Ovid's Changing Worlds*, 27–79.

8 In the introduction to her anthology, *Elizabethan Minor Epics*, Elizabeth Story Donno writes, "when from his quarters at Lincoln's Inn, Lodge rushed his small volume of 'unperfit Poems' to the printer, he inaugurated not only a new Elizabethan genre but also a new standard of poetic achievement" (6).

9 The loudest applause is that of Julius Caesar Scaliger, who demands, "who can learn enough to speak adequately about Ovid, much less to dare reprove him?" James, however, responds, "The record of critical opinion, as Scaliger well knew, raises the opposite question: who among critics doubts his entitlement to judge Ovid and find him wanting?" ("Ovid and the Question of Politics in Early Modern England," 343).

10 On Marlowe as "the first Western poet in any language to make Ovid's career pattern *literally* his own," see Cheney, *Marlowe's Counterfeit Profession*, 49. Cheney continues, "While Renaissance writers such as Golding and Shakespeare busied themselves with either the moralized or the eroticized Ovid, Marlowe arrived with an Ovid that transcends this dichotomy.

Marlowe's new Ovid is an Ovid with a 'literary career' – a poet who presents himself with a multigenre career pattern, a political ideology, a sexual orientation, and a vision of the poet's vocation and sense of destiny" (51).

11 See Peter Knox, "A Poet's Life," in *A Companion to Ovid*, ed. Knox, 3–7.

12 On the broader implications of this shift, see pp. 49–50.

13 For an analysis of this speech as a palimpsest of Ovidian texts and translations (and for a favourable view of Marcus), see Cheney, *Shakespeare's Literary Authorship*, 65–73.

14 For Lynn Enterline, Philomela's weaving "proves every bit as persuasive as the tongue [she] once hoped would 'move the very rocks to consciousness' ... It moves her sister, Procne, to terrifying action. The tapestry then extends the confusion between the 'speakable and the unspeakable' to another person ... because the crime conveyed in these marks resists the 'indignant words' Procne seeks with her 'questing tongue'" (*Rhetoric of the Body from Ovid to Shakespeare*, 5). Philomela's tapestry, of course, is literally a "text," from the Latin verb *texere* (to weave); see the *OED*, s.v. "text, n(1)."

15 Barkan, *Gods Made Flesh*, 246.

16 The Folio stage direction specifies, "she takes the staff in her mouth, and guides it with her stumps" (4.1.75, s.d.).

17 Spenser, *The Faerie Queene*, ed. Hamilton, 714–18, but see Syrithe Pugh, *Spenser and Ovid*, for an alternative account of Ovid serving Spenser already in 1579 as "the presiding genius" of *The Shepheardes Calender* (12).

18 In the *Daphnaïda*, Spenser adapts Ovid's Alcyone by intertextual way of Chaucer's *Book of the Duchess*. In the *Muiopotmos*, he reprises the tapestry-weaving contest between Arachne and Minerva from the *Metamorphoses*.

19 R.W. Maslen writes, "the men who raped [Lavinia] have subjected Ovid's text to a ... damaging exegesis. They have used it, in fact, as a kind of rapists' instruction manual" ("Ovid in Early Elizabethan England," in *Shakespeare's Ovid*, ed. Taylor, 16). Maslen does not differentiate, however, between Aaron as "tutor" and Chiron and Demetrius as students.

20 *OED*, s.v. "plot, n(1)." 1a, 3a, 4, 6.

21 Bull, *The Mirror of the Gods*, 357.

22 Throughout the play, Shakespeare takes pains to establish a range of allusive capacities, from the Clown who mistakes "Jupiter" for "gibbet-maker" (4.3.79–80) to Aaron himself. Toward the clownish end of this spectrum, Demetrius compares his mother to Ovid's vengeful Hecuba (1.1.135–41), from a passage in the *Metamorphoses* identified by Enterline as among the texts most commonly assigned by humanist pedagogues, as a "'mirror' or 'example' for pupils to imitate" (*Rhetoric of the Body*, 25). To be sure,

Demetrius's invocation of Hecuba is at least more relevant than Titus's delusional identification with Virgil's Aeneas – and will continue to inspire more learned Shakespearean characters like Lucrece and Hamlet – but his textbook allusion is superseded by Aaron's expert Ovidian technique. On the *Metamorphoses* generally as "the Bible of a tradition – read, reread, translated, illustrated, moralized, reborn," see Leonard Barkan, *The Gods Made Flesh*, 1.

23 Ibid., 244.

24 Ovid's verb, *resolvere*, can also refer to the repayment of a debt (Lewis and Short, s.v. "resolvere," v. 1.B.2), underscoring the precision of Philomela's vengeance. Already in the *Metamorphoses*, however, retaliatory balance proves impossible to sustain, since Itys's innocence resembles too closely that of Philomela herself; as she had cried out for her father while Tereus cut out her tongue, so Itys's final cries are for his mother (*Met.* 6.555, 640). In an uncanny sense, Philomela's original vengeance against Itys is already "worse than Philomel," in that she cuts her nephew's throat (*iugulum*), whereas Tereus had refused to cut hers when she offered it (553, *iugulum parabat*).

25 Shakespeare's source is Livy, but see Waith's note to 5.3.36–8.

26 David Bevington observes, "The Andronici are driven to the limits of verbal and visual speech and still find those means of expression too short of what they feel" (*Action is Eloquence*, 31). That metamorphosis and its promised escape not only lie beyond the reach of any allusive re-enactment, but indeed become more unthinkable with each lost limb or voice is a logical extension of this claim.

27 Bate, *Shakespeare and Ovid*, 28.

28 Dolven, *Scenes of Instruction*, 44.

29 Ovid's term for "wings" is *pennis* (the ablative plural employed twice at *Met.* 6.667–8), and it is difficult not to ascribe to Shakespeare an allusive pun on "pen" and "penis": a pen is precisely what Lavinia lacks, or as Chiron jeers, "Write down thy mind, bewray thy meaning so, / An if thy stumps will let thee play the scribe" (2.4.3–4).

30 Following William Keach (see *Elizabethan Erotic Narratives*, xvi–xvii), I employ the anachronistic generic term epyllion for the indispensable clarity it lends to critical discussions of the many mid-length, generally erotic and Ovidian narrative poems of the late Renaissance.

1. Impotence and Stillbirth: Nashe, Shakespeare, and the Ovidian Debut

1 Meres, *Palladis tamia*, 286r–v. Meres's comparisons are modeled on a well-known passage in Quintilian's *Institutio oratoria* (10.1.85 ff.).

2 On the relationship between the *Isle of Dogs* fiasco and *Lenten Stuff*, see
  Lorna Hutson, *Thomas Nashe in Context*, 250–1.
3 In the sixteenth century, Meres's verb, "to worry," could mean "to seize
  by the throat with the teeth and tear or lacerate; to kill or injure by biting
  and shaking," referring to hunting dogs (*OED*, "worry, v." 3a). On the
  allegorical association of Actaeon's hounds with everything from rabies to
  ingratitude, see Conti, *Mythologiae*, 6.24.
4 Nashe's editor Ronald McKerrow observes that "Of classical authors
  Ovid is by far the most frequently used," and enumerates specific allusions, noting further that Nashe's "indebtedness to the *Metamorphoses*
  cannot be measured by his actual quotations, for he constantly refers to
  stories therein contained ... It is somewhat surprising to find only about
  a dozen quotations from [Virgil], as against the hundred odd from Ovid."
  ("Nashe's Reading," in *Works of Thomas Nashe*, 5:133–4). Though approximate, such quantifying remains suggestive; if Spenser in his *Faerie Queene*
  and Shakespeare in *Titus Andronicus* stage an allusive competition between
  Virgil and Ovid as poetic authorities, in Nashe's work this contest has
  already been decided. A more precise sense of Ovid's significance to Nashe
  emerges from Sean Keilen's reading of the letter appended to the 1591
  edition of Sidney's *Astrophel and Stella*: "Nashe's phrase in the final paragraph, 'Such is the golden age wherein we live,' appears to be a translation
  of a line from the *Ars amatoria* – '*Aurea nunc vere sunt saecula*' (2.277). As
  best I can tell, this is the first reference by an English writer to the English
  Renaissance as a golden age" ("English Literature in its Golden Age," in
  Forms of Renaissance Thought, ed. Barkan, Cormack, and Keilen, 52).
5 See *Lenten Stuffe*, in *Works* 3.195.
6 On the alternate title, see Katherine Duncan-Jones, "City Limits: Nashe's
  'Choise of Valentines' and Jonson's 'Famous Voyage,'" 248.
7 The explicit content of the *Choice* has given many critics pause. McKerrow's statement in the "Doubtful Works" section of his landmark edition
  says it all: "There can, I fear, be little doubt that this poem is the work of
  Nashe" (*Works*, 5:141). Contemporary indictments of Nashe's *Choice* by
  Gabriel Harvey and Joseph Hall, however, along with John Davies's later
  reminiscence (discussed below), make the poem's attribution to Nashe all
  but certain, despite his own equivocating self-defence later in the quarrel
  with Harvey. The pertinent texts are quoted by David Frantz in "'Leud
  Priapians' and Renaissance Pornography," 159–62, and by Stapleton in
  "Nashe and the Poetics of Obscenity," in *Thomas Nashe*, ed. Brown, 32–3.
8 As Stapleton observes, "The far-ranging periodic sentence at the beginning
  of the *Choise* ... recreates the whole of the protagonist's world in miniature
  by way of details (the seasons, ritual dancing and mating, place-names) ...

and echoes Chaucer's *General Prologue* not a little in tone, wrought couplets, cataloging, and even the number of lines in the first sentence (eighteen)" ("Poetics of Obscenity," 316).

9 Jonathan Crewe observes, "In 'The Choice of Valentines,' Nashe stages what he calls a 'shift' to the city. In doing so, he continues to assign ontological priority to pastoral and to the poetic ideal, thus conferring by implication a diminished or 'fallen' character upon the verse of the city." (*Unredeemed Rhetoric*, 48). Ian Frederick Moulton, however, takes issue with the characterization of the *Choice's* green-world as pastoral, asserting that "the rustic sexuality of the beginning of the poem is described in terms both nostalgic and parodic, and is at no point presented as a serious alternative to the experience of the brothel. Its genealogy is more Chaucerian than classical, and the atmosphere evoked is that of a medieval English feast-day, not of pastoral *otium*" ("Transmuted into a Woman or Worse," in *Thomas Nashe*, ed. Brown, 64). All references to Nashe's *Choice* are to McKerrow's edition, and will be cited parenthetically by line number.

10 Latin quotations from the *Amores* are from the Loeb edition, but I have provided Marlowe's contemporary translations, entitled *All Ovids Elegies*, as they appear in *The Complete Works of Christopher Marlowe*, ed. Gill, vol. 1 (cited parenthetically in the text with the abbreviation *AOE*).

11 Davies, "The Papers Complaint, compild in ruthfull Rimes Against the Paper-spoylers of these Times," in *The Scourge of Folly*, line 232. The relevant section is quoted by McKerrow in Nashe, *Works*, 5:153.

12 Drayton remarks that "surely Nashe, though he a Proser were, / A branch of Lawrell yet deserues to beare" ("Elegy to Henry Reynolds, of Poets and Poesie," ll. 112–13, quoted by McKerrow in Nashe, *Works*, 5:153).

13 Sasha Roberts notes that "*Venus and Adonis* was Shakespeare's 'bestselling' work during his lifetime, running to an astonishing ten editions by 1617 and a further five reprints by 1636" (*Reading Shakespeare's Poems in Early Modern England*, 2), and discusses its popularity as "an erotic sourcebook" for manuscript miscellanies (84).

14 Moulton notes that "Nashe largely rejects the mythologizing of passion in favour of the matter-of-fact sexual world of the *Amores*" ("Transmuted into a Woman," 68). Moulton also provides the most detailed discussion of the poem's extant texts (59–60).

15 McKerrow (*Works*, 5:397–8) discusses this manuscript and its cipher (Dyce MS 44).

16 On Nashe's debt to Maximianus, and the likelihood of the misidentification with Gallus, see Stapleton, "A New Source for Thomas Nashe's *The Choice of Valentines*," 17–18.

17 The Dyce compositor likewise eliminates much of Thomalin's earlier
   rhetorical embellishment. Stapleton discusses the *Choice* as a Chaucerian
   fabliau, "something like *The Reeve's Tale* in treatment if not in material"
   ("Poetics of Obscenity," 316).

18 According to the *OED*, "scot and lot" can refer to the settling of a tavern
   bill ("scot, n(2)." 2a, 3). On the *Choice* as "explicit about male sexual inadequacy and female sexual autonomy," see Moulton, "Transmuted into a
   Woman," 61.

19 Davies, "Papers Complaint," in *The Scourge of Folly*, line 232.

20 Roberts discusses Davies's "ambivalent" charge against *Venus and Adonis*
   as pornography, arguing that Davies's "account of what women get up to
   in 'their Closset-games' is as much the occasion for titillation as rebuke"
   (*Reading Shakespeare's Poems*, 33). This reading may further apply to
   Davies's indictment of the "dampned *Dildo*" later in his "Paper's Complaint." See also Roberts's discussion of Margaret Bellasis's 1630s manuscript miscellany, which includes a version of the *Choice* lacking the dildo
   passage (182).

21 The sonnet, then, is in keeping with Nashe's later attitude toward Ovid
   in such prose works as *The Unfortunate Traveller*, characterized by a free-
   ranging but irreverent usage of Ovidian material, which "shows us the
   degradation to which such a name can be subjected" (Ossa-Richardson,
   "Ovid and the 'Free Play with Signs in Thomas Nashe's *The Unfortunate
   Traveller*," 955).

22 D.C. Feeney discusses Ovid's own deployment of this strategy: "The
   Jupiter-like status of Augustus, and especially his Jovian wrath, with full
   apparatus of bolt and fire, are insistent themes in the exile poetry. From
   exile Ovid … challenges the implacable Princeps to be like a god in more
   than anger, and relent by showing clemency" (*Gods in Epic*, 222).

23 See Stapleton on Nashe's esteem for Ascham, and on the *Choice* as "a veritable example of *imitatio*, whether we limit ourselves to some of Ascham's
   principles, or if we apply his very broad ideas more generally to literature"
   ("Poetics of Obscenity," 311).

24 Quoted by Frantz, "Leud Priapians," 161.

25 Quoted by Stapleton, "Poetics of Obscenity," 313.

26 On Nashe's *Choice* and its attendant sonnets as a response to the "career
   fictions of Marlowe and Spenser," see Cheney, *Reading Sixteenth-Century
   Poetry*, 251–2.

27 While the other myths are better known, Ovid's passing reference to
   Crocus and Smilax at *Met.* 4.283 illustrates ironically the overabundance of
   floral metamorphoses in his poetry.

28 Although the half-finished *Fasti* complements the *Metamorphoses* at many junctures, it remains unclear which poem Ovid composed first. See Knox, "Poet's Life," 6.

29 G.W. Pigman distinguishes between the complex apian metaphor as employed by Seneca – requiring not only the gathering from others' rhetorical gardens but also the digestion and transformation of those flowers into something new – from the simple flower-sampling recommended by Macrobius in the *Saturnalia*, and one could argue that Ovid indulges in the latter form of imitation in the passage I have quoted from the *Fasti* (see "Versions of Imitation in the Renaissance," 4–11). Flora's self-aggrandizement, however – the ironic manner in which she gathers floral metamorphoses without transforming them – depends upon Ovid's prior transformations of *florilegia* in the *Metamorphoses*, and Ovid himself is the chief victim of her acquisitive horticulture. However much credence we lend the *Fasti*'s Flora, then, Ovid remains eminently suited to the Renaissance conception of transformative imitation, or as Pigman quotes from Petrarch's *Familiares*, "Take care that what you have gathered does not long remain in its original form inside of you: the bees would not be glorious if they did not convert what they found into something different and something better" (1.8.23, quoted by Pigman, 7).

30 On the glut of Ovidian elements adorning Italianate Renaissance gardens and especially Kenilworth, where the Duke of Leicester entertained Elizabeth in 1575, see Michael Leslie, "Spenser, Sidney, and the Renaissance Garden," 7–8. Hester Lees-Jeffries observes, "It is not surprising, given their liminality and their blurring of the boundaries between art and nature, that many Renaissance gardens and fountains drew on Ovid's *Metamorphoses* for their imagery and controlling narratives" (*England's Helicon*, 10).

31 On Adonis as representative of Shakespeare's "own Ovidian career in response to the Virgilian Spenser," see Cheney, *Reading Sixteenth-Century Poetry*, 262–3.

32 Hulse, *Metamorphic Verse*, 143.

33 Shakespeare, *Venus and Adonis*, ll. 1165–76, in *Complete Sonnets and Poems*, ed. Burrow, 235. Subsequent references to *Venus and Adonis* in this section are to this edition, provided parenthetically by line number.

34 In his introduction, Burrow further observes that "Red and white were burned into the imaginations of Londoners in 1593: those infected with the plague in the city carried red wands to warn passers-by; in the country they carried white" (ibid., 15). Plague-wands aside, red and white are likewise blazoned on England's national flag. On Reynolds, and for extensive

excerpts from his zany letters, see Katherine Duncan-Jones, "Much Ado with Red and White," 479–90.

35 The poem's earlier variations on verdancy foreshadow ironically the "Green-dropping sap" of Adonis's floral state. Apostrophizing her beloved's lips, for example, Venus prays, "O never let their crimson liveries wear, / And as they last, their verdour still endure, / To drive infection from the dangerous year" (506–8), incoherently implying that Adonis's lips have changed from red to green. Editors have responded to this crux with everything from the replacement of "verdour" with "virtue" to the re-definition of "crimson" as something short of red (see Anthony Mortimer, "'Crimson Liveries' and 'Their Verdour'"). Venus's chromatic confusion, however, corresponds to her impulse to associate Adonis with a landscape properly (but not permanently) green, and prefigures the irony of her own impetuous act of cropping the flower at the end of the poem, foreclosing any remaining chance that his "verdour still endure."

36 Although Shakespeare's red and white would have registered as spent Petrarchan conventions, the poem's vivid colours have roots in the *Metamorphoses* as well. Ovid's Orpheus, narrating the Adonis myth, describes Venus's cultivation of a blood-red flower (*flos de sanguine concolor, Met.* 10.735). Although Ovid's version of the myth provides Shakespeare with ample raw material for his imitation, the flower's parthenogenesis at the end of the epyllion more precisely recalls Apollo's lamentation over Hyacinthus earlier in Orpheus's song, in which a sympathetic nature responds to Apollo's divine sentiment, without requiring anything like Venus's bubbling witches' brew of nectar and blood. As the blood of Hyacinthus "ceased to be" (*desinit esse, Met.* 10.211), so the mangled corpse of Shakespeare's Adonis vanishes decorously, hence the allusion links Shakespeare's narrative to the homosexual song of Orpheus, undermining his own coercively heterosexual Venus. As Richard Halpern writes, "Ironically, the first half of Shakespeare's Ovidian poem depends on the denial of a wished-for 'metamorphosis'" ("'Pining Their Maws,'" in *Venus and Adonis: Critical Essays*, ed. Kolin, 380).

37 See also Michael Pincombe, "The Ovidian Hermaphrodite," in *Ovid and the Renaissance Body*, ed. Stanivukovic, 155–70. Lauren Silberman discusses the tensions between the Venus and Adonis story as a "myth of the hunt" and as the "Hermaphrodite [who] figures the union of opposites" (*Transforming Desire*, 49).

38 Bate, *Shakespeare and Ovid*, 51.

39 The anomalous form of Spenser's catalogue stanza, with a missing or truncated central line, makes the omission obvious (see Hamilton's note to 45.3–4).

40 Comparing the two poems, Judith Anderson cautions against a "critical tradition [which] has too often assumed rivalry or anxiety as the only possible relation between poets and precursors," and recontextualizes Shakespeare's engagement with Spenser, such that "the relation of the epyllion to the epic looks less like parody and critique and more like dialogue and complement" (*Reading the Allegorical Intertext*, 204). Anderson likewise focuses on the inherent ambivalence of Spenser's flower-catalogue, remarking, "Appropriately, the flowers of metamorphosis, at once of death and life, of mutability and perpetuity … also *contain* … the jealousy, self-enclosure, grief, and despair variously found in the culturally fertile myths of Hyacinthus, Narcissus, Amaranthus, and all other sorts of floral metamorphees" (218). On the Garden of Adonis more generally as a site for Spenserian ambivalence, replete with "allusions to death and imprisonment, images seemingly out of place in the poet's own myth of imaginative fertility," see Susanne Wofford, *Choice of Achilles*, 347–51.

41 On Reynolds's view that "the poem was about himself, and revealed the Queen's sadistic-erotic desire to attract and humiliate him," see Duncan-Jones, "Much Ado with Red and White," 489–90. On Southampton, see Patrick Murphy, "Wriothesley's Resistance," in *Venus and Adonis*, ed. Kolin, 323–40. For allegorical readings equating Adonis with the sun, a grain of wheat, etc., see Conti, *Myth.* 5.16.

42 Essentially, I am arguing that Bate's claim that Shakespeare's poem "moves *towards* an etiology of love's anguish" should be rendered absolute (*Shakespeare and Ovid*, 58, emphasis mine). For Shakespeare's best-known variation on Venus's hysterical theme, see Sonnet 120.

43 See Bate, *Shakespeare and Ovid*, 59.

44 Shakespeare, *Sonnets and Poems*, ed. Burrow, 173–4.

45 Coppélia Kahn argues that key to the poem's success was Shakespeare's shrewd appeal to "a self-consciously literary audience … with a specialized literary taste for the poetry of Ovid" ("Venus and Adonis," in *Cambridge Companion to Shakespeare's Poetry*, ed. Cheney, 72–5).

46 Of course, Shakespeare relies heavily on sources other than Ovid for *Lucrece*, and in any case, if we take the "barren land" unthriftily "eared" in *Venus and Adonis* to have been the *Metamorphoses* in particular, rather than the Ovidian corpus in general, then arguably he makes good on his promise to head for greener intertextual pastures by turning to the *Fasti*. Shakespeare would have consulted the latter poem – more erudite and ostensibly more mature than the *Metamorphoses* – in Marsus's edition, which spins Ovid's myth of Lucretia toward Livy's "historical" account (see Burrow's introduction to *Sonnets and Poems*, 48–50). In a well-known marginal

note, Gabriel Harvey observes, "The younger sort takes much delight in Shakespeares Venus, & Adonis: but his Lucrece, & his tragedie of Hamlet, Prince of Denmarke, haue it in them, to please the wiser sort" (*Marginalia*, ed. Smith, 232).

47 On Shakespeare's recapitulations of precepts from Ovid's *Ars amatoria* in *The Taming of the Shrew* and *As You Like It*, among other comedies, see James, "Shakespeare's Learned Heroines in Ovid's Schoolroom," in *Shakespeare and the Classics*, ed. Martindale and Taylor, 66–85.

2. Shadow and Corpus: The Shifting Figure of Ovid in Chapman's Early Poetry

1 "*Richard Stapleton* to the Author," in *The Poems of George Chapman*, ed. Bartlett, 51, ll. 1–2, 5; "*Tho: Williams* of the inner Temple," ibid., ll. 13–14.

2 "I.D. of the middle Temple," in *Poems*, 52, ll. 5–9, 12–14; Bartlett identifies the poet of this and the following sonnet as Davies (52n).

3 Chapman, *Ovids Banquet of Sense*, in *Poems*, 3.8–9. All references to Chapman's works are to Barlett's edition and are provided parenthetically; in the case of the *Banquet* by stanza and line with the prefix *OBS*, and in that of the *Shadow* by line with the prefixes *HN* and *HC* for the "Hymnus in Noctem" and "Hymnus in Cynthiam," respectively.

4 The commonplace epigraph to *Venus and Adonis* is from *Amores* 1.15.35–6: *vilia miretur vulgus; mihi flavus Apollo / pocula Castalia plena ministret aqua* (*Sonnets and Poems*, ed. Burrow, 173, "Let the common herd be amazed by worthless things; but for me let golden Apollo provide cups full of the water of the Muses").

5 See, for example, Plotinus's *Enneads* (cf. 5.8.26–8, 32–4), though Chapman derived his Neoplatonism more immediately from Ficino (see Martin Wheeler, "*Ouids Banquet of Sence* and the Thrill of the Chase," 325).

6 Shakespeare again provides a representative example, having choreographed *Venus and Adonis* around the pun on "venery." See Edward Berry, *Shakespeare and the Hunt*, 55.

7 My terms here may recall Harold Bloom's *Anxiety of Influence* (14–16), but the notes to the *Shadow*, which do not correspond to any of Bloom's "revisionary ratios," in fact mark one limit of imitation itself; in several of Bloom's arcane senses, the *Shadow* is an Ovidian poem, but its notes are an instance of Chapman's calculated misrepresentation of himself, not a "misreading" of Ovid.

8 Snare, *The Mystification of George Chapman*, 156, 166.

9 See Schoell, *Études sur l'humanisme continentale en Angleterre à la fin de la Renaissance*, 21–42. The *Mythologiae* was first published in 1567 in Venice,

and many editions followed, though scholars have yet to resolve which one Chapman used.

10 *Sans une exception, toutes les citations d'auteurs grecs et latins sont extraites de la Mythologiae* (ibid., 37).

11 In the introduction to their translation, Mulryan and Brown identify particular echoes of Conti in works by Spenser, Lodge, Nashe, Florio, Bacon, Marston, Drayton, Daniel, Jonson, Sandys, Burton, Browne, and Milton, as well as Chapman (*Myth.* xxxvi–xliii).

12 Marston may have had Chapman's *Shadow* in mind when he mocked the practice of recycling passages from the mythographers as a shopworn trade secret:

> O darknes palpable! Egipts black night!
> My wit is stricken blind, hath lost his sight.
> My shins are broke, with groping for some sence
> To know to what his words haue reference …
> Reach me some Poets Index that will show …
> *Natalis Comes*, thou I know recites …
>
> (Marston, "Satyre 2" of *Certaine Satyres*, in *The Poems of John Marston*, ed. Davenport, ll. 21–4, 26, 28)

Like his contemporaries, Marston uses Conti's Latin alias, Natalis Comes. Ever ironic, Marston ridicules both the actual cause of the *Shadow*'s obscurity – extremely contrived "reference" – and its author's pretention to a trendy mythographic obscurantism, for any "Poets Index" will make "Egipts black night" as plain as day. Hence, the satire does not expose Chapman so much as play upon the transparency of his professional posture, in a variation on the generic imperative to conceal particular identities beneath fictional caricatures. In a parenthetical understatement, Mulryan and Brown note that Marston was "no mean cribber of Conti himself" (*Myth.*, xxxvii).

13 Conti declares, "We will not bother with interpretations about men changed into trees or bodies devoid of sense or of reason, unless they have some demonstrable worth" (*Myth.* 1.1; but see the many entries listed under "Ovid" in the index to Mulryan and Brown's edition).

14 Chapman's glosses on *HN* 392 and *HC* 117, 120, 130, 418, 422, and 509 all derive from *Myth.* 3.18, in the midst of which Conti quotes *Met.* 8.270–8 and *Fasti* 1.387–8.

15 In his concise treatment of Meleager's nemesis, the Calydonian Boar, for instance, Conti cites Ovid three times, but Chapman forgoes any reference, though he complains that his contemporaries are "transformd to

Calydonian bores" and recounts the metamorphosis of his own Euthymia into an even larger boar (*HN* 84). Chapman's allusion to "th' Ætolians" in the latter instance reveals how carefully he read the *Mythologiae*, for Conti's initial treatment of Diana (*Myth.* 3.18) does not mention Ætolia; he only locates the myth much later (7.3, again from the *Metamorphoses*), whence Chapman's epithet. Ovid likewise goes unmentioned when Chapman adapts his catalogue of dogs from Conti's discussion of Actaeon (*Myth.* 6.24; *Met.* 3.206–25).

16 When describing pagan sacrifice, for instance, Conti twice quotes from the *Metamorphoses*, which he compares unfavourably to analogous moments in Virgil's poems (*Myth.* 1.10 and 1.11). On the other hand, Conti's promotion of Ovid to a quantitative (if not qualitative) allusive parity with Virgil, alongside Orphic and Homeric materials, produces a composite centre of authority, contrasting with the predominantly Virgilian foundations of earlier humanist mythography. Boccaccio in particular had relied on post-Augustinian interpretations of the *Aeneid* for his defence of poetry in the *Genealogia gentilium deorum* (see *Boccaccio on Poetry*, trans. Osgood, 67–9). While Chapman makes little direct use of any mythographer other than Conti, Ovid's gradually increasing authority, in proportion to that of Virgil, necessarily affects the Elizabethan poet's intertextual posture.

17 See pp. 76–7.

18 The closest analogue is probably Jonson's *Poetaster* (1601), which situates the disinterested satirist Horace decorously between the culpable license of Ovid and the unapproachable eminence of Virgil. Jonson's Horace, who repeatedly expresses his animus against the city of Rome and prefers the more authentic countryside offstage, is a dramatic cousin to Chapman's *Shadow* persona, who longs to return to ostensibly pure Greek origins, so as to escape an English poetry bastardized from decadent Roman models (i.e., Ovidianism). I discuss *Poetaster* in the conclusion.

19 Chapman did translate four apocryphal Virgilian epigrams for his 1612 volume, *Petrarchs Seven Penitentiall Psalms*.

20 *Institutio oratoria*, trans. Butler, 10.1.88.

21 *Nutricia*, in Poliziano, *Silvae*, trans. Fantazzi, ll. 434–9.

22 Ibid., cf. ll. 703–19.

23 Sandys, "The Life of Ovid," in *Ovid's Metamorphoses Englished*, ¶.

24 On Nashe's own sense of this problem, see pp. 36–8.

25 For Gosson's attack, see *The Schoole of Abuse*, 2; for Sidney's defense, see *The Defence of Poesy*, in *The Major Works*, ed. Duncan-Jones, esp. 238–40. Sidney does not so much authorize Ovidianism directly as imply that classical poets are to be evaluated case by case, rather than dismissed *en masse* according to Gosson's traditional misinterpretation of Plato's prohibition

of poets from his ideal republic. Sidney resolves that Plato urges the elimination merely of the "abuse" of poetry, rather than the banishment of poets themselves, having "found fault that the poets of his time filled the world with wrong opinions of the gods, making light tales of that unspotted essence" (239). While this claim would seem to condemn Ovid as the chief propagator of pagan mythology, Sidney pointedly omits any reference to the *Metamorphoses* here, instead quoting from Scaliger's *Poetices*, which refutes the appeal to Plato and famously defends Ovid in particular. On Scaliger's judgment, see James, "Ovid and the Question of Politics in Early Modern England," 343.

26 The conclusion of the *Defence* exemplifies Sidney's allusive balancing act, as he pronounces curses upon any recalcitrant reader unsympathetic to poetry, yet declares, "I will not wish unto you the ass's ears of Midas" (*Defence*, 250); that is, he alludes unmistakably to Ovid's damning allegory of poor taste while ostensibly reserving his own judgment. The *Defence* was enjoying a posthumous revival in the spring of 1595, as printers vied for the rights to publish long-circulated manuscripts. See Duncan-Jones's headnote to the *Defence* (ibid., 371).

27 I use the term "ambivalence" in the sense of a "coexistence in one person of contradictory emotions or attitudes (as love and hatred) towards a person or thing … a balance or combination or coexistence of opposites; oscillation, fluctuation, variability, etc." (*OED*, s.v. "ambivalence, n.").

28 Darryl Gless describes the poem's critical heritage as "a welter of violently contrasting and mutually exclusive interpretations" ("Chapman's Ironic Ovid," 21), while Raymond Waddington observes, "The critics divide endlessly, like Ramist dichotomies, over the question of whether Ovid rises to a spiritual epiphany or sinks in sensual debauch," before declaring that he himself has "opted for the 'descent' reading" (*Mind's Empire*, 115). Early on, Douglas Bush identified "Ficino's discussion of 'Ratio, Visus, Auditus, Olfactus, Gustus, and Tactus'" as Chapman's main source for the *Banquet*'s Neoplatonic focus; see *Mythology and the Renaissance Tradition*, 204n13; cited also in Bartlett, *Poems*, 49n. In his 1961 article, "The Banquet of Sense," however, Frank Kermode made a powerful case for interpreting Chapman's poem as ironic, influencing all subsequent commentators. Almost immediately, Donno found that Kermode "errs, largely through a too-conventional interpretation of the figures in the poem" (*Elizabethan Minor Epics*, 13), preferring the Neoplatonic reading. Other proponents of the more positive reading include Rhoda Ribner, "*Ovid's Banquet of Sense* and the Emblematic Tradition," Louise Vinge, "*Ovids Banquet of Sence*: Its

Sources and Theme," and more recently, Wheeler, *"Ouids Banquet of Sence and the Thrill of the Chase."*

29 On Julia's transgression, see Tacitus, *Annals*, trans. Jackson, 1.53.

30 *OED*, s.v. "ruin, n."

31 Ibid., s.v. "ardor, n." 1, 3.

32 Compare Shakespeare's employment of the banquet of sense motif in *Venus and Adonis*, ll. 433–50.

33 See Bush, *Mythology and the Renaissance Tradition*, 204n13. For Jerald Jahn, this passage demonstrates that Chapman's "Ovid lacks … the knowledge with which to moderate his ascent at its natural zenith," and resolves the poem as a "tragedy of natural aspiration" ("Chapman's *Enargia* and the Popular Perspective on *Ovids Banquet of Sence*," 21).

34 *OED*, s.v. "chapman, n." 2, 4. Waddington identifies the pun as "a private joke for [Chapman's] audience of cognoscenti" (*Mind's Empire*, 133).

35 Gerald Snare observes, "If the narrator is providing a guide for us … he does so in a profoundly ambiguous way. His rhetoric, of course, is as elaborate as Ovid's, as extended, as if possessed by a poetic frenzy analogous to those which continually possess Ovid. Moreover, his epic warnings are as erotically charged as Ovid's self-descriptions" (*Mystification of George Chapman*, 129).

36 Chapman's Niobe tableau is thus an admonitory "moniment" in the sense Spenser often applies, as at *FQ* 5.8.45.3 (*OED*, s.v. "monument, n." 5b). See pp. 96–7.

37 On Chapman's fascination with anamorphic figuration, see Stephen Clucas, "'To Rauish and Refine an Earthly Soule': Ficino and the Poetry of George Chapman," in *Marsilio Ficino: His Theology, His Philosophy, His Legacy*, ed. Allen and Rees, 440–2.

38 Corynna's "loose robe of Tynsell" recalls Spenser's Acrasia: "All in a vele of silke and siluer thin, / That hid no whit her alablaster skin" (*FQ* 2.12.77.4–5).

39 Gless, "Chapman's Ironic Ovid," 32.

40 See Snare, *Mystification of George Chapman*, 121–2.

41 Not only would "Flora's" fit the meter of the stanza just as well as the surprising "Chloris[']," but prototypes for Chapman's *locus amœnus* – most immediately Spenser's Bower of Bliss (cf. *FQ* 2.12.50) – generally refer to the mature goddess of flowers, rather than to the obscure virginal nymph. Bull notes Flora's further association with prostitutes (*Mirror of the Gods*, 211, 352), which may have contributed to Chapman's preference for the Greek maiden-name, already invoked in the *Shadow of Night* (*HN* 181).

Miriam Jacobson discusses further variations on the Chloris/Zephyrus myth in "The Elizabethan Cipher in Shakespeare's *Lucrece*," 345–6.

42 On Botticelli's treatment of the myth, see Edgar Wind, *Pagan Mysteries in the Renaissance*, 115–17.

43 Nor could Chapman have derived any direct association of Flora with Chloris from Botticelli's own source, Poliziano's *Stanze*, which does not include the Greek name (see *Stanze*, ed. Quint, viii).

44 Conti, *Myth.* 6.13, referring to Pausanias's *Description of Greece*, 2.21.9. That Chapman consulted Conti (now among other sources) for his *ekphrasis* is clear. Conti cites Pausanias, for example, on the anamorphic nature of the Niobe simulacrum on Mount Sypilus, and for the detail that Niobe wept only in summer (*Myth.* 6.13), both of which Chapman imports, though Conti also dwells on Ovid's testimony, including lines from the *Heroides* (20.105–6, whence Chapman's adjective "*Mygdonian*" at *OBS* 3.3) and the *Epistulae ex Ponto* (1.2.29–30). On the other hand, although Conti provides multiple lists of Niobe's children, none of them match Chapman's memorial list in the fifth stanza of the *Banquet*, even in combination. Further details in Chapman's adaptation of the myth, such as the bloodiness of Niobe's tears, seem original to the *Banquet*.

45 Later in the poem, as the narrator – suddenly an overcautious *praeceptor amoris* himself – warns Ovid not to introduce himself to his beloved, he argues that "the Thicket *Floras* hands hath set / To hide thy theft, is thinne and hollow harted" (42.7–8), reverting to the goddess's more traditional and problematic name.

46 *Hero and Leander*, in Chapman, *Poems*, ed. Bartlett, 6.287–91.

47 In 1616, Chapman made one last pass at the myth of Hero and Leander, publishing a translation of the Greek version as *The Divine Poem of Musaeus*. In his preface, Chapman calls the Greek original "the incomparable Loue-poem of the world," and emphatically rejects any connection between his translation and Marlowe's version: "When you see *Leander* and *Hero*, the Subiects of this Pamphlet; I perswade my self, your preiudice will encrease to the contempt of it; eyther headlong presupposing it, all one; or at no part matcheable, with that partly excellent Poem, of Maister *Marloes* … [T]he VVorkes are in nothing alike; a different Character being held through, both the Stile, Matter, & inuention." (A7r–8v). By reascribing the myth to the legendary Musaeus, rather than to Marlowe, Chapman seeks to divorce himself from his early "collaboration," and finally executes on Marlowe's literary corpus the suspended sentence meted out to the *Banquet*'s ghost of Ovid.

3. Ovid in the Godless Poem: Allusive Rebellion in Edmund Spenser's Legend of Justice

1 Lyne, *Ovid's Changing Worlds*, 129; Fletcher, *The Prophetic Moment*, 93; Burrow, "Original Fictions: Metamorphoses in *The Faerie Queene*," in *Ovid Renewed*, ed. Martindale, 101–3.

2 Syrithe Pugh's 2005 study, *Spenser and Ovid*, for example, begins with a reading of *The Shepheardes Calender* as "Spenser's New *Fasti*," and discusses the 1596 *Faerie Queene* as a variation on Ovid's late poetry of exile. In *Spenser's Ovidian Poetics* (2009), M.L. Stapleton reads Spenser's imitations in light of earlier English translations by poets like George Turberville and Thomas Churchyard.

3 Wilson-Okamura, "Errors about Ovid and Romance," 220–1.

4 As he revisits and reconfigures his own work, Spenser adapts a process of "double allusion" familiar to his contemporaries and, according to Patrick Cheney, already adapted by Marlowe, who "uses an obvious classical text to exploit the less obvious text of a (living) colleague" (*Marlowe's Counterfeit Profession*, 18, n. 36; in his note, Cheney traces a short genealogy of the "double allusion" concept from its classicist roots). Cheney maintains, "Marlowe's intertextuality does not target simply the dead Ovid, the dead Virgil, or the dead Theocritus, but England's living Virgil [i.e., Spenser]. Marlowe contextualizes his diachronic imitation of classical poets in a synchronic imitation of a contemporary" (ibid., 71). Essentially, I read Spenser as reproducing this Marlovian effect, though he himself remains the "target" of his networks of "double allusion."

5 Including, of course, allusive patterns and career models beyond the Ovidian. Vital to my argument, as to all intertextual readings of Spenser, is a constant sense of Ovidianism's interplay within, against, and alongside other allusive networks, especially the Virgilian and Augustinian. For a wide-ranging account of this interplay, see Patrick Cheney, *Spenser's Famous Flight*, 56–62; for a focused interpretation of Busirane's tapestries in the 1590 *Faerie Queene* as an example of such interplay, see John Watkins, *Specter of Dido*, 167–74.

6 See pp. 63–4.

7 Many scholars have explored the multifarious Ovidian voice, but D.C. Feeney's extended discussion of the argument between the heretical Pirithous, who does not believe in metamorphosis, and the devout Lelax, who maintains that the gods' power is "boundless and without limit," is especially helpful. Feeney identifies the episode as a nexus between poet

and reader, in which the fictional contest requires our adjudication: "Readers tend to be either Lelax or Pirithous," Feeney claims, as he works to resist the skeptic's easy impulse to "side with Pirithous" against the reality of the metamorphic gods (*Gods in Epic*, 229–32). At stake for Feeney is the reader's affirmation of Ovid's prerogative as a poet to have his universe both ways; our judgment between these minor characters reflects the credence we lend to Ovid's poem – not to the details of the mythological narrative per se, but to the authority of poetic fictions as commentaries on our lived experience. Spenser's similar gambit for his reader's judgment should become apparent over the course of this chapter, though the result might be less of a draw.

8 This is not to deny the pivotal status of the *Muiopotmos* in the development of Spenser's poetry. I limit my claim here to the subtlety and circumspection of its intertextual content. On the *Muiopotmos* as "a world in which the stark tableaux of epic poetics must give way to the intricately woven tapestries of romance," see Ayesha Ramachandran, "Clarion in the Bower of Bliss," 81). On the poem as a political allegory developed around competing allusions to Virgil and Ovid, with Ovidianism ultimately bested, see Robert Brinkley, "Spenser's *Muiopotmos* and the Politics of Metamorphosis."

9 Fletcher describes Proteus as "the daimon who controls much of what happens in Books III and IV… By denying Proteus his claim to authority over Florimell, over the principle of flourishing life and its image, beauty, Spenser allows himself to come to her rescue. The poet's *persona*, opposed to Protean guile, becomes the shapeshifter the poem needs" (*Prophetic Moment*, 93–4).

10 Of course, Busirane's triumphant Cupid has countless prototypes and analogues, but Spenser's emphasis on his title – "And vnderneath his feet was written thus, / *Vnto the Victor of the Gods this bee*" (3.11.49.1–2) – points most directly to the *victor* acknowledged by Ovid at *Am.* 1.2.50.

11 Lyne notes, "The classic *topoi* of [Ovid's] loving *personae* become so familiar that they barely need a specific source (something which, interestingly, gradually becomes true of both Ovid and Petrarch)" ("Love and Exile after Ovid," in *Cambridge Companion to Ovid*, ed. Hardie, 291).

12 On Spenser's androgynous Venus, see Wind, *Pagan Mysteries*, 211–17. Hamilton cites *Colin Clout*, ll. 800–2 (4.10.41n).

13 Another way to think about Book 4's Venus is as a *topos* or commonplace, in Stephen Hinds's sense that she "invokes [an] intertextual tradition as a collectivity, to which the individual contexts and connotations of individual prior instances are firmly subordinate" (*Allusion and Intertext*, 34).

Characteristic of Book 4, such *topoi* reflect Spenser's new emphasis on the harmony and interdependence of friendship as a social virtue; in these cases, the ultimate allusive source for any narrative element – a goddess's attributes, for instance, or a temple's furnishings – matters less than that element's suitability for redistribution within new allegorical contexts. On the other hand, it is easy to overstate the diffusive effect of even the most frequented *topoi*, or as Hinds qualifies his own definition, "The so-called commonplace, despite our name for it, is not an inert category in … discourse but an active one, with as much potential to draw poet and reader into, as away from, engagement with the specificities of its history" (40). Spenser's androgyne Venus of Book 4, for example, might lead a 1596 reader back into the "specificities" of the *Metamorphoses* – by way of the Hermaphroditus reference at the end of the 1590 version of *The Faerie Queene* – rather than outward into more nebulous Neoplatonic readings.

14 On Proteus as a "figure of the superstitious or popular imagination which may once have been a fresh cultural force but can no longer be taken seriously unless it is revised," see Harry Berger, Jr, *Revisionary Play*, 213–14.

15 Locating Spenser in the wider romance tradition, Patricia Parker writes, "Ariosto's reliance on continual narrative deferral and on the romance proliferation of different story lines is both continued and transformed in Spenser's version of *dilatio*" (*Inescapable Romance*, 7–8). For Parker, Spenser's Proteus plays an ambiguous role in the dilatory process, on the one hand "reduced" to villainy "despite his many changes of shape," but on the other, as "the host of the marriage of the Thames and Medway, an emblem for its boundless promise of fertility" (98). I argue here that Proteus's latter, ostensibly positive aspect is in effect an extension of his terminally reductive role in Spenser's poem.

16 As Barkan observes, "For all its emphasis upon the blurring of clear categories, metamorphosis is as much concerned with reduction and fixity as with variability or complexity" (*Gods Made Flesh*, 66).

17 Spenser's rhetoric here may echo Golding's: "If God to me a hundred mouthes with sounding tongues should send, / And reason able to conceyve, and thereunto should lend / Me all the grace of eloquence that ere the Muses had, / I could not shew …" (Golding, 8.688–91). The "many mouths" *topos* also serves as Hinds's example of the concept (see note 13, above). Jonathan Goldberg notes that Proteus himself is "curiously (significantly?) absent from the list of sea gods," and associates his invisibility with that of Elizabeth, who rules over this imperial canto unseen, "present in all the forms that represent power: triumph, genealogy, sea dominion, and map" (*Endlesse Worke*, 144).

18 Ovid helps to establish Apollo's ironically poor medical reputation in his myth of Coronis (*Met.* 2.618), and the "King of Leaches" ordinarily has no power over lovesickness. Spenser offers a more characteristic assessment earlier in Book 4: "Such was the wound that *Scudamour* did gride; / For which *Dan Phebus* selfe cannot a salue prouide" (4.6.1.8–9).

19 Some specifics: in Book 6, Cupid punishes Mirabella offstage, and the Graces dance on Acidale for Colin Clout, "whom they of them selues list so to grace" (6.10.20.5), but in neither instance have the gods intruded upon the narrative; rather, Spenser's questing knights have brushed against narrative tangents still incorporating the divine. Indeed, the immediacy with which the Graces vanish upon seeing Calidore gives us a sense of the new disconnect between the poem's allegorical characters on the one hand and the numinous gods and nymphs of classical tradition on the other; in a sense, the pagan gods come to inhabit Faerieland while avoiding the poem. The main exception to the godlessness of the poem's final third is the Hermetic Isis of 4.7, but Isis only moves and acts in Britomart's dream (and even within the dream, the predominant verb is "seemed," at 5.7.13.1, 14.2, and 15.3). The priest's interpretation, moreover, mediates between the inset dream in which Isis acts and the narrative in which Britomart acts. Spenser thus takes pains to limit even Isis's direct involvement, exactly the opposite narrative approach to his incorporation of Proteus's prophecy into Marinell's story in Books 3 and 4. To be sure, the gods re-emerge prominently in the *Cantos of Mutabilitie*, but from 1596 to the *Cantos'* publication in 1609, the gods, as agents, drop out of Spenser's poem as soon as Proteus cedes Florimell back to the narrative in 4.12.

20 Berger, *Revisionary Play*, 202.

21 The Roman poet thus diverges from the earliest tradition, recorded in Hesiod's *Works and Days* (ll. 106–201), which identifies five ages, inserting "a god-like race of hero-men" between bronze and iron. In this "nobler and more righteous" age occurred the various Greek mythic cycles, up to the fall of Troy, and thus it would include all of the *Metamorphoses* until the rise of Rome. Spenser would have had access to Hesiod's account via mythographic redactions, but like Ovid he chose to exclude it in favour of a constantly degenerating schema.

22 The well-known sixteenth-century cycle of illustrations by Bernard Saloman and Virgil Solis depicts the restoration scene; see the University of Virginia's online collection, "Ovid Illustrated" (http://ovid.lib.virginia.edu/ovidillust.html#cycles).

23 *Pace* David Lee Miller, who cautions against a categorical reading of the Pyrrha and Deucalion allusion. Spotting a pun in Spenser's participle

"degender[è]d," lengthened due to its position at the end of the alexandrine, Miller suggests, "Perhaps they have simply been degender-read, slandered by the golden-age fantasies that authorize this discourse of historical pessimism, underwriting its ability to discover in men the worst that 'may ... be red'" ("Gender, Justice, and the Gods in *The Faerie Queene*," 22).

24 Sandys's 1632 translation restores the lines' original sense, "Hence we, a hardy Race, inur'd to payne: / Our Actions our Originall explayne" (*Ovid's Metamorphoses Englished*, 10). In his commentary, Sandys further interprets the stone-throwing passage in terms of Christian salvation, concluding, "So the giuing vs hearts of flesh instead of those of stone, is meant by our conuersion" (33).

25 Naseeb Shaheen detects echoes in the proem of Mt. 24.29, Isa. 13.10, and Joel 2.10 (*Biblical References in The Faerie Queene*, 139), but the key distinction is intratextual, in that Spenser's biblical allusions, especially to Revelation, were clear throughout the first book of the *Faerie Queene*, but are now so remote as to lose themselves in syncretism.

26 Hamilton's note to 1.Pr.4.9 defines "dearest dread" as "the Godesse whom [Spenser] beholds with fear and reverence" and glosses the line with a reference to Isa. 8:13, "Sanctifie the Lord of hostes, and let him be your feare, and let him be your dread." Isaiah's prophecy, however, proceeds to describe the Lord "as a stombling stone & as a rocke to fall vpon" (8:14), better befitting the "awfull dread" of Book 5.

27 Spenser recreates Elizabeth's carefully maintained ambiguity of gender in the stanza's c-rhymes, "gotten/soften/often" (the f's presumably unpronounced). The rhyme-words appear feminine, insofar as they close each line with an additional unstressed syllable, but the "-en" suffix is routinely syncopated elsewhere in *The Faerie Queene* to fit the meter, which in this case would convert the feminine endings to metrical masculinity. This ambiguity follows from the dual source of the softening tears, "gotten" on the male Cupid by his "sweete smyling mother"; the latter description in turn prefigures the hermaphroditic Venus who laughs "with amiable grace" as she permits Amoret's abduction from her Temple (4.10.56.1–4). The final c-rhyme of Book 5's proem, by contrast, is emphatically masculine: "thrall/all/Arte-gall." For a different reading, see Richard McCabe, who argues that in the Legend of Justice, Spenser endorses Ficino's portrayal of justice as bisexual, and expresses the fear that "a female monarch will upset the balance, effectively emasculating her ministers by blunting the phallic edge of Justice's 'sword'" (*Spenser's Monstrous Regiment*, 93).

28 Pugh locates the critical moment in *The Faerie Queene*'s "contest between Virgilian and Ovidian poetics" earlier, arguing that Book 1 arrives at "a condemnation of Virgilian poetics on moral, political, and religious grounds, and a rereading of Ovid as a counter-Virgilian poet, exponent of a set of values more amenable to Spenser's poem …" For Pugh, Book 3 resolves any remaining conflict: "In the book ostensibly closest to Elizabeth and to Virgilian justification of her rule through the prophetic depiction of her ancestral descent, the Ovidian values of the Garden of Adonis displace and marginalize the political ends of Virgilian epic …" (*Spenser and Ovid*, 6–7). Notably, the critical trend has been to locate the key transition – from "the Virgilian model on which Spenser particularly relied" to an Ovidian self-revisionism – progressively earlier in Spenser's career. For Richard Helgerson, writing in 1983, it is the late *Fowre Hymnes* volume, not *The Faerie Queene*, which elicits the comment, "No wonder if Spenser saw himself less as a new Virgil and more as the Ovid of the *Tristia*, abandoned by his friends for his *carmen et error*" (*Self-Crowned Laureates*, 75, 86).

29 Pugh notes the contrast between the proem to the Legend of Justice and Virgil's fourth eclogue, identifying the latter with the comic conclusion to Spenser's Legend of Friendship (*Spenser and Ovid*, 210).

30 Abraham Fraunce provides the standard "star-read": "Then did Astræa leaue the polluted earth, and setled her selfe betweene the Starres called Leo and Libra, the Lyon and the Balance, couering her face in the cloudes for griefe to behold such impietie" (*Third part of the Countesse of Pembrokes Yvychurch*, 9).

31 At *Georgics* 1.33–5, Virgil writes, *Erigonen inter Chelasque sequentis / panditur (ipse tibi iam bracchia contrahit ardens / Scorpios et caeli iusta plus parte reliquit)* ("between the Virgin and the grasping Claws, a space is opening (lo! for you even now the blazing Scorpion draws in his arms, and has left more than a due portion of the heaven!)"). Compare Ovid, *Met.* 2.195–7: *est locus, in geminos ubi bracchia concavat arcus / Scorpius et cauda flexisque utrimque lacertis / porrigit in spatium signorum membra duorum* ("There is one place where the Scorpion bends out his arms into two bows; and with tail and arms stretching out on both sides, he spreads over the space of two signs"). In his provocative reading of Book 5's "decorous" zodiac, David Lee Miller asks rhetorically, "Is the text not asking us to think about the gap between Leo and Virgo?" ("Gender, Justice, and the Gods," 23); I argue here that this question should be extended to the gap between Virgo and Libra.

32 Spenser returns to this set of allusions when he compares the Souldan's runaway horses to those of Phaethon, terrified by the "vgly craples" of the "monstrous Scorpion" (5.8.40.3–4). In other words, later in the Legend of

Justice, the space Virgil created for Augustus's apotheosis as Libra reverts to Ovid's image of the gargantuan *Chelae* of Scorpio. See pp. 88–9.

33 McCabe, *Spenser's Monstrous Regiment*, 215.

34 On Mercilla's iconographical overload, see Jane Aptekar, *Icons of Justice*, 13–18, 58–69. Aptekar finds that, "In detail after detail, Spenser's description of Mercilla corresponds with the emblematists' queenly representations of the royal virtues of justice, equity, magnanimity, clemency, and so forth. In detail after detail, too, naturally, Spenser's Mercilla resembles the Queen Elizabeth whom Renaissance illustrators and portrait painters saw: a lady heavily laden with symbolical accoutrements" (58). I argue here that despite and beneath the orthodox symbolism, Mercilla's claim to the throne of justice is troubled by the continued absence of Astraea; see Rebeca Helfer, *Spenser's Ruins and the Art of Reflection*, 262.

35 *OED*, s.v. "let, v(1)." 12a and "let, v(2)." 1a. On the pun, see Burrow, *Epic Romance*, 133. Aptekar notes, "Spenser lets his queen have it both ways: at the same time that her rival is safely dead, Jove-struck, as it were, she herself is a paragon of the mercy poured down from 'th'Almighties' judgment seat" (*Icons of Justice*, 18).

36 Richard Hardin elaborates, "Like Phaethon, who attempted to usurp the position of Apollo, god of justice, and was destroyed, the Souldan (whose name suggests a pun on *sol* 'sun'+*dan* 'master') is felled by Arthur, the true sun of justice he thought to control" ("Adicia, Souldan," in *Spenser Encyclopedia*, 7). The interpretation of the Souldan and his arsenal as Philip II and the Armada dates back to Upton's 1758 edition of *The Faerie Queene*, as Hamilton notes (5.8.28–45n., see also the notes to stanzas 37, 40, and 45).

37 Neither myth figures prominently in the *Metamorphoses*, though at *Amores* 3.2.15–16, Ovid recalls how the tyrant Oenomaus tried and failed to kill Pelops in a chariot race, and at *Heroides* 9.67–8, Deianira reminds Hercules of Diomedes and his flesh-eating mares, as she mocks her husband for having permitted Omphale to dress him as a woman (a source for Spenser's Radigund episode, completed in the preceding canto).

38 Carol Rupprecht notes how a similar stanza of pronominal confusion, during Britomart's duel with Radigund (5.7.33), "suggests Britomart's confrontation with and conquest of her shadow, the unacknowledged and undermining tendencies within herself" ("Radigund," in *Spenser Encyclopedia*, 580–1).

39 The iconographic tradition splits evenly on the question of whether the solar chariot remains in one piece, as in Ovid, or is shattered by the lightning. Michelangelo's drawing and Giulio Romano's ceiling fresco in the Palazzo Te, for example, retain the unbroken chariot, while the Flemish tapestry

cycle now in the Musée de la Renaissance and Hendrick Goltzius's engraving of Phaethon in freefall both exemplify the artistic impulse to depict an exploding chariot whenever the opportunity arises.

40 In his commentary, Sandys calls Hippolytus's suffering "vndeserved," noting that "the chast youth suffers for anothers vnchastety. But virtue, though afflicted for a time, can never be finally suppressed." He does refer to an alternative version by "some authors," according to which Virbius was a "cunning Imposter," but there is no trace of this in Spenser (*Ovid's Metamorphosis Englished*, 523–4).

41 Throughout this chapter's arguments regarding sympathy, I am indebted to Burrow's assertion that *The Faerie Queene* is "rootedly hostile to the manipulation of authority through the pretence of loving concern ... And this hostility to pity is encoded in its structure" (*Epic Romance*, 120). Burrow's Spenser, by resisting scenes of pity authorized by his own sources (e.g., Tasso's *Gerusalemme liberata*), challenges "the Queen's disposition to mercy," especially in Ireland, and insists instead upon "the razing of rebellion, and the social practices which give rise to it, ... in order 'to reduce thinges into order of Englishe lawe'" (130, quoting *View*, ed. Maley, 142). I argue further that Spenser constantly tempts his readers, his monarch, and himself to sympathize with precisely those characters afforded no pity in the poem's narrative, through allusions expressly designed to trigger such sympathies, and despite our sense that a rigorous allegory of justice should offer no room for pity at all. Spenser derives this allusive practice from Ovid's myths of dismemberment and annihilation, which indeed comprise the majority of Book 5's allusions; as they proliferate, these Ovidian allusions increasingly compel our misplaced sympathies for the unjust. By the climax of the Legend of Justice, then, we should recognize that a rigorous allegory must not only incorporate counterintuitive sympathies for "rebellious" subjects – never properly to be pitied – but must concede the futility of resisting all such sympathy in the pursuit of law and order.

42 On Spenser's recombination of Ovidian myths in the *Mutabilitie* cantos see Richard Ringler, "The Faunus Episode," in *Essential Articles*, ed. Hamilton, 289–98.

43 Ovid's own myth derives from Virgil, *Aen*. 7.761–82, according to which Diana reconstructs Hippolytus and hides him in Egeria's grove, "that there alone, amid Italian woods, he might live out his inglorious days" (*solus ubi in silvis Italis ignobilis aevum / exigeret*). Virgil likewise reports Jove's punishment of Aesculapius for resurrecting Hippolytus.

44 My thanks to Denis Feeney for this reference. While Horace's ode resonates in the lamentations of Spenser's Diana and her nymphs, the

unrecognizability of the Souldan's remains is carefully Ovidian, in that Euripides and Seneca – the principal alternative classical sources for the tragic Hippolytus myth – do not so mangle his corpse. Such details matter because they permit us to locate the exact moment at which Spenser abandons even the allusion to Ovid's Hippolytus, as he repudiates the divine agency by which Diana reassembles the unrecognizably mangled Hippolytus and bestows immortality upon him. The nothingness that is left of Spenser's Souldan may well be an echo of Horace's ode, but it is primarily a function of the "stonie age" of Book 5; this is what Hippolytus's fate would have been in a world without metamorphosis.

45 While Spenser specifies no physical arborification for his "wooddy nymphs," his pun on "wood" (that is, driven mad) points us to Ovid's rationale for the Heliades' original metamorphoses.

46 Dolven, *Scenes of Instruction*, 214. Fittingly, *munera* is Ovid's word for the useless "offerings" of tears, which the Heliades shed over the tomb of their brother Phaethon (*Met.* 2.341).

47 Joseph Campana writes, "In *The Faerie Queene*, we are continually invited to feel the physical sympathy, the affective resonance, awakened whenever we make contact with a vitality central to lived experience, a vitality Spenser found most palpable in moments of intense suffering" ("Spenser, Suffering, and the Energy of Affect," 46).

48 For Berger's classic use of the term "conspicuous irrelevance," see *The Allegorical Temper*, 120–60; especially pertinent to my claims here is Berger's account of Spenser's unlikely allusion to the amorous, doomed Penthesilea while introducing his own chaste and invulnerable Belphoebe (124–8).

49 Greenblatt, *Renaissance Self-Fashioning*, 175.

50 Spenser takes advantage of his stanza form to make this transference seamless: Arthur erects his monument in the first three lines of 5.8.45, at which point the enjambed b-rhyme of the fourth line signals Adicia's first glimpse of her husband's armour.

51 Samient, of course, is never just a messenger in these episodes. Once Arthur and Artegall accept her unsubstantiated report that her mistress's enemy Adicia has had her assaulted without provocation (5.8.22–4), she colludes with the knights to entrap her foes, posing as a damsel in distress, helping first to lure the Souldan out of his castle, then Adicia, and finally Malengin. In contrast, none of the murderous women recalled in 5.8.47 were the professed enemies of their victims. Regarding their common crime of infanticide, we might consider further that except for the infant Artegall, kidnapped by Astraea, no children inhabit the barren landscape of Book 5; whereas Book 1's Orgoglio had shed the "bloud of guiltlesse

babes, and innocents trew" (1.8.35.6), Adicia practices no such injustice even in her fury.

52 Ino's madness refers to *Met.* 4.481–530, where she throws herself and her son from a cliff while fleeing her insane husband (who has just murdered their other child), but Ovid nowhere describes her "when with knife in hand / She threw her husbands murdred infant out." There are many myths of "raging Ino" and her infanticidal tendencies, including an alternate version treated at length by Ovid – not in the *Metamorphoses* but at *Fasti* 3.853–76 – according to which Ino frames her stepchildren for her own crime of spoiling the food supply, though she does not murder them with a knife. In apparent consternation, Lotspeich argues that Spenser follows Conti's "several confusing versions of the story" (*Classical Mythology in the Poetry of Edmund Spenser*, 72). Most accounts, however, describe the gods' intervention to save Ino from suicide, metamorphosing her into the sea-goddess Leucothoë and her son into the sea-god Palaemon (as Spenser reports at 4.11.13.4–6; see *Met.* 4.531–42). Allusive confusion is thus to be expected when it comes to Ino, but whatever Spenser's source, her deification makes her a singularly poor prototype for Adicia, who becomes a beast, though indeed like all versions of Ino, Adicia attempts suicide in the following stanza (5.8.48.3–4).

53 Cora Fox, *Ovid and the Politics of Emotion*, 98.

54 My thanks to Leonard Barkan for this latter observation. Medea's escape from both metamorphosis and destruction is almost unique among the mortal characters of the *Metamorphoses*: as she flies off in her own chariot, pulled by her own dragons, there is a clear contrast to Phaethon, unable to control the solar horses.

55 On the gate to the Bower of Bliss, Spenser offers a more balanced version of the myth, indicting Jason's "falsed fayth, and loue too lightly flitt" alongside Medea's bloodier crimes (2.12.44.7, 45.6–9).

56 On the destabilizing implications of Medea's multiple identities for Ovid and his readers, see Barchiesi's discussion of her epistle in the *Heroides*: "literary consciousness diffracts the identity of mythical personae. It is difficult to say how far this Medea – seen through Apollonius and Euripides, Ovid's tragedy and Ovid's elegiacs – is still *one*" (*Speaking Volumes*, 113).

57 The Loeb editor, Arthur Wheeler, glosses the etymological pun: "Ovid derives Tomis (Tomi) from τέμνω, 'to cut.'" Both Boccaccio (*Genealogia* 4.12) and Conti (*Myth.* 6.7) note the derivation.

58 Like his contemporaries, Spenser turns frequently to such mythographers as Boccaccio and Conti, but his more concerted imitative constructs – like this densely allusive stanza – remain in dynamic tension with the Ovidian

source. Spenser may easily have found an annotated and allegorized condensation of the Medea story in the *Mythologiae* or elsewhere, but it is his readiness to extract individual elements from such conglomerates, and to recombine them with allusions to other myths, which actually constitutes the Ovidian poetics, never simply the poet's encyclopedic knowledge of myths, nor the relative frequency of his use of them. This caution could come anywhere in any account of Spenser's engagement with Ovid; I have chosen to place it here because my effort to determine the stakes of Spenser's discarding of the Medea allusion entails a claim for his sensitivity, not only to the disparate sources of her myth, but indeed to its development throughout the Ovidian corpus.

59 McCabe, *Spenser's Monstrous Regiment*, 3–4.

60 For an alternative account of Spenser's Ovidianism, according to which "the author streamlines his ancient model by imposing his conceptions of form, sometimes distorted, on stories that threaten to metamorphose beyond their boundaries," see Stapleton, *Spenser's Ovidian Poetics*, 134.

61 In other words, I read Spenser as projecting (fearing as well as hoping for) an ideal reader, capable of following his allusions to their fullest extent, while anticipating a community of far less perfectly learned readers. Giorgio Pasquali wrote long ago, "The poet may not be aware of reminiscences, and he may hope that his imitations escape his public's notice; but allusions do not produce the desired effect if the reader does not clearly remember the text to which they refer" (translation and quotation from Gian Biagio Conte, *Rhetoric of Imitation*, 24–5). Leaving aside the often unmeasurable degree of the poet's consciousness of reminiscence (though I assume Spenser to be peculiarly conscious in this regard), I embrace the possibility that the "desired effect" of many of Spenser's allusions in Book 5 of *The Faerie Queene* lies precisely in the hope that they will be misinterpreted or even wholly ignored by some readers.

62 Fox, *Politics of Emotion*, 98.

63 Bate discusses the rhetorical convention of adapting Ovid's Hecuba as "'a mirror' of woefulness" (*Shakespeare and Ovid*, 20).

64 In the 1590 *Faerie Queene*, for example, Spenser distances himself from his own portrayal of Adonis with the phrase, "sooth it seemes they say" (3.6.47.1).

65 See McCabe, *Spenser's Monstrous Regiment*, 63–70. On the woods as the "perfect place for Adicia to change her shape," see Lyne, *Ovid's Changing Worlds*, 128.

66 I extend to the Adicia episode Paul Alpers's claim that "Malbecco's transformation represents not a change in him, but a terrible remaining what he

is" (*Poetry of "The Faerie Queene,"* 389). Fox likewise compares the metamorphoses of Adicia and Malbecco as examples of "an Ovidian aesthetic" (*Politics of Emotion*, 103).

67 In the Latin, only thirty lines separate this leonine, regal Hecuba from the "mad bytch" to which Spenser likens Adicia before transforming her into a tiger.

68 To be sure, the Malengin episode suggests several topical readings. Michael O'Connell argues for an Irish context, claiming, "Malengin, who changes his shape like Proteus in the *Odyssey*, portrays the shiftiness of the Irish guerillas who effectively eluded the English forces … Spenser assigns him the 'glib,' the long bushy style of hair worn by Irish men, and the rugged cloak which doubled as bed and blanket" ("*Faerie Queene*, Book V," in *Spenser Encyclopedia*, 282). Cyndia Clegg, on the other hand, asserts that Malengin "can be associated with the Jesuit mission [in England] in several respects … [His] Protean aspect parallels the Jesuits' use of disguise." ("Justice and Press Censorship in Book V of Spenser's *Faerie Queene*," 251, 253).

69 Contrast Book 6, in which Calidore's transparent pastoral disguise parodies the facility with which characters were able to disguise themselves earlier in the poem. Such earlier proteans include not only the god Proteus, but also Archimago as Redcrosse and Duessa as Fidessa, or the lump of snow crafted by the witch into the surprisingly durable False Florimell.

70 Such shapes signal a loss of character agency throughout Ovid's poetry. Arborification and petrification are so commonly the static products of metamorphosis that no reader can be unfamiliar with them (e.g., the Heliades, Myrrha, Battus, everyone Perseus meets), but Spenser's emblems of flight could also refer to similarly reductive Ovidian motifs. Several of the *Metamorphoses'* bird-myths culminate in natural animosities between bird species, which then fly out of the poem and into the world we recognize (e.g., Nisus and Scylla). The fox, surprisingly, gets the worst treatment of all in a remote corner of the Ovidian corpus, wrapped in hay by a peasant boy and set afire to run yelping through the fields (*Fasti* 4.691–712). Malengin's final transformation into a hedgehog, however, has no parallel in Ovid.

71 Spenser, *View*, 66.

72 Ibid.

73 Willy Maley, *Spenser Chronology*, 14–15. McCabe, however, casts doubt on the assumption that Spenser witnessed O'Brien's execution, which "occurred in 1577, three years prior to Spenser's officially documented arrival in Ireland," and argues instead that Irenaeus reiterates the libel of Irish blood-drinking originating with Giraldus Cambrensis (*Spenser's Monstrous Regiment*, 60).

4. The Post-Metamorphic Landscape in Drayton's *Endimion and Phoebe* and *England's Heroical Epistles*

1 *English Literature in the Sixteenth Century*, 533.
2 Broad similarities remain, of course, between the *Epistles* and Ovid's *Heroides*, as well as passages Drayton has evidently derived from the original. Geraldine Howard's epistle to the Earl of Surrey, for example, ends with the demand that he return from overseas, recalling Penelope's epistle to Odysseus in the *Heroides*. But as Alison Thorne observes, "Drayton's remaking of Ovid in *EHE* is clearly no mere exercise in literary pastiche, still less an attempt to render a canonical Latin text faithfully into the vernacular tongue. Rather, in the competitive and renovatory spirit of early modern theorizing of *imitatio*, it entails a bold transposition of the *Heroides'* basic scenario of abandoned women lamenting the loss or treachery of their lovers into an alien cultural system with its own mores, discursive habits, literary conventions and legendary past" ("'Large complaints in little papers': Negotiating Ovidian Genealogies of Complaint in Drayton's *Englands Heroicall Epistles*," 371).
3 Alessandro Barchiesi describes Ovid's generic intervention as "'elegiac' incisions into the narrative bodies of epic, tragedy and myth" (*Speaking Volumes*, 33).
4 See Andrew Hadfield, "Michael Drayton's Brilliant Career," 141.
5 Raphael Lyne quotes Alexander's sonnet, as well as William Browne's 1612 description of Drayton as "our second Ovid" (*Ovid's Changing Worlds*, 151–2 and n.). Notably, however, Alexander's sonnet first appears in the fourth edition of the *Epistles* (1600), while the first edition (1597) presents only the all-purpose commendatory verse of "E. Sc." [Edmond Scory], who characterizes the volume as containing "The secret Passions of a wittie Lover" ("To M. Michael Drayton," line 12, in *The Works of Michael Drayton*, ed. Hebel, 2:132). Scory's poem in fact provides no evidence that he has read the *Epistles*, and applies better to Drayton's earlier work, especially to *Ideas Mirrour* (1594). Throughout this chapter, all references to Drayton's poetry are to Hebel's edition, except where otherwise noted, and are provided parenthetically by the number of the epistle and line number(s), or with the prefix *EP* in the case of *Endimion and Phoebe* (I have retained the archaic spelling for the poem's title, but adjusted to the more familiar "Endymion" when discussing the character).
6 Stephen Gosson, for instance, condemns Ovid for "his cunning in the inceste of Myrrha, and that trumpet of Baudrie, the Craft of love," while praising Augustus for banishing the poet (*Schoole of Abuse*, 2). See

Dympna Callaghan, "The Book of Changes in a Time of Change," in *Companion to Shakespeare's Works*, ed. Dutton and Howard, v. 4, 33–4.

7 Hadfield, "Brilliant Career," 129–30.

8 *OED*, s.v. "banquet, n(1)." 2.

9 On the epyllion as a "rite of passage" or "proving ground" for new poets (or for poets who would be seen renewing their careers), see Brown, *Redefining Elizabethan Literature*, 116–29. Brown notes further, "The epyllia tend to be dedicated to individuals or groups that have links with the author's youth," citing Lodge, Chapman, and Weever (119). Other examples of the genre include Thomas Edwards's *Cephalus and Procris* (1595), John Marston's *Metamorphosis of Pygmalion's Image* (1598), Thomas Cutwode's *Caltha Poetarum* (1599), Cyril Tourneur's *Transformed Metamorphosis* (1600), John Weever's *Faunus and Melliflora* (1600), John Beaumont's *Metamorphosis of Tobacco* (1602), and Francis Beaumont's *Salmacis and Hermaphroditus* (1602).

10 So, for example, Lodge recounts his Scylla's metamorphosis in a dozen lines after devoting a thousand to amorous complaint, Tourneur reserves his absurd unicorn for a single stanza despite the title of his poem, *The Transformed Metamorphosis*, and Beaumont includes the inevitable transformation of Hermaphroditus almost grudgingly at the end of his *Salmacis*, tersely paraphrasing Ovid's Latin.

11 See Burrow, *Epic Romance*, 184–6, where Drayton features prominently among the "inglorious Spensers."

12 Endymion's sleeping apotheosis is an alternative to the metamorphoses punctuating rival epyllia. Garrett Sullivan, discussing Sidney's *Arcadia*, observes that in romance "sleep transports and transforms the sleeper, reconfiguring his identity and recalibrating his relation to the passions" (*Sleep, Romance and Human Embodiment*, 63).

13 Lodge, Thomas, *Scillaes Metamorphosis* (1589), in *Elizabethan Minor Epics*, ed. Donno, 123.6.

14 The main exception, Marsyas, is flayed alive by Apollo at *Met.* 6.382–400.

15 The setting of Endymion's myth reminds us immediately of Ovid's Narcissus, but the latter's flower was white (*Met.* 3.510), not purple, as in the case of Shakespeare's Adonis. See above, chapter 1, note 35.

16 As Vertumnus, for example, seeks to seduce Pomona (*Met.* 14.698–771).

17 In addition to a hymnal, *Harmonie of the Church* (1593), Drayton had previously published *Idea the Shepheards Garland* (1593) and the sonnet sequence *Ideas Mirrour* (1594). The latter two volumes had established him under the pastoral sobriquet of Rouland, emulating Spenser's Colin Clout.

18 Brown, *Redefining Elizabethan Literature*, 125–6.

19 As Lyne observes, "Drayton writes in a post-Spenserian milieu, emulating his predecessor's exploits, and *Poly-Olbion* can be seen as a work written in the aftermath of *The Faerie Queene*." Noting further that "Drayton is influenced partly by a Spenserian Ovid," Lyne bypasses *Endimion* to focus instead on the *Epistles* as "an early foray" into the shared intertextual "territory" of Ovidianism (*Changing Worlds*, 142, 151). As I argue in this chapter, however, to English readers of the 1590s the *Epistles* would have seemed less an "early foray" than a decisive annexation of rich and largely unoccupied intertextual territory.

20 Marlowe, *Hero and Leander*, in *Works*, vol. 1, ed. Gill, ll. 137, 141–4, 154–5.

21 This conflation of the Petrarchan and Ovidian traditions is hardly Drayton's innovation; the *Metamorphoses*, after all, had broadly informed Petrarch's *Rime Sparse*, and motifs like the all-conquering Cupid or the unrequited lover's languishment are common to both traditions, which were further admixed by poets from Jean de Meun and Chaucer through Sidney and Spenser.

22 Citing this passage, Lyne writes, "While *England's Heroicall Epistles* derive directly from the *Heroides*, the text that Drayton most often implicitly maligns is the *Metamorphoses*. Ovid's works explicitly about love, the *Amores* and the *Ars Amatoria*, cannot be ignored, but it is his book of changes that provides the dangerous erotic values lamented by Matilda" (*Changing Worlds*, 157).

23 In Drayton's earlier treatment, *The Legend of Matilda the Faire* (1594), the doomed heroine had complained of the tyrant's advances in specifically Ovidian terms: "A Beast, a Byrd, a Satyre in the shade, / A flood, a fire, a Serpent and a Swaine" (*Matilda*, ll. 647–8). Such protean harassment recalls Spenser's rapacious but impotent tyrants – especially the enchanter Busirane and Proteus himself – in the 1590 *Faerie Queene*.

24 Ordinarily, this critique of the rhetoric of seduction as broadly Ovidian would hardly be fresh or consequential; after all, Gosson was indicting the *Ars amatoria* as "that trumpet of Baudrie" back in 1579. In Drayton's case, however, the extension of the *Epistles'* trans-historical satire of the English court to include the "Ovidian master-trope of metamorphosis" has further nationalist implications (Thorne, "Large Complaints," 376). Hence, Drayton's Queen Katherine, raised in France, ironically mocks the assumption of an Ovidian persona as a French affectation, testifying to English cultural supremacy in having abandoned such rhetoric (11.61–74).

25 *Pace* Efrossini Spentzou, who argues that the putative authors of Ovid's *Heroides* instantiate an alternative female presence and voice within the

male-dominated epic tradition. Spentzou's contention that "the heroines' struggle for control over their own destinies is really these feminine literary figures' effort to (re)write their stories, against the will of the classical authorities" challenges a masculinist bias in the reception of Ovid's *Heroides* – a challenge which may, with care, be extended to studies of Renaissance epistolarity (*Readers and Writers in Ovid's Heroides*, 28–9). Distilling such an *écriture féminine* from the *Epistles*, however, proves proportionally less plausible to the extent that Drayton restores the masculine perspective to parity within the epistolary genre.

26 On Chapman's recapitulation of myths involving Diana, see pp. 55–7.

27 George Puttenham's bewildering discussion of "historical poesy" offers an instructive introduction to the difficulties of distinguishing between contemporary historical writing and poetry; see *The Art of English Poesy*, ed. Wigham and Rebhorn, 128–31. In most cases, historical events are construed as examples for present behaviour and policy, without regard to questions of accuracy or strict attention to form.

28 Clark Hulse argues that Drayton sought to distinguish his own work from that of contemporaries, especially Daniel, as early as the *Legends* of 1593–6. For Hulse, *Matilda* "introduces the term 'legend' by way of rebuking Daniel's *Rosamond* for the false devotional language that was an aspect of the poem's Petrarchism" (*Metamorphic Verse*, 227–8).

29 The commentary follows each epistle, in the tradition of Spenser's *Shepheardes Calender*, with its glosses by the mysterious "E.K." Drayton's commentator (there is no reason to preclude Drayton's own authorship) mines well-known chronicles like Stow's *Annales*, which provides a typical version of the Rosamond legend:

> Rosamond the faire daughter of Walter, Lord Clifford, Concubine to Henry the 2 (poysoned by D. Elianor as some thought) died at Wodstock, where K. Henry had made for her an house of a wonderfull working, so that no man or woman might come to her, but if hee were instructed by the king, or such as were right secrete with him touching the matter. This house after seene was named Labyrinthus, or Dedalus worke, which was thought to be an house wrought like unto a knotte in a garden, called a Maze, but it was commonly sayde, that lastly the Queene came to her by a clewe of thredde, or silke, and so dealt with her, that shee lived not long after … (*Stow*, ed. 1592, 219)

30 Daniel, *Complaint of Rosamond*, in *Complete Works*, ed. Grosart, ll. 47, 9–10; hereafter cited parenthetically by line, with the prefix "*Comp.*"

31 The historian William Camden, however, declares that Woodstock Labyrinth, built to hide Rosamond "out of the sight of his iealous *Juno* the

Queene … is nowhere to be seene at this day" (*Britain*, ed. 1610, 375). The semi-apocryphal status of the Labyrinth's ruins locates Drayton's epistle in the Spenserian tradition, recalling the complaint of the ghostly Genius of Verulamium in *The Ruines of Time* (1591).

32 Daniel's Rosamond refers to the "innumerable wayes" of Henry's "stately Pallace," echoing Ovid's *innumeras … vias*, but makes no reference to the Meander (*Comp.* 470–2). Drayton's commentator identifies the Meander geographically and observes that its "intricate Turnings, by a Transumptive and Metonymicall kind of speech, [are] called Meanders," but he does not mention the *Metamorphoses* (1.89n).

33 On *hyperbaton*, see Richard Lanham, *Handlist of Rhetorical Terms*, 86. The emphatic redundancy of "But yet still" complements the inverted syntax of "walke I," producing a small labyrinth of a line. Lyne observes of Rosamond, "The maze comes to symbolize her entrapment within a terrifying circle of sin and reminders of sin, mainly gleaned from myth" (*Changing Worlds*, 160).

34 On the mythological content and erotic aspects of *cassoni*, see Bull, *Mirror of the Gods*, 38.

35 Boccaccio discusses Amymone briefly in his *Genealogia* (2.25).

36 Barkan, *Gods Made Flesh*, 223.

37 Bull, *Mirror of the Gods*, 37.

38 The illuminations accompanying the Bodleian manuscript of Clément Marot's 1534 French translation (MS. Douce 117) present a standard, frame-by-frame depiction of the narrative, in contrast to Daniel's truncated *ekphrasis*.

39 By modernizing the text, Hebel spoils the orthographic pun; I quote here from the second (1598) edition of *Englands Heroicall Epistles*, 4[ʳ].

40 For transcriptions of contemporary eyewitness accounts, see Leslie, "Spenser, Sidney, and the Renaissance Garden." Christine Coch notes further that Nonsuch featured a labyrinth with unusually high hedges, and her reading of Spenser's Bower of Bliss episode in relation to the garden informs my sense of its significance to Drayton (see "Trials of Art," 52–9).

41 Barchiesi, *Speaking Volumes*, 30.

42 Fulkerson, *Ovidian Heroine as Author*, 12.

43 On allusions to Medea in Book 5 of *The Faerie Queene*, see pp. 103–8.

44 "Ovid's *Heroides*, Drayton and the Articulation of the Feminine," 391. Clarke concurs with Hardin, who asserts, "The general plan of the *Heroical Epistles* … is to show divine Providence guiding England through a troublesome past into a glorious present under Elizabeth" (*Michael Drayton and the Passing of Elizabethan England*, 48).

45 Clarke, "Articulation of the Feminine," 396.
46 Cobham's treasons would have resonated at the end of the sixteenth century, as the aging Elizabeth had frequently been accused of usurpation (by Catholic supporters of Mary Stuart) and implicitly censured for failing to provide a suitable heir (by Protestant foes of James Stuart, including Spenser). Jean Brink detects bias toward non-Stuart claimants to the throne at the end of the first edition of Drayton's *Epistles* ("Michael Drayton and John Donne," 54).
47 *Elizabeth I and her Age*, ed. Stump and Felch, 484. Louis Montrose writes, "Although the verbal portrait drawn by de Maisse frankly registers the ravages of age, it eschews the opportunity for maliciously misogynistic commentary that his private medium allowed him" (*The Subject of Elizabeth*, 232). On imputations of witchcraft, see Carole Levin, "Gender, Monarchy, and the Power of Seditious Words," in *Dissing Elizabeth*, ed. Walker, 78–9.
48 For Elizabeth's exclamation, "I am Richard II, know ye not that?" upon learning that the Essex plotters had hired the Lord Chamberlain's Men to perform Shakespeare's tragedy, see *The Shakspere Allusion-Book*, ed. Ingleby et al., 100. In another famous instance, King James of Scotland demanded that Spenser be punished for depicting his mother Mary Stuart as Duessa in *The Faerie Queene* (see Mark Eccles, "James I of England," in *Spenser Encyclopedia*, 409).
49 While Medea fails to assassinate Theseus, she does escape: *effugit illa necem nebulis per carmina motis* (*Met.* 7.424, "But Medea escaped death in a dark whirlwind her witch songs raised").
50 Enterline, *Rhetoric of the Body*, 25–6.
51 Jonson, "The Vision of Ben. Ionson, on the Muses of his Friend, M. Drayton," 29–32.
52 See Jonson's prefatory verses to Chapman's *Georgicks of Hesiod* ("To my worthy and honour'd Friend," in Herford and Simpson, *Ben Jonson*, 8:388–9, ll. 1–3) and his famous praise of Shakespeare as superior to "all, that insolent Greece, or haughtie Rome / Sent forth, or since did from their ashes come" ("To the Memory of my Beloved," 39–40).

5. The Brief Ovidian Career of John Donne

 1 "The Apprenticeship of John Donne: Ovid and the Elegies," 419. Robin Sowerby notes that Ovid's elegies in particular "have a clear generic relation to those of Ovid." (*The Classical Legacy in Renaissance Poetry*, 303). More recently, Burrow writes, "Ovid enabled writers from the period to sound

respectably learned even while they described undressing with their mistress – as Donne does in 'To his Mistress Going to Bed'" ("Re-embodying Ovid: Renaissance Afterlives," in *Cambridge Companion to Ovid*, ed. Hardie, 304).

2 Marotti, *John Donne, Coterie Poet*, 44. Marotti quotes Roma Gill, "*Musa Iocosa Mea*: Thoughts on the Elegies," in *John Donne: Essays in Celebration*, ed. Smith, 47.

3 Ibid., 54.

4 George Herbert, "Jordan (1)," ll. 13–15, in *The English Poems*, ed. Wilcox, 200.

5 "An Elegie upon the death of the Deane of Pauls, Dr. Iohn Donne: By *Mr. Tho. Carie*" in *The Poems of John Donne*, ed. Grierson, ll. 61–70. Carew's elegy was published among many others to Doctor or Dean Donne in the posthumous 1633 edition of the poems, including Sir Thomas Browne's provocatively-titled "To the deceased Author, Upon the *Promiscuous* printing of his Poems, the *Looser sort*, with the *Religious*." See also Laurence Lerner, "Ovid and the Elizabethans," in *Ovid Renewed*, ed. Martindale, 121.

6 "To Sir Edward Herbert, at Juliers," in *The Poems of John Donne*, ed. Grierson, ll. 1–2, 9–12, responding to "The State progress of Ill," in *The Poems English and Latin of Edward Lord Herbert of Cherbury*, ed. Smith, ll. 125–6. Herbert's satire is dated August 1608, and his "Satyra Secunda" of the following month notably plays upon the trope of metempsychosis, as the process by which English travellers are reborn as French dandies.

7 On the term *praeceptor amoris*, see Introduction, note 5. Stapleton helpfully distinguishes the persona of the *Amores* from that of the *Ars amatoria*:

> Few [critics] discuss the 'student,' Ovid's speaker in the *Amores*, but he merits attention as an original character in elegiac poetry whom medieval and Renaissance poets imitated and revised extensively. He is a truly 'unreliable narrator' who discovers his own foolishness in a sequence of love poems, a megalomaniac who becomes everything he despises. I shall name him *desultor Amoris*, despite his protest to the contrary: 'non sum desultor Amoris' (*Am.* 1.3.15) … *The desultor* seems designed to have been the student of the *praeceptor*, a relationship noted as early as the twelfth century. (*Harmful Eloquence*, 7–8)

While I feel Stapleton slightly overstates the turpitude of Ovid's amorous persona, I agree that in the *Amores* Ovid pointedly portrays the abysmal failure of the very precepts he had offered in the *Ars*. If I conflate the *desultor* of the *Amores* with the *praeceptor* of the *Ars* in this chapter, it is because I read Donne as subordinating such a nuanced distinction to the priority of repudiating Ovidian authority in general.

8 Texts of the epigrams are from Grierson's edition, 75, as are all further references to Donne's poetry, cited parenthetically by line number(s). The editors of the Donne *Variorum* estimate that "Donne's active period as a writer of epigrams ... would appear to have spanned, roughly, the last decade of the sixteenth century," indicating that the epigrams were "among Donne's earliest poems." The three mythographic couplets, however, did not appear among the earliest sequence of nine epigrams, which scholars ascribe instead to an intermediate sequence around 1596, and were not as frequently copied into period manuscripts as several others. See the Donne *Variorum*, vol. 8, ed. Stringer, 14–15. According to M. Thomas Hester, Donne's epigrams were highly regarded; William Drummond commented, "If he would, [he] might easily be the best epigrammatist we have found in *English*," and Ben Jonson wrote, in his own epigram to Donne, "Who shall doubt, *Donne*, where I a Poet bee, / When I dare send my *Epigrammes* to thee? / That so alone canst judge, so'alone dost make" (both cited in Hester, "Donne's Epigrams: A Little World Made Cunningly," in *The Eagle and the Dove*, ed. Summers and Pebworth, 80).

9 Even Donne's other epigrams fit more comfortably into his poetic output in the 1590s than the three mythographic couplets. "The Antiquary" and "A Licentious Person," for example, blend into the longer satires and share themes with "The Calme" and "The Storme."

10 Rosalie Colie notes that "epigrams were miniature versions of greater kinds," with epitaph serving as the miniaturized form of tragedy (*Resources of Kind*, 68).

11 *Heroides* 7 ends: *hoc tantum in tumuli marmore carmen erit:* / PRAEBUIT AENEAS ET CAUSAM MORTIS ET ENSEM; / IPSA SUA DIDO CONCIDIT USA MANU (*Her.* 7.194–6, "let this brief epitaph be read on the marble of my tomb: FROM AENEAS CAME THE CAUSE OF HER DEATH, AND FROM HIM THE BLADE; FROM THE HAND OF DIDO HERSELF CAME THE STROKE BY WHICH SHE FELL"; compare also Phyllis's epitaph at *Her.* 2.145–8). Ovid's epitaphs – not strictly paradoxes – draw attention to the irony of suicide as a form of female agency, all other agency (*causae*) remaining masculine. Donne's adaptations read more like riddles: "cruell frinds, by parting haue ioynd here."

12 Hester, "Little World," 82.

13 Hester remarks, "In his epigrams (as in his lyrics) the movement is toward the compression of the speaker's utterance into as small a space as possible, almost to reduce the poem to a phrase or even a word. This, of course, is a given of the genre ... In most cases, the Donne epigram (or lyric) does just the opposite of 'elaborating' on a motif or metaphor" ("Little World," 90).

The myths Donne has chosen to compress into epigrams, however, are already elaborate, each having been treated at great length both by Ovid himself and by his many commentators and imitators. By way of epigrammatic contrast to the mythographic couplets, Donne devotes eight lines to lampooning the periodical *Mercurius Gallobelgicus*, six to the burning ship, and four to the falling wall.

14 Indeed, Donne's mythographic epigrams may be read as a literary variation on the long visual tradition of retrofitting dilatory Ovidian texts within the miniscule frames of emblematic woodcuts. Paul White argues that "the 'pluritemporalité' technique [was] particularly well suited to illustrating the *Heroides* … Ovid's heroines exist in a narrative in which past, present, and future events collapse together, subsumed by the immediacy of passion" (*Renaissance Postscripts*, 101).

15 In the gray area between the mythographic couplets and the *praeceptor* of Donne's elegies, we find the lesbian persona of "Sapho to Philaenis." Donne's authorship of this epistle has been disputed, but for H.L. Meakin it is quintessentially Donnean, "outdoing Ovid and his fellow Inns of Court wits with one stroke by writing a lesbian epilogue to Ovid's heterosexual love poem between Sappho and Phaon, the ferryman" (*John Donne's Articulations of the Feminine*, 90). I agree with this reading insofar as Sappho's legendary suicide had seemed imminent at the end of *Heroides* 15, and Donne's epistle thus resurrects her in spite of Ovid (though Ovid's authorship of *Heroides* 15 was likewise doubted even in the Renaissance). In other words, while the Latin original tends away from erotic elegy and toward funeral elegy, Donne's "epilogue" pushes the tradition in the opposite direction. The autoeroticism of "Sapho to Philaenis," however, falls short of the reciprocation of sexual desire, and the persona's resonance with Ovid's Narcissus bodes ill for her survival. Hence, I read this poem as a less-radical departure from the Ovidian tradition than Meakin, though on the other hand I find Stapleton's characterization of "Sapho to Philaenis" as "male fantasy and wish-fulfillment" reductive ("'Why should they not alike in all parts touch?': Donne and the Elegiac Tradition," 1). See also Lyne, "Intertextuality and the Female Voice after the *Heroides*," 310–15.

16 Hence, Donne ignores or avoids Conti's account in the *Mythologiae*, where Plato fails to appear, but Ovid is quoted twice (*Myth.* 8.11).

17 Scholars have long noted the influence of *Amores* 1.4 and 1.5 on two other early elegies by Donne, "Fond woman," and "Come, Madam, come," though Stella Revard questions the extent of that influence in "Donne and Propertius: Love and death in London and Rome," in *Eagle and the Dove*, ed. Summers and Pebworth, 69.

18 Of course, a great many poetic lovers, most of them Petrarchan, have encountered such tempests, and Donne mocks them as well, but his imitative stake in this particular elegy of Ovid's is also uniquely large, for he engages it again in "The Indifferent" (from the *Songs and Sonnets*, and thus probably post-dating Donne's Ovidian period), the first stanza of which testifies to the persona's capacity to "love both faire and browne," etc. (1). Though this statement recalls Ovid's *candida me capiet, capiet me flava puella, / est etiam in fusco grata colore Venus* (*Am.* 2.4.39–40, "A fair white skin will make prey of me, I am prey to the golden-haired, and even a love of dusky hue will please"), Donne's attitude in "The Indifferent" again insinuates superiority over his less adept precursor. Whereas Donne "can love her, and her, and you and you, / ... can love any, so she be not true" (8–9), his persona's volition contrasts starkly with the passivity of the Ovidian lover, signaled in the Latin by deponent and passive verbs like *uror* and *capior* (*Am.* 2.4.12, 13, "I am set on fire," "I am captured"). This masochistic element of Ovid's erotic posture does not translate easily to Donne's zero-sum bedroom.

19 On the self-destructive promiscuity of Ovid's persona in the *Amores*, see Stapleton, *Harmful Eloquence*, 23.

20 On the conflation of Ovidian and Petrarchan conventions, Enterline writes, "Because of Petrarch's persuasive rendering of metamorphosis as the melancholy condition of a writing and desiring self, Elizabethan poets – be they Petrarchan or anti-Petrarchan – habitually read Ovid and Petrarch together, playing one off the other for different effect (ranging from satiric to tragic)" (*Rhetoric of the Body*, 23). See also Enterline's complementary chapters on John Marston's *Metamorphosis of Pygmalion's Image* and Shakespeare's *Rape of Lucrece* as "profoundly different" approaches to the intertextual blend of Ovid and Petrarch (ibid., 152).

21 See Stapleton, *Harmful Eloquence*, 22–3.

22 For a positive reading of "Love's Progress," see Ilona Bell, "Oral Sex and Verbal Tricks – John Donne and Renaissance Sexual Practice," 45–76. Bell rejects the traditional reading of the poem as "a misogynistic screed," reinterpreting Donne's erotic map as a guide not to desultory intercourse, but rather to the mutual pleasures of oral sex. Instead of an implied audience of witless acolytes, Bell imagines a brighter coterie, claiming that "'Love's Progress' teaches poets and lovers and lovers of poetry how to do better. Donne's verbal journey entices us to circle back, recalculate, and begin anew, again and again." But while Bell's exuberant reading recasts the notorious elegy as celebrating progressive sexuality, her sense of the poem's satirical content seems insupportably limited: "[Donne] directed

his satire at scientists whose ideological anxieties led them to monstrously distort the implications of their own findings … 'We err,' Donne writes, warning his readers to beware erroneous premises and claims that 'injure women' and men too" (75). Thus restricting Donne's satirical target to a small set of continental "new anatomists," Bell sacrifices much of the poem's cultural relevance and fine-tuned ambiguity – for example, any notion that the poem is self-satirical, or might indict rather than applaud the reader's degree of erotic sophistication. Ultimately, there seems little reason why "Love's Progress" cannot imply a dual readership – the few who "get it" versus the majority who do not – nor present an ambiguous persona who serves simultaneously as the sexually omniscient *praeceptor* and the pedant whose delusions of mastery reflect his culture's decadence. Stapleton traces the Ovidian origins of this latter persona, whom he terms the *desultor amoris*, in "Donne and the Elegiac Tradition," 2–4.

23 *Conversations with Drummond*, 1:136.

24 Ibid., 151. In fact, Donne completed 520 lines of the *Metempsychosis* – far more than could fit on "but one sheet" – of which lines 51–70 indicate that the sinful soul's final host will be English, precluding Calvin as a candidate. The errors, of course, may be due to Drummond's reportage.

25 So, for example, Cyril Tourneur gave his 1598 epyllion the reflexive title of *The Transformed Metamorphosis*, and the terms were likewise interchangeable in the particular context of Ovid; the *OED* cites Richard Eden's 1555 translation of Peter Martyr, referring to the *Metamorphoses* as "Ouide his transformations" (s.v. "transformation, n." 1a). Donne himself uses the terms appositionally in a 1626 sermon (see p. 177).

26 On resisting the "temptation" to identify Pythagoras's speech directly with Ovid's "genuine authorial voice," see Alessandro Barchiesi, *Speaking Volumes*, 62–9. Barchiesi further observes, "vegetarianism … in Ovid's time rarely failed to elicit ironic responses" (62–3).

27 See Janel Mueller, "Donne's Epic Venture in the *Metempsychosis*," 123–5.

28 So, for example, Donne draws upon Budaeus's sixteenth-century edition of pseudo-Philo's *Iudaei antiquitatum biblicarum liber* for the name of "Adams fift daughter Siphetecia" (457); see W.A. Murray, "What Was the Soul of the Apple?," 143. Donne's preface is reprinted in Grierson's edition, 293–4.

29 Mueller, "Epic Venture," 123.

30 Feeney explores the problematics of the *Metamorphoses*' closing panegyric, which he finds "certainly … very tempting to read ironically" (see *Gods in Epic*, 210–24).

31 Kenneth Gross notes that the stanzas of the *Metempsychosis*, though "pointedly mirroring those of Spenser's *Faerie Queene*," introduce "a less

interwoven, more abrupt rhyme-scheme than Spenser's" ("John Donne's Lyric Skepticism," 371).

32 Shakespeare, *A Midsummer Night's Dream*, 5.1.24, 26.

33 Josephus, *Works*, trans. Lodge, 6. Mueller includes the disclaimer, "in suggesting that the *Metempsychosis* can profitably be viewed in the light of the *Metamorphoses*, I am not undertaking to establish Donne's indebtedness to Ovid in any specific point" ("Epic Venture," 113–14).

34 Indeed, while Donne's primary allusion is to Josephus's account of "Seth's pillars," the line's secondary resonance might just as readily allude to Horace's famous boast of having "finished a monument more lasting than bronze, more lofty than the regal structure of the pyramids" (*Odes* 3.30.1–2; *Exegi monumentum aere perennius / regalique situ pyramidum altius*) as recall Ovid, who recycles Horace's verb (*exegi*). For Donne's purposes in the *Metempsychosis*, such a proliferation of allusive referents is an advantage, rather than a hindrance, as he pursues his own claim to superlative poetic authority; both Horace and Ovid are left in the dust beneath the dust of Seth's pillars. For more on Donne's indirect allusive style, see M.L. Stapleton, "Donne and the Elegiac Tradition," 4–5.

35 Of course, this is not always how Ovid employs his aetiological metamorphoses, which sometimes bear little relation to the myths in which they are embedded, but medieval and early modern traditions of moralizing the *Metamorphoses* tend to overemphasize precisely this correlation between ultimate form and innate essence. Hence Golding, in the preface to his 1567 translation, verges on denying the physical aspect of metamorphosis entirely, as when he observes of Circe's bestial victims, "Not that they lost theyr manly shape as to the outward showe, / But for that in their brutish brestes most beastly lustes did growe" (Golding, "Preface," 99–100). Andrew Feldherr considers the ideological stakes and hidden ambiguities of this sense of metamorphosis as "an emphatically final process," the victims of which "do not lose the enduring aspects of their being, rather they take on a form that reveals them" ("Metamorphosis in the *Metamorphoses*," in *Cambridge Companion to Ovid*, ed. Hardie, 171).

36 Hence the botanist John Gerard feels compelled to debunk such "doltish dreames," though even he appears mesmerized by the folklore surrounding the mandrake, recognizing its reputation as a fertility drug, and recommending it as a soporific (*Herball*, 280–2).

37 Marotti discusses the topical allegories of the *Metempsychosis* as part of "a general vocabulary of disappointment"; see *John Donne, Coterie Poet*, 128–33. On the identification of Cecil as the "great soule" and of Essex as the whale in this interlude, see Martin van Wyk Smith, "John Donne's

'Metempsychosis,'" 141–52. More recently Richard Dutton has extended such topical readings to Jonson's *Volpone*; see "Jonson's Metempsychosis Revisited," in *Ben Jonson and the Politics of Genre*, ed. Cousins and Scott, 146–55.

38 Admittedly, such passages may comprise instances of a *topos*, short of allusion even in the least direct sense of that term; hence Carey, while recognizing the origin of Myrrha's fallacy in Ovid's myth, calls it "hackneyed property," appropriated by "hordes of harmless pedants and clergymen" writing Neo-Latin elegies (*John Donne: Life, Mind & Art*, 237). On the other hand, the increased stakes of Donne's redeployment of the *topos* – previously justifying mere promiscuity in the elegy "Change," but by the *Metempsychosis* excusing incest – suggests an allusive movement toward rather than away from Ovid's incestuous Myrrha.

39 Carey, otherwise the most sensitive reader of the *Metempsychosis*, implausibly describes this passage as "among Donne's most delicate and tender things" (157).

40 Gross briefly tracks Donne's poetic evolution from the insouciant soul of the *Metempsychosis* to the active persona of the mature lyrics, observing that the former "is eerily passive, whereas the lyric poems stage a restless work of making" ("Donne's Lyric Skepticism," 373).

41 Hence, Donne's revised and reformed "Progress of the Soul" (published as *The Second Anniversary* in 1612) looks "Up, up ... / Up ..." with anaphoric emphasis (ll. 339–66).

42 Donne, *Devotions upon Emergent Occasions*, ed. Raspa, 99.

43 *The Sermons of John Donne*, ed. Potter and Simpson, 6:56; see also Donne's sermon of February 12, 1618, 2:170–1. On the surprising frequency of Ovidian allusions in early modern English sermons, see Stapleton, "Marlowe's Ovid: The 'Elegies' in the Marlowe Canon," 10–12.

44 *Sermons*, 7:135.

45 While Jonson's ongoing anxiety over the Ovidian label and compulsively antagonistic response in some sense corresponds to what Harold Bloom terms "*askesis*, or a movement of self-purgation" (*Anxiety of Influence*, 15), my overall argument's distance from Bloom's Freudian model should be apparent from this discussion of Donne's fundamentally political attitude towards his own participation in Ovidianism as an early modern cultural phenomenon. As I read his poetry, Donne is never under Ovid's direct influence as a precursor, but instead constantly recalculates his various audiences' perceptions of his attitude toward Ovid, taking into account such personal contingencies as the necessity of reconciling with powerful friends and patrons following his mid-career disgrace, and the ongoing concern – intermediate between public networking and private

correspondence – involved in the development and maintenance of a coterie audience.

46 *Letters*, ed. Hester, 21–2.

47 Carew, "Elegy," ll. 95–8; "Priest" may be a pun on "press'd," as both compulsion to servitude and publication.

48 Compare Walton's epigraph to the early editions of *The Poems of J.D.*, in which the image of the young Jack Donne on the frontispiece – a reproduction of the Hilyard miniature, dated 1591 – gives way to the text of Donne's poems, which record his reformation over the course of a lifetime:

> This [i.e., Donne's portrait] was for youth, Strength, Mirth, and wit
>   that Time
> Most count their golden Age; but t'was not thine.
> Thine was thy later yeares, so much refind
> From youths Drosse, Mirth, & wit; as thy pure mind
> Thought (like the Angels) nothing but the Praise
> Of thy Creator, in those last, best Dayes.
> Witnes this Booke, (thy Embleme) which begins
> With Love; but endes, with Sighes, & Teares for Sins.

Walton's sentiment aptly describes the 1635 volume, in which the *Songs and Sonnets* appear first among the poems, whereas the 1633 first editions begin with *Metempsychosis*, better fitting Carew's account of the transformation of "Flamen" into "Priest" (even in the 1635 edition, the epistle to the *Metempsychosis* appears in the front matter, though the poem itself is relegated to the volume's middle).

49 On Donne's lifelong attachment to the doctrine of the body's reconstitution and reunification with the soul on Judgment Day, see Ramie Targoff, *John Donne, Body and Soul*, 117–18. Targoff, however, dismisses the *Metempsychosis* as an "early poem," and classes its titular doctrine among those "theories about the soul that [Donne] considered … no more than occasional interests – ideas that he found amusing or convenient for particular purposes, but never entertained as serious possibilities" (8). Yet Donne had once taken metempsychosis seriously enough to write his second-longest poem about it; only *The Second Anniversary*, also entitled "The Progress of the Soule," is (slightly) longer.

Conclusion: "It sticks strangely, whatever it is"

1 Jonson, *"Prœludium,"* in Chester, *Loues Martyr*, 177–8. In his 1616 Folio *Works*, Jonson reprinted the poem as part of *The Forest*, slightly revised and

again followed by the "Epode." For the minor differences between the two versions, see *Ben Jonson*, ed. Herford and Simpson, 8:107–8.

2 See pp. 48–9.

3 Katherine Maus argues that Jonson's "tastes, though unexceptionable, do not simply duplicate those of his contemporaries. He fails to share, for example, the enthusiasm for Ovid which so marks the work of Edmund Spenser, Christopher Marlowe, William Shakespeare, and John Donne" (*Ben Jonson and the Roman Frame of Mind*, 4).

4 Carew, "Elegie," ll 63–4, 66–7.

5 Jonson closed his *Epigrams* with the mock-epic "On the Famous Voyage," exploring the Thames as a sewer. *Eastward Ho*, which Jonson co-wrote, and which ran afoul of the Jacobean authorities, involves a similar project. See Katherine Duncan-Jones, "City Limits: Nashe's 'Choise of Valentines' and Jonson's 'Famous Voyage'": 258–62.

6 On Nashe's apologetic sonnet, see pp. 34–6.

7 The primary sense of the title, of course, is that of "a prelude or introduction," but the word may also refer to "a series of notes played before a piece of music" (*OED* s.v. "preludium, n.").

8 The debate goes back at least to Swinburne, but Alan Sinfield provides a helpful summary of the opposing arguments in *Shakespeare, Authority, Sexuality*, 40–3, before concluding that Ovid must be banished from the play because he "challenges the material power of fathers and husbands at its ultimate patriarchal reference point, Caesar" (52). This cultural materialist reading works surprisingly well with the present paragraph's ultimately psychoanalytic claim that Jonson can neither resist putting Ovid at centre-stage nor kicking him offstage. I do not believe, however, that Jonson's latent Ovidianism is entirely or even primarily psychological, as I explain below. In his introduction to the Revels edition of the play, Tom Cain provides the clearest statement of the play's central critical problem, observing that "If ... 'the essential plot' concerns Ovid, then we are left with a long, eventful and ideologically important last act in which he is not referred to, even by implication; if the 'essential plot' is that of Horace, then the main protagonist does not appear until Act III, and plays only a minor part in Act IV, to re-emerge in the last act" (3).

9 *Chloridia: Rites to Chloris and her Nymphs*, in Jonson, *Complete Masques*, ed. Orgel, 462. Jonson's epigraph quotes *Fasti* 5.222.

10 See *Timber*, 2424–7, where Jonson affirms of poetic inspiration, "This the *Poets* understood by their *Helicon*, *Pegasus*, or *Parnassus*, and this made *Ovid* to boast: *Est, Deus in nobis; agitante calescimus illo: / Sedibus æthereis spiritus ille venit* ("There is a god inside us; we are stimulated by

his motions: / This spirit comes from heavenly regions"). Combining sentiments from the *Ars amatoria* (3.549–50) and *Fasti* (6.5), this Ovidian testimony to poetry's divine origins, corroborated by a line from Lipsius, serves as a local climax in *Timber* and caps Jonson's discussion of poetic furor.

11 Jonson writes, "I feele my griefes too, and there scarce is ground, / Vpon my flesh t'inflict another wound" ("To Heaven," ll. 21–2), echoing *Met.* 6.388 (*nec quicquam nisi vulnus erat*, "Nought else he [Marsyas] was than one whole wounde" [Golding, 6.494]), as well as *Epistlae ex Ponto* 2.7.41–2 (*sic ego continuo Fortunae vulneror ictu, / vixque habet in nobis iam nova plaga locum*, "so am I wounded by the steady blows of fate until now I have scarce space upon me for a new wound").

12 "Upon Ben Jonson," ll. 25–32, in *Poems of Edmund Waller*, ed. G. Thorn Drury, 30.

13 Greene writes, "Center and circle become symbols, not only of harmony and completeness but of stability, repose, fixation, duration, and the incompleted circle, uncentered and misshapen, comes to symbolize a flux or a mobility, grotesquely or dazzlingly fluid" ("Ben Jonson and the Centered Self," 326). Ann Christensen, however, offers a thoughtful corrective to Greene's overly neat division of Jonson's work into centred poems and uncentred comedies, focusing on the poems' portrayal of women "as both mistress of the household and subordinate to her husband," and arguing that "the dissolute and disbanded households of Jonson's comedies are in fact adumbrated in the poems" ("Reconsidering Ben Jonson and the 'Centered Self,'" 1–2).

Bibliography

Alpers, Paul J. *The Poetry of "The Faerie Queene."* Princeton, NJ: Princeton University Press, 1967.

Anderson, Judith H. *Reading the Allegorical Intertext: Chaucer, Spenser, Shakespeare, Milton.* New York: Fordham University Press, 2008.

Aptekar, Jane. *Icons of Justice: Iconography & Thematic Imagery in Book V of "The Faerie Queene."* New York: Columbia University Press, 1969.

Armstrong, Alan. "The Apprenticeship of John Donne: Ovid and the *Elegies.*" *English Literary History* 44, no. 3 (1977): 419–42.

Baldwin, Thomas Whitfield. *William Shakspere's Small Latine & Lesse Greeke.* 2 vols. Urbana: University of Illinois Press, 1944.

Barchiesi, Alessandro. *Speaking Volumes: Narrative and Intertext in Ovid and Other Latin Poets.* Edited and translated by Matt Fox and Simone Marchesi. London: Duckworth, 2001.

Barkan, Leonard. *The Gods Made Flesh: Metamorphosis and the Pursuit of Paganism.* New Haven, CT: Yale University Press, 1986.

Bate, Jonathan. *Shakespeare and Ovid.* Oxford: Clarendon Press, 1993.

Beaumont, Francis. *Salmacis and Hermaphroditus.* London, 1602.

Beaumont, John. *The Metamorphosis of Tobacco.* London, 1602.

Bell, Ilona. "Oral Sex and Verbal Tricks—John Donne and Renaissance Sexual Practice." *John Donne Journal* 29 (2010): 45–76.

Berger, Harry, Jr. *The Allegorical Temper: Vision and Reality in Book II of Spenser's "Faerie Queene."* New Haven, CT: Yale University Press, 1957.

– *Revisionary Play: Studies in the Spenserian Dynamics.* Berkeley: University of California Press, 1988.

Berry, Edward I. *Shakespeare and the Hunt: A Cultural and Social Study.* Cambridge: Cambridge University Press, 2001.

Berry, Lloyd E., ed. *The Geneva Bible: A Facsimile of the 1560 Edition.* Madison: University of Wisconsin Press, 1969.

Bevington, David. *Action Is Eloquence: Shakespeare's Language of Gesture.* Cambridge, MA: Harvard University Press, 1984.

Bloom, Harold. *The Anxiety of Influence: A Theory of Poetry.* 2nd ed. New York: Oxford University Press, 1973.

Boccaccio, Giovanni. *Boccaccio on Poetry: Being the Preface and the Fourteenth and Fifteenth Books of Boccaccio's "Genealogia Gentilium Deorum" in an English Version.* Translated by Charles G. Osgood. New York: Liberal Arts Press, 1956.

– *Genealogy of the Pagan Gods, Books I–V.* I Tatti Renaissance Library. Translated by Jon Solomon. Cambridge, MA: Harvard University Press, 2011.

Brink, Jean R. "Michael Drayton and John Donne." *John Donne Journal* 27 (2008): 49–66.

Brinkley, Robert A. "Spenser's *Muiopotmos* and the Politics of Metamorphosis." *English Literary History* 48, no. 4 (1981), 668–76.

Brown, Georgia. *Redefining Elizabethan Literature.* Cambridge: Cambridge University Press, 2004.

Bull, Malcolm. *The Mirror of the Gods: Classical Mythology in Renaissance Art.* Oxford: Oxford University Press, 2005.

Burrow, Colin. *Epic Romance: Homer to Milton.* Oxford: Clarendon Press, 1993.

– "Original Fictions: Metamorphoses in 'The Faerie Queene.'" In *Ovid Renewed: Ovidian Influences on Literature and Art from the Middle Ages to the Twentieth Century*, edited by Charles Martindale, 99–119. Cambridge: Cambridge University Press, 1988.

– "Re-embodying Ovid: Renaissance Afterlives." In *The Cambridge Companion to Ovid*, edited by Philip Hardie, 301–19. Cambridge: Cambridge University Press, 2002.

Bush, Douglas. *Mythology and the Renaissance Tradition in English Poetry.* Minneapolis: University of Minnesota Press, 1932.

Callaghan, Dympna. "The Book of Changes in a Time of Change: Ovid's *Metamorphoses* in Post-Reformation England and *Venus and Adonis*." In *A Companion to Shakespeare's Works, Vol. 4: The Poems, Problem Comedies, Late Plays*, edited by Richard Dutton and Jean E. Howard, 27–45. Malden, MA: Blackwell, 2006.

Camden, William. *Britain: or A chorographicall description of the most flourishing kingdomes, England, Scotland, and Ireland.* Translated by Philemon Holland. London, 1610.

Campana, Joseph. "On Not Defending Poetry: Spenser, Suffering, and the Energy of Affect." *PMLA* 120, no. 1 (2005): 33–48.

Carey, John. *John Donne: Life, Mind & Art.* New York: Oxford University Press, 1981.

Chapman, George. *The Divine Poem of Musæus: First of all Bookes.* London, 1616.

– *The Poems of George Chapman*. Edited by Phyllis Brooks Bartlett. New York: Modern Language Association of America, 1941.

Cheney, Patrick. *Marlowe's Counterfeit Profession: Ovid, Spenser, Counter-Nationhood*. Toronto: University of Toronto Press, 1997.

– *Reading Sixteenth-Century Poetry*. Chichester, UK: Wiley-Blackwell, 2011.

– *Shakespeare's Literary Authorship*. Cambridge: Cambridge University Press, 2008.

– *Spenser's Famous Flight: A Renaissance Idea of a Literary Career*. Toronto: University of Toronto Press, 1993.

Chester, Robert. *Loues Martyr*. London, 1601.

Christensen, Ann C. "Reconsidering Ben Jonson and the 'Centered Self.'" *South Central Review* 13 (1996): 1–16.

Clarke, Danielle. "Ovid's *Heroides*, Drayton and the Articulation of the Feminine in the English Renaissance." *Renaissance Studies* 22, no. 3 (2008): 385–400.

Clegg, Cyndia Susan. "Justice and Press Censorship in Book V of Spenser's *Faerie Queene*." *Studies in Philology* 95 (1998): 237–62.

Clucas, Stephen. "To Rauish and Refine an Earthly Soule: Ficino and the Poetry of George Chapman." In *Marsilio Ficino: His Theology, His Philosophy, His Legacy*, edited by Michael J.B. Allen and Valerie Rees, 419–42. Leiden, Netherlands: Brill, 2002.

Coch, Christine. "The Trials of Art: Testing Temperance in the Bower of Bliss and Diana's Grove at Nonsuch." *Spenser Studies* 20 (2005): 49–76.

Colie, Rosalie L. *The Resources of Kind: Genre-Theory in the Renaissance*. Edited by Barbara K. Lewalski. Berkeley: University of California Press, 1973.

Conte, Gian Biagio. *The Rhetoric of Imitation: Genre and Poetic Memory in Virgil and Other Latin Poets*. Translated and edited by Charles Paul Segal. Ithaca, NY: Cornell University Press, 1986.

Conti, Natale. *Mythologiae*. Translated by John Mulryan and Steven Brown. 2 vols. Tempe: Arizona Center for Medieval and Renaissance Studies, 2006.

Crewe, Jonathan V. *Unredeemed Rhetoric: Thomas Nashe and the Scandal of Authorship*. Baltimore: Johns Hopkins University Press, 1982.

Daniel, Samuel. *The Complete Works in Verse and Prose of Samuel Daniel*. Edited by Alexander B. Grosart. 5 vols. New York: Russell & Russell, 1963.

Davies, John. *The Scourge of Folly*. London, 1611.

Dolven, Jeff. *Scenes of Instruction in Renaissance Romance*. Chicago: University of Chicago Press, 2007.

Donne, John. *Devotions upon Emergent Occasions*. Edited by Anthony Raspa. Montreal: McGill-Queen's University Press, 1975.

– *Letters to Severall Persons of Honour: A Facsimile Reproduction with an introduction by M. Thomas Hester*. Delmar, NY: Scholars' Facsimiles and Reprints, 1977.

– *Poems, by J.D., with Elegies on the Author's Death*. London, 1633. Facs. Amsterdam: Theatrum Orbis Terrarum Ltd., 1970.

– *The Poems of John Donne*. Edited by Herbert J.C. Grierson. London: Oxford University Press, 1912.

– *The Sermons of John Donne*. Edited by George R. Potter and Evelyn M. Simpson. 10 vols. Berkeley: University of California Press, 1953–62.

– *The Variorum Edition of the Poetry of John Donne*. Edited by Gary A. Stringer et al. 8 vols. Bloomington: Indiana University Press, 1995.

Donno, Elizabeth Story, ed. *Elizabethan Minor Epics*. New York: Columbia University Press, 1963.

Drayton, Michael. *Englands Heroicall Epistles*. London, 1598.

– *Works*. Edited by J. William Hebel, Bernard Newdigate, and Kathleen Tillotson. 5 vols. Oxford: Oxford University Press, 1961.

Duncan-Jones, Katherine. "City Limits: Nashe's 'Choise of Valentines' and Jonson's 'Famous Voyage.'" *Review of English Studies* 56 (2005): 247–62.

– "Much Ado with Red and White: The Earliest Readers of Shakespeare's *Venus and Adonis* (1593)." *Review of English Studies* 44 (1993): 479–501.

Dutton, Richard. "Jonson's Metempsychosis Revisited: Patronage and Religious Controversy." In *Ben Jonson and the Politics of Genre*, ed. A.D. Cousins and Alison V. Scott. 134–61. Cambridge: Cambridge University Press, 2009.

Dymoke, Tailboys (ps. Thomas Cutwode). *Caltha Poetarum: or The bumble bee*. London, 1599.

Eccles, Mark. "James I of England." In *The Spenser Encyclopedia*, edited by A.C. Hamilton et al., 409. Toronto: University of Toronto Press, 1990.

Edwards, Thomas. *Cephalus and Procris*. In *Elizabethan Minor Epics*, edited by Elizabeth Story Donno, 155–79. New York: Columbia University Press, 1963.

Enterline, Lynn. *The Rhetoric of the Body from Ovid to Shakespeare*. Cambridge Studies in Renaissance Literature and Culture 35. Cambridge: Cambridge University Press, 2000.

Feeney, D.C. *The Gods in Epic: Poets and Critics of the Classical Tradition*. Oxford: Oxford University Press, 1991.

Feldherr, Andrew. "Metamorphosis in the *Metamorphoses*." In *The Cambridge Companion to Ovid*, edited by Philip Hardie, 163–79. Cambridge: Cambridge University Press, 2002.

Fletcher, Angus. *The Prophetic Moment: An Essay on Spenser*. Chicago: University of Chicago Press, 1971.

Fox, Cora. *Ovid and the Politics of Emotion in Elizabethan England*. Basingstoke, UK: Palgrave Macmillan, 2009.

Frantz, David O. "'Leud Priapians' and Renaissance Pornography." *Studies in English Literature* 12 (1972): 157–72.

Fraunce, Abraham. *The Third Part of the Countesse of Pembrokes Yvychurch, Entitled, Amintas Dale*. London, 1592.

Fulkerson, Laurel. *The Ovidian Heroine as Author: Reading, Writing, and Community in the Heroides*. Cambridge: Cambridge University Press, 2005.

Gerard, John. *The Herball or Generall Historie of Plantes*. London, 1597.

Gill, Roma. "*Musa Iocosa Mea*: Thoughts on the *Elegies*." In *John Donne: Essays in Celebration*, edited by A.J. Smith, 47–72. London: Methuen, 1972.

Gless, Darryl J. "Chapman's Ironic Ovid." *English Literary Renaissance* 9 (1979): 21–41.

Goldberg, Jonathan. *Endlesse Worke: Spenser and the Structures of Discourse*. Baltimore, Johns Hopkins University Press, 1981.

Gosson, Stephen. *The Schoole of Abuse*. London, 1579.

Greenblatt, Stephen J. *Renaissance Self-Fashioning: From More to Shakespeare*. Chicago: University of Chicago Press, 1980.

Greene, Thomas M. "Ben Jonson and the Centered Self." *Studies in English Literature* 10 (1970): 325–48.

Gross, Kenneth. "John Donne's Lyric Skepticism: In Strange Way." *Modern Philology* 101 (2004): 371–99.

Hadfield, Andrew. "Michael Drayton's Brilliant Career." *Proceedings of the British Academy* 125 (2004): 119–47.

Halpern, Richard. "'Pining Their Maws': Female Readers and the Erotic Ontology of the Text in Shakespeare's *Venus and Adonis*." In *Venus and Adonis: Critical Essays*, edited by Philip C. Kolin, 377–88. New York: Garland, 1997.

Hardin, Richard F. "Adicia, Souldan." In *The Spenser Encyclopedia*, edited by A.C. Hamilton et al., 7–8. Toronto: University of Toronto Press, 1990.

– *Michael Drayton and the Passing of Elizabethan England*. Lawrence: University Press of Kansas, 1973.

Harvey, Gabriel. *Gabriel Harvey's Marginalia*. Edited by G.C. Moore Smith. Stratford, UK: Shakespeare Head Press, 1913.

Helfer, Rebeca. *Spenser's Ruins and the Art of Reflection*. Toronto: University of Toronto Press, 2012.

Helgerson, Richard. *Self-Crowned Laureates: Spenser, Jonson, Milton and the Literary System*. Berkeley: University of California Press, 1983.

Herbert, Edward. *The Poems English and Latin of Edward Lord Herbert of Cherbury*. Edited by G.C. Moore Smith. Oxford: Clarendon Press, 1923.

Herbert, George. *The English Poems of George Herbert*. Edited by Helen Wilcox. Cambridge University Press, 2007.

Hesiod. *Hesiod, The Homeric Hymns and Homerica*. Translated by Hugh G. Evelyn White. Loeb Classical Library. London: William Heinemann, 1920.

Hester, M. Thomas. "Donne's Epigrams: A Little World Made Cunningly." In *The Eagle and the Dove: Reassessing John Donne*, edited by Claude J. Summers and Ted-Larry Pebworth, 80–91. Columbia: University of Missouri Press, 1986.

Hinds, Stephen. *Allusion and Intertext: Dynamics of Appropriation in Roman Poetry*. Roman Literature and Its Contexts. Cambridge: Cambridge University Press, 1998.

Homer. *The Odyssey*. Translated by A.T. Murray. Loeb Classical Library. Cambridge, MA: Harvard University Press, 1945.

Horace. *Odes and Epodes*. Translated by Niall Rudd. Loeb Classical Library. Cambridge, MA: Harvard University Press, 2004.

Hulse, Clark. *Metamorphic Verse: The Elizabethan Minor Epic*. Princeton, NJ: Princeton University Press, 1981.

Hutson, Lorna. *Thomas Nashe in Context*. Oxford: Clarendon Press, 1989.

Ingleby, C.M., F.J. Furnivall, and John Munro, eds. *The Shakespere Allusion-Book*. London: Oxford University Press, 1932.

Jacobson, Miriam. "The Elizabethan Cipher in Shakespeare's *Lucrece*." *Studies in Philology* 107 (2010): 336–59.

Jahn, Jerald D. "Chapman's *Enargia* and the Popular Perspective on *Ovids Banquet of Sence*." *Tennessee Studies in Literature* 23 (1978): 15–30.

James, Heather. "Ovid and the Question of Politics in Early Modern England." *English Literary History* 70 (2003): 343–73.

– "Shakespeare's Learned Heroines in Ovid's Schoolroom." In *Shakespeare and the Classics*, edited by Charles Martindale and A.B. Taylor, 66–85. Cambridge: Cambridge University Press, 2004.

– *Shakespeare's Troy: Drama, Politics, and the Translation of Empire*. Cambridge Studies in Renaissance Literature and Culture 22. Cambridge: Cambridge University Press, 1997.

Jonson, Ben. *Ben Jonson*. Edited by C.H. Herford, Percy Simpson, and Evelyn Simpson. 11 vols. Oxford: Oxford University Press, 1925–52.

– *The Complete Masques*. Edited by Stephen Orgel. The Yale Ben Jonson. New Haven, CT: Yale University Press, 1969.

– *Poetaster*. Edited by Tom Cain. Revels Plays. Manchester: Manchester University Press, 1995.

Josephus. *The famous and memorable vvorkes of Iosephus*. Translated by Thomas Lodge. London, 1609.

Kahn, Coppélia. *"Venus and Adonis."* In *The Cambridge Companion to Shakespeare's Poetry*, edited by Patrick Cheney, 72–89. Cambridge: Cambridge University Press, 2007.

Keach, William. *Elizabethan Erotic Narratives: Irony and Pathos in the Ovidian Poetry of Shakespeare, Marlowe, and Their Contemporaries*. New Brunswick, NJ: Rutgers University Press, 1977.

Keilen, Sean. "English Literature in Its Golden Age." In *The Forms of Renaissance Thought: New Essays in Literature and Culture*, ed. Leonard Barkan, Bradin Cormack, and Sean Keilen. 46–74. Basingstoke, UK: Palgrave Macmillan, 2009.

Kermode, J.F. "The Banquet of Sense." *Bulletin of the John Rylands Library* 44 (1961): 68–99.

Kinney, Daniel, and Elizabeth Styron. 2007. "Ovid Illustrated: The Reception of Ovid's *Metamorphoses* in Image and Text." University of Virginia Electronic Text Center. http://ovid.lib.virginia.edu/ovidillust.html#cycles.

Knox, Peter E. "A Poet's Life." In *A Companion to Ovid*, edited by Peter Knox, 3–7. Blackwell Companions to the Ancient World. West Sussex, UK: Wiley-Blackwell, 2009.

Lanham, Richard A. *A Handlist of Rhetorical Terms*. 2nd ed. Berkeley: University of California Press, 1991.

Lees-Jeffries, Hester. *England's Helicon: Fountains in Early Modern Literature and Culture*. Oxford: Oxford University Press, 2007.

Lerner, Laurence. "Ovid and the Elizabethans." In *Ovid Renewed: Ovidian Influences on Literature and Art from the Middle Ages to the Twentieth Century*, edited by Charles Martindale, 121–35. Cambridge: Cambridge University Press, 1988.

Leslie, Michael. "Spenser, Sidney, and the Renaissance Garden." *English Literary Renaissance* 22 (1992): 3–36.

Levin, Carole. "'We Shall Never Have a Merry World while the Queene Lyveth': Gender, Monarchy, and the Power of Seditious Words." In *Dissing Elizabeth: Negative Representations of Gloriana*, edited by Julia M. Walker, 77–95. Durham, NC: Duke University Press, 1998.

Lewis, C.S. *English Literature in the Sixteenth Century, Excluding Drama*. New York: Oxford University Press, 1954.

Lodge, Thomas. *Scillaes metamorphosis: enterlaced with the vnfortunate loue of Glaucus*. London, 1589.

Lotspeich, Henry Gibbons. *Classical Mythology in the Poetry of Edmund Spenser*. Princeton, NJ: Princeton University Press, 1932.

Lyne, Raphael. "Intertextuality and the Female Voice after the *Heroides*." *Renaissance Studies* 22 (2008): 307–23.

– *Ovid's Changing Worlds: English Metamorphoses, 1567–1632*. Oxford: Oxford University Press, 2001.

– "Love and Exile after Ovid." In *The Cambridge Companion to Ovid*, edited by Philip Hardie, 288–300. Cambridge: Cambridge University Press, 2002.

Maley, Willy. *A Spenser Chronology*. Lanham, MD: MacMillan, 1994.

Marlowe, Christopher. *The Complete Works of Christopher Marlowe*. Edited by Roma Gill. 5 vols. Oxford: Clarendon Press, 1987–98.

Marotti, Arthur F. *John Donne, Coterie Poet*. Madison: University of Wisconsin Press, 1986.

Marston, John. *The metamorphosis of Pigmalions Image and certaine satyres*. London, 1598.

– *The Poems of John Marston*. Edited by Arnold Davenport. Liverpool: Liverpool University Press, 1961.

Maslen, R.W. "Myths Exploited: The *Metamorphoses* of Ovid in Early Elizabethan England." In *Shakespeare's Ovid: The "Metamorphoses" in the Plays and Poems*, ed. A.B. Taylor, 15–30. Cambridge: Cambridge University Press, 2000.

Maus, Katherine Eisaman. *Ben Jonson and the Roman Frame of Mind*. Princeton, NJ: Princeton University Press, 1984.

McCabe, Richard A. *Spenser's Monstrous Regiment: Elizabethan Ireland and the Poetics of Difference*. Oxford: Oxford University Press, 2002.

Meakin, H.L. *John Donne's Articulations of the Feminine*. Oxford: Clarendon Press, 1998.

Meres, Francis. *Palladis Tamia*. London, 1598. Facs. New York: Scholars' Facsimiles and Reprints, 1938.

Miller, David Lee. "Gender, Justice, and the Gods in *The Faerie Queene*." In *Reading Renaissance Ethics*, edited by Marshall Grossman, 19–37. New York: Routledge, 2007.

Montrose, Louis Adrian. *The Subject of Elizabeth: Authority, Gender, and Representation*. Chicago: University of Chicago Press, 2006.

Mortimer, Anthony. "'Crimson Liveries' and 'Their Verdour': *Venus and Adonis*, 505–8." *Notes and Queries* 48 (2001): 274–5.

Moulton, Ian Frederick. "Transmuted into a Woman or Worse: Masculine Gender Identity and Thomas Nashe's 'Choice of Valentines.'" In *Thomas Nashe*, ed. Georgia Brown. 329–60. Surrey, UK: Ashgate, 2011.

Mueller, Janel M. "Donne's Epic Venture in the 'Metempsychosis.'" *Modern Philology* 70 (1972): 109–37.

Murphy, Patrick M. "Wriothesley's Resistance: Wardship Practices and Ovidian Narratives in Shakespeare's *Venus and Adonis*." In *Venus and Adonis: Critical Essays*, edited by Philip C. Kolin, 323–40. New York: Garland, 1997.

Murray, W.A. "What Was the Soul of the Apple?" *Review of English Studies* 10 (1959): 141–55.

Nashe, Thomas. *The Works of Thomas Nashe*. Edited by Ronald B. McKerrow. 5 vols. 1903–10. Rpt. Ed. F.P. Wilson. Oxford: Basil Blackwell, 1958.

O'Connell, Michael. "*The Faerie Queene*, Book V." In *The Spenser Encyclopedia*, edited by A.C. Hamilton et al., 280–3. Toronto: University of Toronto Press, 1990.

Ossa-Richardson, Anthony. "Ovid and the 'Free Play with Signs' in Thomas Nashe's *The Unfortunate Traveller*." *Modern Language Review* 101 (2006): 945–56.

Ovid. *Metamorphoses: The Arthur Golding Translation, 1567*. Edited by John Frederick Nims. New York: Macmillan, 1965.

– *Ovid in Six Volumes*. Loeb Classical Library. 6 vols. Cambridge, MA: Harvard University Press, 1969.

Parker, Patricia A. *Inescapable Romance: Studies in the Poetics of a Mode*. Princeton, NJ: Princeton University Press, 1979.

Pigman, G.W. "Versions of Imitation in the Renaissance." *Renaissance Quarterly* 33 (1980): 1–32.

Pincombe, Michael. "The Ovidian Hermaphrodite: Moralizations by Peend and Spenser." In *Ovid and the Renaissance Body*, edited by Goran V. Stanivukovic, 155–70. Toronto: University of Toronto Press, 2001.

Plato. *Euthyphro, Apology, Crito, Phaedo, Phaedrus*. Translated by Harold North Fowler. Loeb Classical Library. Cambridge, MA: Harvard University Press, 1914.

Plotinus. *Enneads*. Translated by A.H. Armstrong. Loeb Classical Library. 7 vols. London: William Heinemann, 1988.

Poliziano, Angelo. *Silvae*. Translated by Charles Fantazzi. I Tatti Renaissance Library. Cambridge, MA: Harvard University Press, 2004.

– *The Stanze of Angelo Poliziano*. Translated by David Quint. Amherst: University of Massachusetts Press, 1979.

Pugh, Syrithe. *Spenser and Ovid*. London: Ashgate, 2005.

Puttenham, George. *The Art of English Poesy*. Edited by Frank Wigham and Wayne A. Rebhorn. Ithaca, NY: Cornell University Press, 2007.

Quintilian. *Institutio oratoria*. Translated by H.E. Butler. Loeb Classical Library. 4 vols. London: William Heinemann, 1922.

Ramachandran, Ayesha. "Clarion in the Bower of Bliss: Poetry and Politics in Spenser's 'Muiopotmos.'" *Spenser Studies* 20 (2005): 77–106.

Revard, Stella P. "Donne and Propertius: Love and Death in London and Rome." In *The Eagle and the Dove: Reassessing John Donne*, edited by Claude J.

Summers and Ted-Larry Pebworth, 69–79. Columbia: University of Missouri Press, 1986.

Ribner, Rhoda M. "The Compasse of This Curious Frame: Chapman's *Ovid's Banquet of Sense* and the Emblematic Tradition." *Studies in the Renaissance* 17 (1970): 233–58.

Ringler, Richard N. "The Faunus Episode." In *Essential Articles for the Study of Edmund Spenser*, edited by A.C. Hamilton, 289–98. Hamden, CO: Archon Books, 1972.

Roberts, Sasha. *Reading Shakespeare's Poems in Early Modern England*. Basingstoke, UK: Palgrave Macmillan, 2003.

Rupprecht, Carol S. "Radigund." In *The Spenser Encyclopedia*, edited by A.C. Hamilton et al., 580–1. Toronto: University of Toronto Press, 1990.

Sandys, George. *Ovid's Metamorphoses Englished, Mythologiz'd and Represented in Figures*. Oxford, 1632. Facs. New York: Garland, 1976.

Schoell, Franck L. *Études sur l'humanisme continentale en Angleterre à la fin de la Renaissance*. Paris: Champion, 1926.

Shaheen, Naseeb. *Biblical References in the Faerie Queene*. Memphis, TN: Memphis State University Press, 1976.

Shakespeare, William. *The Complete Sonnets and Poems*. Edited by Colin Burrow. Oxford: Oxford University Press, 2002.

– *The Norton Shakespeare: Based on the Oxford Edition*. Edited by Stephen Greenblatt, Walter Cohen, Jean E. Howard, and Katherine Eisaman Maus. New York: W.W. Norton, 1997.

– *Titus Andronicus*. Edited by Eugene M. Waith. Oxford: Oxford University Press, 1984.

– *Titus Andronicus*. Edited by Jonathan Bate. London: Routledge, 1995.

Sidney, Sir Philip. *The Major Works*. Edited by Katherine Duncan-Jones. Oxford: Oxford University Press, 1989.

Silberman, Lauren. *Transforming Desire: Erotic Knowledge in Books III and IV of "The Faerie Queene."* Berkeley: University of California Press, 1995.

Sinfield, Alan. *Shakespeare, Authority, Sexuality: Unfinished Business in Cultural Materialism*. Accents on Shakespeare. New York: Routledge, 2006.

Smith, Martin van Wyk. "John Donne's 'Metempsychosis.'" *Review of English Studies* 24 (1973): 141–52.

Snare, Gerald. *The Mystification of George Chapman*. Durham, NC: Duke University Press, 1989.

Sowerby, Robin. *The Classical Legacy in Renaissance Poetry*. London: Longman, 1994.

Spenser, Edmund. *The Faerie Queene*. Edited by A.C. Hamilton. 2nd ed. New York: Longman, 2001.

– *The Yale Edition of the Shorter Poems of Edmund Spenser*. Edited by William A. Oram, Einar Bjorvand, Ronald Bond, Thomas H. Cain, Alexander Dunlop, and Richard Schell. New Haven, CT: Yale University Press, 1989.

– *A View of the State of Ireland*. Edited by Andrew Hadfield and Willy Maley. Oxford: Blackwell, 1997.

Spentzou, Efrossini. *Readers and Writers in Ovid's "Heroides": Transgressions of Genre and Gender*. Oxford: Oxford University Press, 2003.

Stapleton, Michael L. *Harmful Eloquence: Ovid's "Amores" from Antiquity to Shakespeare."* Ann Arbor: University of Michigan Press, 1996.

– "Marlowe's Ovid: The 'Elegies' in the Marlowe Canon." *Marlowe Studies* 4 (2014): 1–31. Accessed August 12, 2013. http://www.academia.edu/3585698/Marlowes_Ovid_The_Elegies_in_the_Marlowe_Canon.

– "A New Source for Thomas Nashe's *The Choice of Valentines*." *English Language Notes* 33 (1995): 15–19.

– "Nashe and the Poetics of Obscenity: *The Choise of Valentines*." In *Thomas Nashe*, edited by Georgia Brown, 309–328. Surrey, UK: Ashgate, 2011.

– *Spenser's Ovidian Poetics*. Newark: University of Delaware Press, 2009.

– "'Why should they not alike in all parts touch?' Donne and the Elegiac Tradition." *John Donne Journal* 15 (1996): 1–22.

Stow, John. *The annales of England*. London, 1592.

Stump, Donald, and Susan M. Felch, eds. *Elizabeth I and her Age*. New York: W.W. Norton, 2009.

Sullivan, Garrett A., Jr. *Sleep, Romance and Human Embodiment*. Cambridge: Cambridge University Press, 2012.

Tacitus, *Annals*. Translated by John Jackson. Loeb Classical Library. Cambridge, MA: Harvard University Press, 1956.

Targoff, Ramie. *John Donne, Body and Soul*. Chicago: University of Chicago Press, 2008.

Thorne, Allison. "'Large Complaints in Little Papers': Negotiating Ovidian Genealogies of Complaint in Drayton's *Englands Heroicall Epistles*." *Renaissance Studies* 22 (2008): 368–84.

Tourneur, Cyril. *The transformed metamorphosis*. London, 1600.

Vickers, Brian. *Shakespeare, Co-Author: A Historical Study of Five Collaborative Plays*. Oxford: Oxford University Press, 2002.

Vinge, Louise. "Chapman's *Ovids Banquet of Sence*: Its Sources and Theme." *Journal of the Warburg and Courtauld Institutes* 38 (1975): 234–57.

Virgil. *Virgil in Two Volumes*. Translated by H. Rushton Fairclough. Loeb Classical Library. 2 vols. Cambridge, MA: Harvard University Press, 1999.

Waddington, Raymond B. *The Mind's Empire: Myth and Form in George Chapman's Narrative Poems*. Baltimore: Johns Hopkins University Press, 1974.

Waller, Edmund. *The Poems of Edmund Waller*. Edited by G. Thorn Drury. New York: Greenwood Press, 1968.

Watkins, John. *The Specter of Dido: Spenser and Virgilian Epic*. New Haven, CT: Yale University Press, 1995.

Weever, John. *Faunus and Melliflora or, The original of our English satyres*. London, 1600.

Wheeler, Martin. "'The Object Where to All his Actions Tend': George Chapman's *Ouids Banquet of Sence* and the Thrill of the Chase." *Modern Language Review* 101 (2006): 325–46.

White, Paul. *Renaissance Postscripts: Responding to Ovid's "Heroides" in Sixteenth-Century France*. Columbus: Ohio State University Press, 2009.

Wilson-Okamura, David Scott. "Errors about Ovid and Romance." *Spenser Studies* 23 (2008): 215–34.

Wind, Edgar. *Pagan Mysteries in the Renaissance*. Rev. ed. New York: W.W. Norton, 1958.

Wofford, Susanne L. *The Choice of Achilles: The Ideology of Figure in the Epic*. Stanford: Stanford University Press, 1992.

Index

www.ingramcontent.com/pod-product-compliance
Lightning Source LLC
Chambersburg PA
CBHW030945051025
33395CB00008B/87/J